THE
NARROWBOAT
GUIDE

THE
NARROWBOAT
A complete guide to choosing, designing
and maintaining a narrowboat
GUIDE

TONY JONES

ADLARD COLES NAUTICAL

BLOOMSBURY

LONDON · NEW DELHI · NEW YORK · SYDNEY

Adlard Coles Nautical
An imprint of Bloomsbury Publishing Plc

50 Bedford Square   1385 Broadway
London   New York
WC1B 3DP   NY 10018
UK   USA

www.bloomsbury.com

ADLARD COLES, ADLARD COLES NAUTICAL
and the Buoy logo are trademarks of
Bloomsbury Publishing Plc

First published 2016
© Tony Jones, 2016
© Photographs Tony Jones and other photographers noted on page 240.

British Library Cataloguing-in-Publication Data
A catalogue record for this book is available from the British Library.

ISBN: PB: 978-1-4081-8802-6
ePDF: 978-1-4081-8803-3
ePub: 978-1-4081-8801-9

10 9 8 7 6 5 4 3 2 1

Designed and typeset by Susan McIntyre
Printed in China by RRD Asia Printing Solutions Limited

Bloomsbury Publishing Plc makes every effort to ensure that the papers used in
the manufacture of our books are natural, recyclable products made from wood
grown in well-managed forests. Our manufacturing processes conform to the
environmental regulations of the country of origin.

To find out more about our authors and books visit www.bloomsbury.com.
Here you will find extracts, author interviews, details of forthcoming events
and the option to sign up for our newsletters.

CONTENTS

INTRODUCTION

I'm probably preaching to the converted here, but a book of this type could only ever begin with a generous appreciation of our country's canals and rivers. From their rugged industrial beginnings and through periods of neglect and abandonment, our waterways networks have survived and ultimately thrived to become the national treasures that they are today. It is only proper that we should be in awe of an infrastructure that has been through so much.

The canals were built around 300 years ago and they are still being used today in much the same fashion as they were then. The locks and the bridges; the sluices and the tunnels and all of the other Victorian technologies that helped to kick-start the Industrial Revolution are not only still working, but they are more popular and more widely appreciated than ever before. Few aspects of the 21st century can lay claim to such an accolade.

Narrowboating is at the very heart of the canal network. Every leisure, lifestyle and commercial activity associated with the waterways has narrowboating to thank for its existence. Today's boating community brings together people of all different types and many different ages and everyone seems to have a different story. But the one thing that brings us together is our love for life on the inland waterways and the joys that it brings.

The main attraction for many is the leisurely pace of boating life. Getting away from the hustle and bustle of the modern world is a very attractive proposition for lots of people and fits squarely into the definition of a leisure activity. Being outdoors and getting close to nature are attractive benefits too, as boating takes you into the heart of some of the most beautiful parts of Britain. Indeed, the waterways system provides respite from even the least salubrious of landscapes as it winds through towns and cities like a ribbon of rural and rustic peacefulness.

The pastime is so seductive for some that it becomes a full-time lifestyle and a boat becomes their home. For all of its inherent aesthetic beauty, the waterways community is one of the most attractive aspects of our canals and one that is missing from many sectors of modern life. Boating is unavoidably sociable as people come together in close enforced proximity. From sharing the workload at locks and bridges to waiting your turn at a water tap, we exist in a space just wide enough for two boats to pass by comfortably and we become a community by default.

The author aboard Nb The Watchman.

The author's boat Nb The Watchman.

Like all communities the boat owners are a patchwork of personalities and profiles. This book offers useful information and advice to everyone considering owning a narrowboat. To make the book easier to read, you'll find handy headings, hints and tips and a wealth of real-life stories, information and experiences from a wide range of boaters and boating professionals. With boat folk being such an eclectic bunch it would be impossible to cover every possible scenario and so don't restrict your reading and research to one specific profile – you might miss something. In fact, why not just read the whole book. Sure, it might take a little time, but we're not in a rush here. Boat folk rarely are. It's not that boating is specifically slow; it's just that the rest of the world is always in such a terrible rush.

1 HOW TO BUY A BOAT

Buying a narrowboat is an exciting process. Even a cursory online search will turn up hundreds of boats at very agreeable prices. The temptation to rush out and buy one immediately is overwhelming, so congratulations for resisting the urge. The fact that you are reading this book means you realise that there is some important research to be done first. But for now, there is no harm in looking!

Purchasing a boat requires patience, diligence, determination and, sometimes, nerves of steel. It is surprising how much variation there is to be had in such a small space and the choices you make now are vitally important. There are so many factors to be considered and many decisions to be made. Let's start at the very beginning.

Boats come in an array of different shapes and sizes.

TYPES OF BOAT

The inherent traits of the inland waterways determine the types of boat that can navigate there. Narrow locks, low bridges and shallow channels dictate a very specific design and so only a few types of craft are commonly seen.

Narrowboats

The canals were built for narrowboats and these are still the most common vessels you will see there. No wider than 6' 10" (2m 8cm), narrowboats are iconic and unique. Given the very specific criteria of their design you could be forgiven for thinking that if you have seen one narrowboat you have seen them all and that any variation will be insignificant. However, there are some enormous differences to appreciate if you have a discerning eye and you will need to understand these before you make a purchase.

Traditional stern (Trads)

Narrowboats with a stern of this traditional design are modelled on the cargo carrying canal boats of old. The stern deck is just large enough for one person to stand to use the tiller, although there is usually just enough space for someone else to stand inside the cabin with the roof hatch pushed back. Trads are popular for a couple of reasons – firstly because the design and lines are reminiscent of the old style working boats, but also because there is more internal secure space.

Narrowboats are almost always 6' 10" wide.

Traditional (trad) stern.

CASE STUDY: THE TRAD STERN

Lou and Aaron
Nb *Bacchus II*
BOAT: TRADITIONAL STYLE NARROWBOAT
LENGTH: 55FT
BUILT: 1988

'We didn't restrict our search strictly to trads, but it eventually became clear as we looked at more boats that trads have some distinct benefits as a live-aboard vessel. We store all kinds of bulky stuff in my engine room. In there you can find tool boxes, a vacuum cleaner, rock climbing gear and a sack of food for our dog – none of which we would like to leave out on a cruiser stern and we certainly don't have space for them inside the main part of the boat.'

Aaron and Reefer on board Nb Bachus II.

Cruiser stern

The cruiser stern was developed with the leisure boater in mind, and given that few of today's boats can carry 20 tons of coal, it could be argued that these are the boats most suited to the modern canal system. With a large back deck there is enough space for several people to enjoy the boating experience together. The engine is usually situated below the back deck and so the bilges there are often subjected to rain-water ingress, but this is easily dealt with using a bilge pump. Liveaboard boaters might also rue the lost internal space on a cruiser stern, but this is by no means a hard and fast rule and many cruiser stern narrowboats are home to liveaboards.

A cruiser stern.

CASE STUDY: CRUISER STERN

Sam

Nb *Knot HRD Work*

'My boat is primarily a floating office for me to work in away from the distractions of home, but it also doubles as a party boat. This is the main reason I made sure I bought a cruiser stern, as I knew there would be regular parties hosted there. We cruise up and down the section of the Bridgewater canal near where I am moored, stopping off at gastro-pubs along the way. A trad or semi-trad stern just would not have been suitable.'

Semi-trad stern

Semi-trads can be described as the best and the worst of both worlds. The semi-trad design has cabin side walls extending all the way back to the stern deck while leaving a section that is not covered by a roof panel. This serves to retain the appearance of a traditional stern, whilst having enough space for socialising, like a cruiser stern. On the downside, semi-trads lack the secure internal space of a trad and it is impractical for fellow boaters to be seated on the rear deck due to the false cabin walls that surround it. You'll need to decide for yourself if a semi-trad is for you.

External features to look for

Although most narrowboats might look the same to the untrained eye, there are some attractive design features to look out for. Buying a pretty boat might cost a little more so it is important to balance your design budget against your boating necessities and aspirations. As with all things, beauty is in the eye of the beholder; but these traits are commonly considered the work of a boat-building craftsman.

Traditional styling is very desirable.

Above: Look for nicely sweeping cabin shapes.

Below: Box square cabins are less desirable.

CASE STUDY: THE SEMI-TRAD STERN

Steve and Eileen
Nb *Sophie*
LENGTH: 57FT
BUILT: 2005

'It seemed the sensible choice when we considered our circumstances. One of the main reasons was because we have a dog who comes boating with us, and we wanted a little protection around the back deck to keep her from falling in. A trad or cruiser stern would not provide this, so it had to be a semi-trad. There are other benefits for us too – there's more space to socialise and having lockers either side of the deck gives your crew somewhere to sit and places to rest mugs of tea and plates of sandwiches. Keeping mooring pins and mallets here is very convenient too, instead of having them on the roof or leaving them on the floor to trip over. Little things like that are surprisingly nice benefits after having had a cruiser stern boat before this one.'

Semi-trad stern.

Nb Sophie.

OTHER BOATS

Wide beam

Wide-beam boats utilise much of the same styling, features and fittings as a narrowboat, but as the name implies, these boats have much more space aboard. Wide beams are very much like floating apartments and wide-beam owners need to make fewer compromises given that they have so much room to play with. Wide beams will often feature baths, widescreen TVs and large self-contained rooms, much to the distaste of purist canal enthusiasts. Despite the purists' protestations these boats are becoming increasingly common as boating becomes ever more popular with the general public and particularly those who wish to live aboard.

Dutch barge

If you aspire to own a pretty boat with both looks and sophistication, you might consider a Dutch barge. Originally imported from Holland as ex-cargo boats or fishing trawlers, many are now renovated for leisure or live-aboard use. These vessels are undeniably pleasing to the eye and even the newer reproduction boats follow a pattern that is largely agreeable. Older original boats with a good fit out will cost you as much as a new build replica and almost always more than a wide beam of comparative age and condition, but for some boaters, it just has to be a barge.

Tug

Another narrowboat design that you will sometimes see is a tug deck. These long fore decks are considered by many as a very attractive feature, despite the space having few practical uses.

Above: Wide beam. Below: Tug

CASE STUDY: LIVING ON A DUTCH BARGE

Brett and Jane are two new liveaboarders who, after much research, decided that only a Dutch barge would do. 'From the very beginning I knew I needed more space than was available on a narrowboat,' said Jane. 'Brett would probably have been fine, but lack of space was always going to be a deal breaker for me.

'We looked at the prices of Dutch barges and wide beams and initially that swayed us towards the latter. In the early days we just didn't appreciate the style differences, looking only at the interior areas. However, once we'd been on a few wide beams we began to be more discerning, going back to look again at a Dutch barge we had seen in the very early days of our research. Although it wasn't quite as wide as our wish list asked for, we eventually decided that the small compromise there would give us a great boat. Now, we don't even miss the extra two feet that we'd hoped to have.

'In addition to the extra space, there are plenty of other things that we love about this boat. The wheelhouse is such a bonus, acting like a

Dutch barge.

conservatory; somewhere to stash wellies, raincoats and coal sacks. The back cabin is a lovely space that is remote to the rest of the living area on the boat and it is a nice hidey-hole. We use it as a workshop and guest room. Add to that the beautiful lines of the hull and the fabulous wooden fit out inside and I'm glad we went for a barge.'

Other boats

Narrowboats, wide beams and Dutch barges make up the great proportion of steel boats you will see on the inland waterways, but other vessels are certainly available and suitable. Plastic and fibreglass cruisers are a common sight and these come in an array of shapes and sizes. For some reason there is very little crossover between the steel and plastic boating camps. Narrowboaters often teasingly refer to plastic cruisers as 'Tupperware' and, in response, narrowboats are mocked as 'sewer pipes'.

You will occasionally see small sail boats, strange looking lifeboats and incongruous fishing vessels, but these are all very few and far between on the canal system. Along with these there is an ever-shrinking contingent of heritage vessels that were usually cargo carrying boats in their heyday. Few of these boats (such as Leeds and Liverpool short boats) ever reach the market, but they are a very tempting proposition if they have been cared for properly. Keep an open mind, but be sure that you know what you want to do with your boat before you decide to go for a more unusual vessel.

GRP cruiser.

Not your usual canalboat – a repurposed lifeboat.

Right and below: Kennet is a historic Leeds and Liverpool short boat, dating from 1947.
Kennet is 62' long, with a 14' 3" beam.

Maximum sizes

The limitations for inland waterways boats are based on a bridge and a lock on the Kennet and Avon canal. The lock will only take boats that are no more than 70ft long by 12ft and 6in wide, although this can be 13ft wide at a push. The bridge has a width of 12' 6" and an air draft of 7' 6". There is also the underwater draft to consider; if the boat is inland only then this will be restricted to around 28–30in to avoid scraping the canal bed. The maximum boat size that allows full access to the entire waterways network is a 57-foot narrowboat with a typical 6' 10" beam. Wide beams are limited by narrow locks that are found in various parts of the network. If you are considering a wide-beamed vessel of any type it is important to remember that your cruising range will be limited by its girth. Be sure to check the beam restrictions in your chosen mooring and cruising locations.

Small boats can be fun.

CONSTRUCTION

Steel hulls

Most of the boats you will find on the canals and rivers system are made from steel. A well-maintained narrowboat will last for decades so long as repairs and maintenance are addressed. You will often see the thickness of steel listed on boat advertisements and brochures as a three-figure ratio with the most common being 10:6:4. These figures tell us the thickness of the steel in different parts of the boat. Here, the bottom plate of the hull is made from steel that is 10mm thick, the hull sides 6mm thick and the cabin 4mm, although many boat builders will use 5mm steel on the cabin sides to avoid the integral frame showing through the external paintwork. Historic boats and some boats by builders at the cheaper end of the market may be made of thinner steel, but that's not to say they should be written off. These boats will still be sturdy enough but they may degrade to the point of requiring repair somewhat sooner.

The quality of steel used to construct modern boats is a frequent topic of conversation since the demise of the British steel industry. Many consider new, imported steel to be inferior but this is not the experience of those who regularly work on boats. 'Steel quality varies widely and the age of it has no relevance,' says Adam Holgate, boat hood fitter at Canvas Man in Yorkshire. 'I work on hundreds of boats each year and drill thousands of holes in boats and you'll find ball bearings and other scrap bits in the steel of boats from all ages. Other boats are built from high quality materials. It all depends on the specific quality of the steel that the builder decided to use.'

Ian Hillsdon from Lambon Boat Builders explains more. 'Occasionally we do get customers who specifically insist that we must use British steel, believing this to be superior. However, that's not true, and insisting on British steel can pose a problem. Most UK steel suppliers import coils from abroad because the British supply chain is difficult to follow. Buying direct from Corus is not an easy option either because we are such a small customer, compared with others that they supply. The quality of steel is not something that should be judged on the country of origin and it is easy to check that your builder is using good quality materials. There are many grades of steel but the standard that most inland boat builders work to is called S275JR, and this will be of uniform quality whether sourced from the UK or abroad.'

Hull bottoms

Most canal boats have a flat-bottomed hull, but some (such as the Springer) have a 'V'-shaped bottom. Boats with V-shaped hulls rock a little more and have a slightly deeper under-water draft, but the practical differences are negligible.

Other materials

You'll also find boats that use wood, glass reinforced plastic (GRP) and even concrete somewhere in their construction. Using these materials can be cheaper than using steel, but many boaters consider them to be either problematic or inferior too. Relatively few boatyards are equipped to cater and care for boats that are not made from steel and it is no coincidence that many boats using these other materials are in poor repair. This is likely because the original owner bought the boat cheaply and sold it on as a bargain when it fell into disrepair. The bargain buyer, being very cash conscious, might not invest in repairs either and so the boats continue to fall into

disrepair and depreciate. There are exceptions to this broad brushstroke rule and there are some very nicely maintained non-steel craft, but narrowboats were always meant to be made from steel and any deviation from this is likely to create headaches at some point.

NEW OR PRE-LOVED

Buying a brand new boat means you can order the exact specification and layout you require. This means you don't have to make any compromises at all and, if you plan and manage the build well, you can end up with the boat of your dreams. Unlike a second-hand vessel, a new boat will come installed with the most up to date technologies and the exterior paint job of your choice. Of course, this all comes at a price, but for those who have enough time and money, the dream is often too desirable to resist.

Depreciation is the biggest downside for new boat purchasers as the value of the boat will drop steeply in the first few years. With each piece of new kit and equipment the final price will rise and so the build will always be a balance between the cost of the features you install and the value they bring.

Choosing the right boat takes time, but it's worth it.

CASE STUDY: COMMUNICATING WITH YOUR BOAT BUILDER

Ian Hillsdon
OWNER OF LAMBON BOATS
DROITWICH SPA, WORCESTERSHIRE

'One of the most important considerations when choosing a boat builder is that you get along. From design to completion, boats are built over a long period of time that can sometimes run well beyond twelve months. Having a good relationship will speed and assist the process enormously. It is a good idea to visit plenty of boatyards and gauge the reception you get when calling cold. Don't be put off by the workshop; boat building is a dirty game and many builders won't have a spotlessly clean office. If you are welcomed and treated congenially then that is a very good sign. Once you have a short list of potential builders you should call again unannounced, or make appointments if you need extra time.

'You don't necessarily need to know the exact type of boat you want, but do make sure that you have a good idea of how you are going to use the boat. The builder will have enough experience to deduce your needs from this description of use and recommend the style and features. To really understand your needs you will need plenty of boating experience. Be sure to at least go on a boating holiday or ten and, if possible, go boating with boat-owner friends. It's no good just sitting on the riverbank and watching the boats go by. It is difficult to design and build a boat for people who are not boaters! Above all, don't be blinkered. Be open to ideas. We've spent years building boats for a living and we can offer a wealth of advice for free, so you'd be daft not to make the most of us.

'We often get weird and wonderful requests and we like to accommodate where these are sensible, but we always advise against commissioning a boat that is too radical. One day you may need to sell the boat and your unusual design preferences won't necessarily suit someone else.

'The most common problem that builders and customers will experience is, predictably, a financial one. Setting a budget is obviously important but you must also allow for extras and the unforeseen. Boat builders are in business and as much as they appreciate your custom they can only build the boat that was quoted for. Additional items outside the agreement, such as delivery, craning, diesel or sign writing must be paid for by the customer, not the builder.

'Sticking to your plan is vitally important too, if you want to stay within your budget. Adding to the specification and redesigning the build once it is underway can be enormously expensive in both labour and materials. Adaptations will always be necessary as even the best made plans and drawings cannot predict the way the build will run in real life. Often the builder will confirm a solution with the customer as these issues arise and often they will absorb the extra cost. After all, they want you to be happy with the boat. However, in certain circumstances these costs may need to be funded by the customer.

'Be sure to nail down every detail of the build and do not be afraid to ask or make checks. Sometimes builders will fail to make things crystal clear because they do this every day. Often the customer's expectations will exceed that which is recognised as an unspoken standard practice. You shouldn't be worried about asking questions or checking details. In fact, we strongly recommend that you do so.'

Ordering a new boat

The first step in buying a new boat is always to decide exactly what you are looking for. This will always mean looking at a large array of boats to determine the features and fittings you need, including not only the equipment and fittings but also the layout and hull shape too. You will be surprised at the amount of variation you can get in such a small space and there are so many configurations to be had. You will need to be exactly sure of what you want before you start to commission the build. Changing your mind will usually be expensive and will always extend the build time; and some changes will not be viable after some stages of the work are completed.

Choosing a builder

Finding a boat builder is a big job in itself. Once you have an idea of the type of shell you want you will need to find the right builder to make it for you. Not all boat builders build the boat from scratch. Some use shells that are made elsewhere and just fit out the interior. Likewise, other companies just do the steelwork. Others do the whole job from start to finish, reducing the potential for problems and incompatibility.

Keep it local

Proximity is also a big consideration as it is wise to choose a boat builder based somewhere local enough for you to visit the project regularly. Consider too that most boat builders have a backlog of work and so your build slot could be a considerable way into the future.

Securing your slot

Once you have chosen a builder and agreed a specification, a small deposit will secure a build slot. From there the payments are sensibly staggered to correspond with specific stages in the build, starting with a relatively large

Tax

Some new build boats are exempt from tax. Typically only large boats will be exempt based on a calculation of volume and on usage. The measurement from the gunwales to the base is used for the calculation and so narrowboats and narrowboat-style wide beams will not be exempt. Larger boats such as Dutch barges or those with a deep hull may qualify but it is important to discuss this with the builder when discussing price. The boat must also be used for liveaboard purposes and be the sole residence; a status that might be temporary and is often subject to interpretation. Be sure to check eligibility before factoring a tax discount into your costs.

Crazy boat ideas

We were recently asked to build a pontoon for a floating Indian restaurant. The customer wanted the boat to be three storeys high but with a very limited beam. We advised that the boat would be unstable and would likely capsize should too many passengers move to one side. His response was that we should not worry about this as he would manage and restrict the movement of the people on board! We imagined spotters in military uniforms telling people to stand still and organising synchronised toilet visits! We did eventually build the boat but convinced the owner that it should not be three stories high.

LAMBON BOAT BUILDERS

payment for the steel and commencement of the major construction work. The final payment will be made when the boat is completed, signed off and handed over. All new boats will come with a warranty that can be relied upon

Visit your boatbuilder regularly to check on progress.

for repairs and snagging issues in the first few years of ownership. This warranty brings peace of mind to new owners as repair costs are largely negated in these early years of ownership, whereas the new owners of second-hand boats will invariably inherit repairs and maintenance costs which can be significant.

CONTRACTS WITH YOUR BUILDER

The British Marine Foundation has a useful standard template contract that most builders and clients will be happy to use. The contract is geared towards the customer (and so it should be) but it also covers the builder too. This contract will include a specification, a drawing of some sort and an agreed payment plan that has been discussed and agreed by both parties. The only risky payment in this contract is the very first payment which is for the steel purchase. After that point, everything produced is the property of the customer.

Check your steel

Steel comes in many different forms. Sometimes it can come in its basic form with the mill scale still attached. Over a period of around two years this mill scale will drop off, so if you are intending to have the boat painted it is best to have the mill scale shot blasted off. This can be done either prior to fabrication or after fabrication by a mobile blaster.

It is important to be aware that boat builders go bust with surprising regularity and even the large established companies are not immune from the curse of bankruptcy. On the other hand, you should not consider smaller companies to be any more vulnerable as there are many small builders that tick along just fine for many decades with no problem at all. Finding a financially stable boat builder is a difficult challenge and can be something of a lottery. The best advice is to check up on your builder and their history as much as possible and make your choices from there.

Top tips for new boat builds

1. Conduct plenty of research to determine the exact specification of the boat you want.

2. Find a builder that specialises in the type of boat you aspire to.

3. Check out your builder thoroughly. Look for one with consistent build quality and good financial credentials.

4. Be sure to use a staged payment structure to pay for your boat.

5. Consider using the standard contract from the British Marine Foundation.

6. Stay in touch with your builder and ask about problems regularly. There will always be issues during any build, but don't let them gather dust – deal with them immediately.

7. Try not to change your mind about any specifications during the build as these will be expensive, time-consuming and occasionally impossible to implement.

8. Be very specific in every communication with your builder. Ambiguity is the source of the vast majority of boat build problems. Make sure the builder understands your instructions – and if you don't understand anything, ask and ask again until you do.

Save money with a sailaway

A sailaway is a boat that is built from new but purchased at a stage of pre-completion. You can buy a sailaway at any one of several different stages and you can normally dictate the stage of completion you would like. For example, you can buy a steel shell that can come with (or without) insulation, running gear, interior fit out, plumbing, electrics, paint job and any other features you care to mention. For those with enough time, skill, money and

patience, a self fit out can be a very economical and rewarding way to get a new boat to your exacting standards. Be aware that fitting out a sailaway to a good standard requires more than a basic competency in DIY as many of the skills you might use in a house will be insufficient when fitting out a boat. Your work will also be subjected to boating specific safety and legal checks, so you should be thoroughly familiar with these and their management before considering a sailaway build. However, sailaway self-builders are amongst the most satisfied of all boat owners as the work requires that you invest a little bit of your soul. You will know your boat inside out and there will be few compromises or surprises – it will be entirely your creation.

BUYING A SECOND-HAND BOAT

Buying a second-hand boat is much like buying a second-hand car. Used boats are cheaper to but you will likely be buying some imperfections and headaches too, some of which might not be noticed until after the sale is completed. This route into boat ownership will invariably require a degree of compromise as you are unlikely to find exactly the boat you are looking for, be it issues with the layout, paint job or specifications. With that said, a little bit of compromise can often buy you a lot of boat that is very close to the one on your wish list at a much lower price.

Do your research

If you are buying a second-hand boat you will need to do plenty of research to ensure you end up with one that is suitable. Read all you can, but there is no substitute for stepping aboard as many boats as possible to compare every feature until you are satisfied that you know what you are looking for. Don't be suckered into buying a 'bargain' until you are quite sure you know what you are taking on and what it will cost to renovate and run. 'Bargain' boats are surprisingly common, so don't be in any rush or worry that you'll miss the deal of the century. There'll be another bargain soon enough.

Those new to boating will need to learn a lot before they are knowledgeable enough to make a good choice. It is frighteningly easy to spend too much money on an unsuitable boat that ends up being an expensive headache. The importance of conducting thorough research cannot be over-emphasised. Hasty decisions are rarely conducive to happy boating. Find out exactly what you are looking for and speak to as many boat owners as you can before deciding on the type of boat you think you want. Once you've compiled a list of features and specifications the search really begins,

but be aware that you will invariably need to compromise at some point.

Buying a second-hand boat is not a scientific process though. Just ask those who have been through it and most will tell you that they bought their boat because they fell in love with it, despite the compromises from their list of ideal specifications. Older boats, like older houses, will always display a degree of character that is inherent with their age and experiences. You'll find that almost every boat you look at will have a feature or character trait that you will not have seen before, some of which will add to the allure of that particular vessel. This is one of the great joys of buying a used boat. Engaging your heart in your purchase process is unavoidable and often commendable, but it is unwise to let your heart rule your head lest you find that the boat you have fallen in love with turns out to be a disaster.

Used boats are an easy way to get started, but be sure to do some research.

Get a survey

It is usually wise to pay for a survey to establish that the boat has no hidden major flaws. For boats over a few years of age a full, out of water survey is advisable, as this will enable the engineer to test the thickness of the hull to determine any corrosion. A full survey will look at the efficacy of the running gear, plumbing, electrics and heating systems as well as giving advice about any other noticeable flaws that can be found. A survey will invariably find things wrong with any boat so you should take independent advice about the severity of the findings and the cost of making right the issues. This can often mean that there is some room for negotiation with the owner, regarding the sale price, if the issues have not been highlighted to you before the survey is conducted.

Be prepared to walk away or to shoulder the costs of any problems the survey finds. Be prepared that some issues might be deal breakers. Be prepared to keep looking. There are plenty of boats out there and yours is amongst them, somewhere. But above all, be prepared to compromise and be realistic and sensible about the boat you are considering, despite what your heart says.

Once you have found the boat of your dreams you'll need to go through the formalities. Your used boat might come with a limited warranty if you buy it from a brokerage, but private transactions will usually be sold as seen. Brokerages will also ensure that the legalities of ownership transfer are taken care of too. If you buy privately be sure to get enough documentation and legal reassurance as this is entirely your own responsibility in this circumstance.

Top tips for buying a pre-loved boat

- Compare lots of boats before compiling a wish list of features and specifications.
- Make sure your finance is in place before negotiating a purchase.
- Brokerage fees are usually paid by the seller so confirm this before you shake hands on the deal.
- Your new boat is unlikely to be in A1 condition and is unlikely to feature the latest technology and kit. Be ready to spend money on repairs and upgrading old equipment once the boat is yours. A list of approximate prices for the most common work can be found in Chapter 8.
- Remember that most novice fit outs and paint jobs will be of poorer quality than those done by professionals.
- Make sure you know what is included in the price and what will be removed from the boat post sale.
- The listed price is very rarely the final purchase price. Haggling is usually to be expected, but be sure to haggle sensibly. The best deals are always the ones where both parties are satisfied by the negotiations.
- Maintaining a good relationship with the previous owner is a good idea as they can be very helpful during the first few months of ownership.

Boat buying season

Like convertible cars, boats are seemingly more expensive during the boating season from April to October.

Ex-hire boats

Some hire companies sell off their older boats as they upgrade their fleet. These can be a bargain and are usually well maintained. They will undoubtedly have taken some punishment during their life in the hire fleet but, as hire companies will usually have the expertise to repair faults as they appear, most of the wear will be cosmetic. It is worth remembering that hire boats' layouts are usually specific to that purpose so be sure that this type of boat is suitable for you.

FINDING A BOAT

Internet

Before you jump in the car and head for the nearest canal it is worth swotting up a little. The quickest and easiest way to do this is on the Internet where there are thousands of boats for sale. Online brokers and boat sales sites feature countless boats for you to compare in all configurations of shape and size and fit out. The sheer number of boats for sale online means that you'll probably find the boat you eventually buy on the Internet.

By browsing boats online you can familiarise yourself with the options available and the terminology inherent in the process. Some sites even feature an information service to help you to decide what suits you best and there is plenty of information in the next part of this book to guide you in these important decisions. For now your aim should be to look at as many different boats as possible so that you get a real understanding of the options that are available.

You can also find narrowboats for sale on auction websites such as eBay where, as with all auctions, you can sometimes land on a bargain. A level of caution is recommended if you're looking at buying a boat by this method however. The competitive nature of auction bidding, coupled with the pressure of bidding against the clock, can cause some buyers to rush in and bid too much. Speed and narrowboats are rarely good bedfellows and the art of purchasing is not usually best rushed. Never buy a boat that you have not inspected in person.

More conventional purchasing methods may be better suited to those new to the world of boating as there is much to consider and negotiate before any money changes hands. It is usually better to leave the high-pressure auction purchases to those with the experience to make quick and accurate buying decisions.

Pros and cons of buying online

Pros

- Plenty of boats to peruse
- You can become familiar with boating features and terminology
- Economic use of search time and money

Cons

- Pictures are not as useful as stepping aboard
- Ads may be out of date or expired
- You may find your ideal boat is many miles away

Boat brokerages

Looking at pictures of boats online is all well and good, but eventually you will need a close look at the real thing. Arranging to view a selection of boats individually will usually incur a serious amount of travel, and so a more efficient way is to visit one of the large boat brokerage companies. With several large brokers located around the country, a visit to one of these enables you to board and inspect several boats at the same time in the same place.

Always view a boat in person before making an offer.

The benefits of stepping aboard to view a boat cannot be over emphasised. You will find that there is a vast amount of variance in the type and quality of boats available within your budget and only viewing them in person will enable you to discern their suitability and value.

Pros and cons of using a brokerage

Pros

- Many boats are available to view in one location
- Opportunity to step aboard and investigate first hand
- All features and facilities will be comprehensively listed by the agent
- Broker ensures smooth sale transition and legality of the transaction
- Finance provision or recommendations available through the broker

Cons

- Fewer boats to view than are available online
- Brokerage has a vested interest in the sale
- Brokerages charge a commission from the seller and so this can increase the asking price

Marinas

Visit your local mooring spot or large marina and speak to the boaters there. They'll often have the most up to date information about the boats that are available locally and they are usually a good source of boating knowledge and experience. Many marinas also have an on-site brokerage facility and you can often find boats for sale there too. Be sure to visit the local marina where you would ideally like to moor your boat. It is possible to kill two birds with one stone by buying a boat from there with the option to take over the mooring too.

Pros and cons of buying via a marina

Pros

- Marina will often know the boats that they have for sale very well
- Good knowledge of boats for sale in the local area
- Possibility of securing a mooring

Cons

- Fewer boats for sale on site
- Possible vested interest issues

Magazines and other publications

Despite the growing popularity of the Internet, many narrowboaters still prefer old school media methods for buying and selling boats. All of the glossy boating mags feature classifieds where you will find a fair collection of boats for sale, as does the popular canal newspaper *Towpath Talk*. Besides, as someone with an interest in boats, you'll likely be buying these magazines anyway. Boat clubs and societies that publish journals and newsletters are another source for boating small ads. These are certainly worth a look if you are in the market as there might just be a bargain on your doorstep.

Pros and cons of using magazines

Pros

- Convenient searching
- Potential to find boats not listed elsewhere

Cons

- Limited number of boats listed
- Small (if any) photographs
- Limited information in listing

Word of mouth

If you're serious about buying a boat then it makes lots of sense to find a trusted mentor with plenty of experience to guide and advise you through the process, and it would be very sensible to consider their recommendations thoroughly. They'll likely know of a handful of boats for sale in their local area and will probably have plenty of information that can help you to discern their suitability and negotiate a fair price. Recommendations from within your expert's network will be similarly useful, and many boaters have a decent-sized boating network to tap into. The waterways community have highly efficient methods of communication and it is very possible that you'll get to hear about boats that are about to go on the market before they are advertised.

In addition to the first degree recommendations you can also ask boaters and boating business owners that you meet on your travels. Again, they'll be aware of local boats for sale and will probably offer information about the boats' heritage and history. Be mindful of any recommenders that have a vested interest in the sale of the boat, but general boat buying caution and thorough research will guard you against most unpleasant surprises.

Pros and cons of using word of mouth

Pros

- Find boats before they are advertised elsewhere
- In depth knowledge of boats' history and heritage
- Expert opinion of the boat that is for sale

Cons

- Possible vested interest concerns
- Hit and miss prospecting style

FIRM UP YOUR DELIVERY DATES

Sam: Nb *Knot Hrd Work*

'I bought an ex-hire fleet boat that I found online. I liked the idea of getting an ex-hire boat as they are invariably well maintained; for example, I know the hull on my boat was blacked (with a protective coating) every year without fail – unlike most boats. Buying the boat was very exciting, but if I had to do it again I would do a few things differently. The first headache I encountered was when the collection date for my boat was postponed. I'd arranged for the boat to be repainted before I took it away and delays at the boatyard delayed my pick-up date by some weeks.

'This had a knock-on effect that I had not thought of at the time, but would be sure to check now. The delay in picking the boat up meant that the waterways' winter maintenance schedule for locks and bridges had begun. I found that I was now stuck on the wrong side of a bridge repair, meaning another delay lasting several weeks.

'Once those issues were sorted it was relatively plain sailing, barring a few lessons on a very steep learning curve. If I were to offer advice to new buyers I would recommend agreeing not only a price, but a delivery date when negotiating a boat sale. I'd strongly recommend finding out how much fuel, water and gas is aboard and how long it has been there. I'd also recommend finding out if your boat is flat bottomed or keeled, particularly if you are moving the boat by road as we were. The transport company will need to bring the right type of stabilising blocks for a keeled hull and won't be best pleased if you previously told them it was flat.'

WHEN SIZE IS EVERYTHING

Phil and Nina: Short boat *Wharfe*

'We liked the idea of having extra space, but we didn't want to buy a wide-beamed narrowboat. Wide-beam narrowboat is something of a contradiction in terms and seemed to spoil the iconic design style that is a narrowboat – a bit like making an E-Type Jaguar estate car.

'In the end we bought a Leeds Liverpool Short Boat as these had the wider beam and interior space we were looking for, but have a specific design and style that makes them perfect for the waterways they were used on. Our mooring is on the Leeds Liverpool Canal so it all seems to have worked out well.'

DO YOUR HOMEWORK WHEN BUYING ONLINE

Steve and Eileen: Nb *Sophie*

'It is often said that your ideal boat will be the second one that you buy, having learned a lot from owning your first boat,' says Eileen. 'This was certainly true for us and so we had a very good idea of exactly what we were looking for when viewing boats online. Having looked at hundreds of potential boats we finally chose six that we wanted to view in person and they were located all over the country.

'We planned a road trip to go see them all and we were really surprised at how different some of them were to what we had expected. It's amazing what you can't tell from a photograph, and remember, we had been very fussy when we had been making our selection. One boat in particular was truly awful. It was dirty, smelly and much shabbier looking than it had appeared in the photographs. The paint job was old and was very poorly done. It was also full of dead flies. This would all have been forgivable and easily remedied, but the asking price was way above what we thought the boat was actually worth.

'Another required a proper look around before we could appreciate how unsuitable it was. There was a white carpet installed, which to us seemed a ridiculous choice for a boat. Sure, we could have replaced it, but there were other issues too, such as a bathroom that was dominated by a full-size bath and having nothing else in the room besides it. The layout was clunky and impractical too. While it ticked all of our boxes from what we could tell from the photos, a quick tour showed that it was nowhere near the boat we wanted.'

REMEMBER WHY YOU ARE BUYING A BOAT

Brett and Jane: Dutch barge *Boadicea*

Brett and Jane originally intended to buy a sailaway or a second-hand boat in need of renovation, but after doing some research they scrapped the idea.

'After looking at a good selection of boats we began to think that a sailaway or renovation was the only way to get the boat that we really wanted,' said Brett. 'I'm pretty handy with a tool kit and so the idea of saving some money and getting a boat we could change to suit our own specifications seemed like a good idea at the time.

'We looked at lots of boats to check if our budget would stretch to the purchase price and the cost of renovation, and very few would be viable purchases. Given that we intended to live aboard we also had to consider the costs of accommodation while the boat was uninhabitable. These proved to be significant.

'However, the real clincher was the amount of stress that would be involved in running a home and fitting out a boat. The amount of work involved would have eaten all of our free time and more. Plus it would delay the ribbon-cutting moment when we could step aboard the boat for good. We decided that one of the main reasons we were buying a boat was for the serenity and slow-paced lifestyle, and doing up a boat had great potential to spoil that notion before we had even begun.'

LEGALITIES, CHECKS AND THE BOAT BUYING PROCESS

Once you have found the boat of your dreams it is time to get serious. There are plenty of hazards along the way between here and the beginning of your life as blissful boat owners and it is important that you get things right.

Sorting the paperwork

Proof of ownership

It doesn't happen often, but sometimes boats are sold fraudulently by people who don't actually own them. Unlike with a car, there is no official ownership document and so it is up to the buyer to reassure themselves that the seller is legitimate. A Bill of Sale is the first place to start. It would be foolish to dispose of such a receipt and so you should be extremely sceptical of any boat and 'owner' that cannot produce one. In addition you should ask to see some paperwork history – old licence invoices, mooring agreements, insurance documents, and invoices for work that has been done. Not only will this convince you of legitimate ownership but it will also give you an indication of the condition of the boat and the level of care the owner has invested in it.

Recreational Craft Directive (RCD) Declaration of Conformity

Since June 1998, all new boats require a Recreational Craft Directive (RCD) Declaration of Conformity when new. This declaration confirms that it has been built to the directive and should list the standards used in the build process. If you have fitted out a new shell yourself the shell requires a declaration when sold to you, but if you use the boat yourself it does not need to comply with the Directive. However, if you sell the boat before five years of it first floating then you will need to issue an RCD Declaration of Conformity before you can sell it. A Declaration of Conformity may be used to licence the boat with the Navigation Authority instead of a BSS Certificate in some circumstances, but if you are fitting the boat out yourself you may need a BSS Certificate (in the absence of a Declaration of Conformity) to licence the boat.

BSS Certificate (sometimes called a BSC or Boat Safety Scheme Certificate)

When a boat is four years old it will require a BSS Certificate to show that it complies with all of the safety requirements of the scheme. A Certificate lasts for four years and a boat cannot be licenced without a current BSS Certificate (or Declaration of Conformity – see above).

Once you have satisfied yourself that the boat and owner are bona-fide then the buying process can start. Predictably, this stage is also fraught with potential pitfalls and it is not

CASE STUDY: THE BOAT BUYING PROCESS – BROKERAGE

Sheila Smith, ABNB BOAT BROKERAGE

'A majority of people who buy a boat will get a survey done before buying. In these circumstances the boat will be withdrawn from sale "subject to survey" allowing you some time to be reassured by the results once the survey is completed. Sometimes the survey will highlight issues that were not apparent when the boat was advertised and this may result in some price negotiation. This can be frustrating for everyone concerned so we always encourage those selling boats to be completely honest about its condition.

'It is the responsibility of the buyer to arrange and pay for a survey. It is not appropriate for a broker to recommend a surveyor, although we can provide you with a list of local surveyors. Some sellers will have a recent survey and they may allow you to look at this instead of paying for a new one. This is a matter of trust between you and the seller, and you should be able to contact the surveyor for reassurance and the possibility of having the survey transferred to you. If a recent survey report isn't available, for the sake of a few hundred pounds you may consider commissioning your own survey for complete reassurance. After all, it could save you many thousands of pounds, so a few hundred is a small price to pay.

'The surveyor will usually need to liaise with the boat owner or the brokerage to gain access. Brokers and local surveyors are usually well acquainted and so communication between these parties is usually slick and efficient. If the boat requires dry dock or crane-lift for an out of water survey, this will need to be timetabled and arrangements made, but again, a good brokerage will be well used to making these arrangements and most of the larger outfits have such facilities on site or nearby.

'From the buyer's perspective, make sure you know how much it is going to cost to complete any repairs, including those that are highlighted in the survey. Balance these against the boat's price tag and be pragmatic. Don't forget that the broker will have priced the boat according to condition and so consideration will already have been made for some obvious defects, such as ageing paintwork and therefore this would not be a reasonable justification for a price reduction. It is easy to fall in love with a boat, and this is something that we encourage because boat buying is such an emotional and joyful experience. There's no need to be hard-nosed. However, make sure that your heart isn't ruling your head and destroying your wallet.'

simply a case of handing over your cash and floating off into the sunset. There is plenty of potential for disappointment and regret, but thankfully both you and the seller can be protected to a great degree and following a tried and tested vending process.

If you are buying from a brokerage, the broker will have pre-written templates and selling agreements to ensure the process goes smoothly and you would be strongly advised to follow their guidance. When buying through a brokerage you might not be able to speak directly to the boat owner so as to protect the interests of everyone involved in the process. A good broker will have the experience and expertise to ensure the transaction flows smoothly and they certainly earn their commission.

Getting a survey

Survey prices depend largely on the size of the boat and the type of survey. The choices are: Full Survey, Hull Survey or In-water/Interior Survey. The cost is likely to be between £300 and £600, depending on boat, location and surveyor.

You can find a surveyor online, in the waterways press or by speaking to local boaters. The *Towpath Telegraph* is often a good source of information and advice.

For a minimal fee, surveyors will often be able to transfer ownership of a recent survey to your name when you have purchased a boat.

PAYING FOR YOUR BOAT

Apart from those with a bank balance healthy enough to pay cash, most boat buyers will need to raise the funds to purchase their new boat. Prospective liveaboard owners will sometimes fund their purchase using the equity they pocket when they sell their land-based house. This was a good option to consider when property prices were appreciating sharply, such as in the late 1990s and early 2000s. However, as house prices began to stagnate and fall, many homeowners realised that they had no equity in their home and so this line of finance was severed.

Others fund their purchase by selling assets such as cars or investment shares, but for many people it is necessary to find a source of finance. Some boat brokerages are also licenced credit brokers, providing finance options from a selection of specialist marine finance companies. Be aware that these finance agreements (or 'marine mortgages' as they are often called) are secured against the purchased asset and you could lose your boat if you default. Some are secured against other assets such as your home, so beware and check the small print before you sign. Another option is an unsecured loan from a bank or other financier. These will rarely be secured against your boat and can often have a comparable interest rate.

Other than these commonly executed methods you will need to get creative. Second jobs, the bank of mum and dad and extreme frugality are options you might wish to consider. Paying in instalments through a private agreement is not unknown, but fraught with risk for both buyer and seller, so be sure to do your homework and be supremely confident if you are to take a more unconventional route to purchase.

The transaction

Once you have seen a survey there may be some negotiation to be done regarding the final price. As with cars and houses, the list price is rarely the final figure. If the owner has fully disclosed the repairs and outstanding work that needs to be done then negotiation will be purely a case of haggling. While there is no typical or standard amount to discount, there are several points that will influence your offer, such as your own financial position, the eagerness of the owner to sell and comparisons with similar boats that you are considering. Factor in the cost and inconvenience of any work to be done and you should be able to come to a mutually agreeable price. Remember that there are plenty of benefits to be had by keeping the previous owner on speed dial as there is always some reason to call them once the boat is yours. A good sales process leaves everybody satisfied with the outcome.

The handover

Every boat has its idiosyncrasies, so some brokerages arrange a handover with the old owner which can be very useful.

If you are buying the boat from a brokerage you will be asked to sign an 'Agreement to Purchase' and will usually have to pay a percentage (around 5–10 per cent) of the purchase price. The agreement outlines the time scales for the sale and any fine details that are relevant. If there is work to be carried out prior to sale it is wise to ensure that these are included in the agreement and provision is made in case the work overruns.

From there it is simply a case of transferring the remaining amount into the seller's account. Sometimes this is done via the broker in order for them to extract their fee, but ownership is never transferred to the buyer until all of the funds have cleared in the seller's account or the broker's client account. Once funds have cleared the seller will complete a Bill of Sale (which you should be sure to keep) and the boat is yours. Only at this point does the boat become your property and you are free to move it, alter it or paint it bright pink, should you so wish.

Congratulations. You are now the owner of a shiny (or not so shiny) new boat. From now on it is your responsibility and you are liable for all of the associated costs. You need to ensure that it is licensed, insured and has a BSS Certificate or RCD Declaration of Conformity. You need to ensure that you are listed as the registered owner with the Canal and River Trust. (This is easily done online.) You'll also need to pay for a mooring and you should consider breakdown coverage if you don't have the requisite engineer skills. Now the fun *really* starts!

SHARED OWNERSHIP

If owning a boat that you will only use occasionally seems like a waste of money then shared ownership could be the answer. Many companies now run shared ownership schemes enabling you to spread the cost of boat ownership. Maintenance expenditure, administration costs and other expenses are divided amongst the syndicate, an arrangement that suits those who wish to minimise the hassle and expense of boating.

There are other benefits too. By purchasing only a part share of a boat, rather than the whole, it's likely you'll be able to afford a better quality boat than you would if you purchased one outright on your own. Also, by spreading the cost of ownership over a long period, your usage costs are considerably less than if you had hired for the same time slots. Of course, this is only true if you keep your share for the long term, but most schemes also allow you to sell your share in the boat to someone else, should you wish to do so.

On the downside, some might feel that the freedom and joy of boat ownership is somewhat diminished if your usage is limited because someone else is using the boat when you want it. Your usage needs to be booked in advance, much as you would for a holiday boat hire. However, if you're the type who likes to pack a case and get boating on a whim, then perhaps shared ownership isn't for you.

Carefree Cruising is a boat share company that has been established since 2002. Owned by boating enthusiasts with many years of experience, the company has 15 different boat syndicates based at Elton Moss Wharf in Cheshire, Welton Haven Marina in Northants and Aston Marina in Staffordshire. Christina Farrall explains the ins and outs of shared ownership.

Our shared ownership scheme is exactly that – you own a share of an actual boat rather than just the entitlement to use it for a period of time as you might find with other 'timeshare' like schemes. You can own your share for as long as you like and sell your share whenever you want to, after your first year. We offer a comprehensive management service that means that you can enjoy your boat without the stress of being involved in the boat's administration.

'Our usage calendar enables flexible cruising. You decide what time of year you wish to use the boat and for how long and we will help you find a share that suits you. Each syndicate rotates the picking order annually, which means that you're not restricted to the same time slot every year. Co-owners are also encouraged to keep in touch with each other and adjust the calendar to swap usage slots if they would like to.

'Each syndicate has its own dedicated bank account and the size of the expenditure budget is decided at the syndicate AGM. Each part owner pays only their relative proportion of the narrowboat's annual running costs. This would typically reduce the running cost per week's ownership to around £375, making it cheaper than narrowboat hire. This covers all aspects of the boat's running costs including winter maintenance and our management fee, you just have to pay for the pump-out and diesel at the end of your trip.

CHRISTINA FARRALL, CAREFREE CRUISING

Shared ownership FAQ

How many owners will I share my boat with?
Typically there will be 12 to 14 syndicate members. This will vary slightly depending on the number of weeks individuals hold. The syndicate is limited to a maximum of 16 owners.

How much does it cost?
Prices start from as little as £1000 per share. This buys a two-week share in the off-peak season that is being sold by an existing syndicate. For a two-week share in a brand new boat you'll pay around £4000. That's just a small selection of the options we offer and it is a good idea to speak to us directly so that we can find the best option for your individual circumstance.

What happens if I want to book the same weeks as someone else in the syndicate?
The best way to avoid disappointment is to buy the right type of share in the first place. Boating is addictive and it is easy to covet more time and better slots than you have originally purchased. We have different types of share depending if you want high season, off season or school holidays.

Once you're part of a syndicate the picking order is rotated each year, maximising the availability of the exact dates you want. We've found this to be the fairest and most efficient way to ensure everyone gets the boating experience they want. (Believe it or not, some companies even allocate usage by picking dates out of a hat!) You even have the chance to swap and change your allocation. Co-owners are regularly in touch with others in the syndicate and there is generally some give and take in the calendar.

What about repairs?
Repairs and maintenance are paid for from a maintenance fund, into which all syndicate

A busy day on the canal.

members contribute depending on their share size. Accidental damage is paid by the responsible party and the boat is fully insured.

How are the perishables paid for, such as fuel and gas?

Each user must make sure the boat is ready for the next by cleaning the boat, refuelling, pumping out the toilet and refilling the water tanks. Gas bottles are changed when they are empty and paid for from the syndicate fund.

Will my boat be painted in the corporate livery of the share scheme company?

Some shared ownership companies do this, but we do not. The boats are named and painted to the specifications of the co-owners in the syndicate. They look like any other privately owned boat on the waterways system. Our boats are also a much higher specification than any hire boat. Hire boats need to withstand quite rough usage by novices who do not have vested interest in looking after the vessel, so hire companies are understandably mindful of this when fitting out their boats. Our boats are cared for by the people who own them and so they are fitted out and maintained to a much higher spec with washer driers, dishwashers, solid oak floors and granite worktops being standard features on all of our new boats.

2 TRYING IT OUT: HIRE BOAT HOLIDAYS

Hiring a boat is a tried and tested stepping-stone towards boat ownership and many boat owners will have caught the boating bug in exactly this fashion. Hiring a boat is highly recommended to anyone considering buying a boat of their own. By spending some time aboard you can fully appreciate the highs and lows that ownership involves and hiring is an easy and enjoyable way to accomplish this.

FINDING A GOOD HIRE COMPANY

Choosing the right hire boat company will largely depend on where you want to explore and you'll likely find a handful of choices in most areas. Once you have chosen a location then a little research can help you to decide which hire company suits your needs best.

History

Find out how long the hire company has been in business. A long history of hiring is usually a good indicator that they offer a good service.

It's a good idea to visit the hire site to view the boats and meet the staff as the quality of both can vary greatly. If you're new to boating then you'll be reliant on the staff for instruction and support so it is worth checking them out before you hand over any money. View the boats for cosmetic wear and tear and general maintenance too as these can be a good indicator of the service you are likely to receive.

Learning how everything works.

Back deck training before you set off is the foundation stone of a good hire-boat holiday. Not only should you ensure that you get good instruction, but it is also important that you listen well and ask questions if necessary. 'Instructing hirers is a fine balance between giving them enough instruction to stay safe and happy, and overloading them with too much information.' So says Andrew Bestall from Snaygill Boats in Skipton. 'It goes without saying that everything we tell you during the instruction session is important, so it's vital

Be sure to choose the right kind of hire boat for your needs.

that you listen to it all. Yes, you might be excited because you're off on your jollies with your mates, but this is the serious bit. Please pay attention! And don't be afraid to ask questions. We won't bite!'

The back deck instruction must deliver enough information to ensure your boating holiday is safe and much of its content is required by law. They are obliged to explain what can go wrong and what you can do to avoid it. It might sound a little scary, but statistically these accidents rarely happen. Following the instructions you are given and using common sense will keep you safe from all but the most random dangers.

Find out what facilities are available aboard the boat. You might want a good old wood-burning stove, only to find that some companies eschew

them for safety reasons. What type of toilet will you find on board, and is it to your liking?
A radio, TV and DVD player might be important, although in reality you'll often struggle to get a good TV signal. Good hire companies know that it is often the little things that can make or break a boating holiday. From storing your suitcases so that you don't have to take them with you to offering baby cots or cot-sided beds – the details matter. Some companies will even hire out bikes, wet weather gear and all sorts of other additional services.

Car parking availability is an important consideration too. Although many hire centres have ample parking, some restrict the number of vehicles that can be parked on site. Some have no parking facilities at all, leaving you with the cost of long-term parking added to your holiday.

Check what's included

- The fine print in the hire agreement is usually worth reading.

- Check if your fuel usage is included in the hire cost, or if you will be charged for it on your return.

- Does the hire cost include a damage waiver insurance to safeguard you against any bumps, scrapes or broken windows? Most hire companies include this in the cost but some don't so it is worth checking.

- Bedding, towels and other sundries are usually included, but again, check this is the case before setting off for your trip.

- Does the company offer a 24-hour call out service? It's unlikely you'll need it, but if you do need it you'll be sorry if it isn't available.

- Can you take pets on board, and is there a charge for this?

- What is their cancellation policy? You'll usually find that you will be required to pay in full in all but the most extreme circumstances.

- Arriving late will often mean you miss part of your holiday, particularly if you do not arrive until after the hire base is closed.

- Returning the boat late after your holiday will always be very expensive.

GETTING OUT AND ABOUT

Boat handling can be daunting if you have never done it before, but as long as you follow the simple safety advice there's not really much to worry about. If you're new to hiring it makes sense to start with a smaller boat to make life easier, rather than loading your holiday with stress by trying to master a bigger boat. You'll soon get used to handling these smaller vessels

Hire boats at their mooring.

and will likely wonder why you didn't go for a bigger boat, but avoiding stress is surely an important part of enjoying your holiday.

If you already have some experience of boating, then sometimes the opposite is true. 'A six berth is fine for six people, but it is better for four!' suggests Jo Dortona from Snaygill Boats. 'The extra storage space and wiggle room can make all the difference, particularly if you're part of a group.'

As with any British holiday, the weather will always be a factor and you should always be ready for it to rain at any time of year. It is said that there is no such thing as bad weather, only inappropriate clothing, and this is particularly true of boating as there is still good fun to be had. Bear in mind that wet weather boating can be a slippery business; so take care, but otherwise, go for it! There'll be much less boating traffic for a start and you will often find that you have the water to yourself.

Windy weather is a different matter. Boating is easy enough while you are underway, but

41

A narrowboat holiday can be most convivial.

manoeuvring for mooring, locks, bridges and turning around can be a nightmare when it is windy. The best advice if it is really windy is to moor up, hunker down and entertain yourself by watching other boats proceeding sideways past you.

Getting into the groove

The most important thing that you should remember as a hire boater is that it is not a race. Leaving behind the customary rush of modern lifestyles is vitally important if you are to enjoy your hire boat holiday and so you should have no need for speed, high revving engines or that stressful feeling that you are going to be late. Make no plans further ahead than the next few hours and favour the

least taxing option when faced with a choice. Planning your journey is useful, but be ready to dispense with the idea that you must make it to a specific place by a specific time if things don't go to plan, because invariably something will happen to disrupt your plans.

While we are on the subject of speed and rushing, it would be remiss not to mention the bugbear of many boaters – the speed at which one passes moored boats. Hire boaters are often accused of speeding past moored boats, despite the fact that many non-hirers are similarly guilty. Your hire company will invariably inform you to slow down past moored boats, but how slow is slow enough? The problem is usually one of perception. New boaters are often inclined to go

Narrowboating – a very British holiday.

faster than is necessary, acceptable or allowed, and so from their perspective, they will have slowed significantly. To the experienced (and stationary) moored boater, the passing boat will still be going way too fast.

Bear in mind that slowing the engine at the last moment will not be sufficient. Boats do not decelerate like cars and it takes a while for your boat to slow to a reasonable passing speed, so be sure to slow down way in advance. Remember that it is the water your boat is pushing that disrupts the moored boats on the bank-side, not your revs or your speed per se.

The fool-proof means of slowing sufficiently is to slow down incrementally, starting the process

very early. By the time you reach the moored boat you should aim to be just above tick-over; the point where the gears leave neutral and the engine has just kicked in to turn the propeller. Your boat and the water around you will be going slowly enough to keep everyone happy and there can be no complaint.

The worst boaters?

Hire boaters are often unfairly besmirched for their poor handling skills, with the blame being laid at the feet of the hire company and the amount of instruction that new hirers receive. Complainers would do well to remember that they were once new to boating and that we all had to learn at some point in the past. Without the hire boat industry it is likely that the canal system could not survive and so perhaps the complainers should be thanking, encouraging and helping hirers instead. Indeed many regular boaters are of the opinion that hire boaters are not the worst offenders for lack of courtesy on the canal. That honour perhaps lies with the occasional 'weekend boater' profile. These have likely owned a boat for several years and so feel like old-hand experts, but use their boat too rarely to become practised or proficient. While hirers are usually humble enough to admit their errors, 'weekenders' often have a higher opinion of their boat handling than is warranted. Perhaps more courtesy, consideration and friendliness is required from all who use the waterways network, whether hirers, owners, expert or novice. After all, the tranquillity and beauty of boating is valuable to us all and complaining is hardly conducive.

Jo Dortona, Snaygill Boats

Curfew

Running your engine before 8am and after 8pm is frowned upon and against the guidelines issued by the Canal and River Trust.

HIRE BOATING FAQ

Q. How much does it cost to hire a boat?
A. It very much depends on how many people are hiring, how many berths you require, how long you want to hire for and the time of year you want to hire. It's a good idea to know how many people, what size boat you want and when you want to hire before you contact the hire company. It's a question our receptionists dread if the caller doesn't know the answer to at least some of the qualifying questions.

Many narrowboat owners are former hire boaters.

Hiring during the off-season autumn months can be a most tranquil and beautiful holiday.

Our small 'day boats' with no sleeper facilities can cost as little as £125 per day.

If you're looking for a midweek short break for up to four people early in the season, you'll spend around £460.

For the same boat during the high season you'll pay around £670.

If you want a bigger boat for up to six people, during high season for a whole week the cost is nearer £1450.

(Prices correct at time of going to press)

Q. Can I go boating if I am disabled or elderly?
A. Of course! Depending on your mobility and ability you might need to press-gang some crew to help with mooring, locks or bridges, but as long as you can get on and off the boat OK then you'll be fine. Boating generally requires two able-bodied people, but a single-handed experienced boater can deal with most aspects of boating alone. Let the hire company know in advance and they will be able to advise you regarding access.

Q. Do I need holiday insurance?
A. Yes. Hire companies cannot offer travel insurance. The boat is usually covered by a damage waiver but travel/holiday insurance is vital to cover for theft, injury, cancellation or other issues. It is often forgotten by hirers.

Q. Can I bring my pet?
A. Most hire companies allow this although some charge an extra cleaning premium. Dogs are usually fine aboard but we do not recommend bringing cats or other animals. In our experience cats will often disappear if they can escape the boat and some are never seen again. It's just not worth it.

Slowing down and easing back is the key to a good hire boat holiday.

Q. Do we need to bring bedding or towels?
A. We provide both bedding and towels, but a few companies do not. It's worth checking.

Q. How about kitchen equipment? Is that included too?
A. Ours are fully fitted, but if you're unsure, just ask. You should be able to see an inventory of what is on board the boat.

Q. Can I bring my straighteners/curlers/ microwave/power hungry appliance?
A. We strongly recommend that you leave them at home.

Q. What if I can't live without my George Forman Grill?
A. If you *must* bring appliances such as this we strongly advise that you consult with your hire company. They'll tell you the best means to use it without running out of power. Best of luck with that.

Q. Do you provide life jackets?
A. Yes, all hire companies must provide life jackets.

Q. How far can we get?
A. That depends on many factors – experience, how much crew you have, the weather and, most interestingly, how quickly you relax into the boating philosophy. Boating is all about the journey, not the destination! If you really must know, you can look at a waterways map and approximate 15 minutes for each mile, lock and swing bridge. It's a very rough estimation but that's boating for you.

Smaller day boats are fun and easy to manoeuvre.

Q. We broke one of the boat windows by accident. Is it going to cost us a lot of money?
A. Not usually as most companies have insurance to cover accidental damage. Some don't, however, so it is worth checking.

Q. Actually, we broke the window because we were drunk and messing around. Are we still covered?
A. Ah! No. Accidental damage is insured but if the damage was caused by misuse then there will be a charge.

Q. So, you wouldn't recommend us getting drunk and messing around?
A. Nope. Have fun, but if you misuse the boat, cause damage or distress to other boaters then we'll reclaim the boat and your holiday is over.

Q. OK we'll be sensible, but is it easy to break or damage the boat?
A. Not if you're sensible. Keep an eye on the display dials, take your time and use your common sense. If you're in charge of the boat or the locks, stay sober. Going too fast and over-heating is the most frequently experienced problem. And don't cruise at night. There's no need and it's no fun.

Q. What do you get called out for most?
A. When hirers lock the keys inside the boat.

47

Top tips for enjoying your hire boat holiday

Buy and use a waterways map

Following your progress on the map means you will always know where you are, making it easier to plan your stops, shopping trips and your visits to pubs and restaurants. It is also vital to know where you are if you break down or have a problem as the hire company will need to find you. And if you call them out, stay where you are until they arrive!

Shower while the engine is running

Water pumps and shower drainage gulpers have power hungry motors. A common mistake is for everyone on board to shower when they moor up after a day's cruising before setting out for the evening. This will likely mean that you run out of power later on in the evening when you return to the boat. The solution is to shower earlier in the day, or at least to leave the engine running until everyone is showered.

Pack your stuff away before setting off

When you first get on the boat, put your stuff away and leave your cases at the hire centre if possible. At the beginning of each cruising day, pack away any kit so that you aren't stepping over it or around it while you're underway. Boats get very untidy very quickly and this can be a real pain if you don't stay on top of it.

Use every tap you come across

Keep your water tank topped up wherever possible. You never know where the next one will be.

Know your winding hole

This is not so important if you are on a circular route, but vital if you need to turn the boat around to get back to base on time. Your waterways map is your friend.

A waterways map is a vital piece of kit.

Keep an eye on the kids

Statistically, any boy between the age of 10 and 15 years old will get wet at some point in the holiday. (Yes, it is usually the boys.)

Pay attention during the hire instruction talk

This cannot be emphasised enough.

Get a little sneaky practice

Hiring a small 'day boat' before you go out on a larger vessel is a very good idea. Day boats are small and really easy to handle; and once you have that experience then steering a larger boat is much easier. With little day boat practice you will look like a gifted boat-handling natural to those who don't know you had some practice beforehand.

Do less shopping

Don't bother bringing loads of groceries on board. Your best bet is to eat out whenever possible to avoid the cooking and washing-up chores. Keep fresh produce shopping to a minimum because the fridge will be quite small and the freezer will probably be a tiny ice box. You might like to have your shopping delivered to the hire base to save handling it twice.

Bring less stuff

The boat is unlikely to be near a convenient place to unload your car, meaning you'll have to carry anything you bring for some distance.

Safety first

A torch and good shoes are a must, ideally hiking shoes, but certainly something non-slip with a sensibly low heel. When you leave the boat to go to the pub or to the restaurant it will be light and you will be sober. When you arrive back you might be tipsy and it will be dark. Staggering around in heels without a torch isn't recommended.

Kids on board should always wear a lifejacket.

Call for help if you need it

If you're worried or if you think there is a problem, call the hire base for advice. They'll put you straight or sort you out. Don't be shy, they're there to help.

Use utilities sparingly

Water, gas and electricity power are not on infinite feed like they are at home. Think about what you are going to do with the rubbish you produce too.

Sturdy boots and a hand torch are boating essentials.

The Narrowboat Guide

Be ready to forget your itinerary

Use it only as a guide. Plan ahead by a few hours at most. Stop to smell any roses you might encounter. Explore nice places for as long as you like. Spend time meeting new people and don't be in a rush to get going. This is the best of boating. There's no hurry!

Play fair

There's plenty of work to be done so make sure you do your fair share. Whether it is steering, working locks and bridges or just cooking and washing up; find some task and do your bit. Boats are small and petty issues can become disproportionately frustrating when people are in such close proximity. There's nowhere to go if you need space, so do your bit and do your best to get along.

Choose your cruising crew carefully

There's no en-suite aboard a boat and so toileting, changing clothes and showers are less private than you might be used to. It's all part of the fun but a little planning and consideration can go a long way. Close company for a week or more can test the best of friendships, so plan carefully, be considerate and have a back-up plan if necessary. Above all, be ready to forgive and forget. It's probably not a big deal in the grand scheme of things.

Plan ahead

If you have elderly or disabled crew members, it might be worth letting the hire base know in advance of your arrival. If you're lucky they might ensure that the boat is waiting in one of the more accessible mooring spots on site to make access easier.

Leave the candles at home

Boats rock and the candles can easily become a fire risk. Be very careful with disposable barbecues too. Don't light them on the boat as this will burn the paint and be sure to keep them raised off any grass surface.

Hire boat holiday checklist

- **Torch** – preferably a head torch so that hands are free
- **Boating clothes** – they could get ripped or stained
- **Wet and/or cold weather clothes**
- **Spare clothes** – in case you fall in
- **Suitable footwear** – waterproof walking boots are the best choice
- **Summer kit** – Shades, sunglasses, bug spray and sun tan lotion
- **Entertainment** – Music/DVDs/Books for those quiet evenings when you're moored out of town
- **Emergency numbers** – particularly the hire boat company's number
- **Map and local guides** – most hire companies provide these, but better safe than sorry
- **Easy-to-prepare food** – you don't want to spend ages cooking and eating out is always preferable
- **Mobile phones and chargers** – including car chargers as most boats run on 12v power
- **Dog kit** (if necessary) – treats, lead, poo bags, food, bowls, lifejacket
- **Camera** – to capture the endless beauty. Dawn and dusk are particularly beautiful on the inland waterways
- **Fishing gear** – If that's your thing. Be sure to get a licence from the post office beforehand
- **Bicycle** – if this is allowed (you may need to protect the paintwork on the roof)

Tony's towpath tales: Why are they dressed as pirates?

I'm sitting aboard my boat writing this chapter, looking out of my window at the boats going past on the Leeds and Liverpool Canal in Kildwick, near Skipton. It's near the end of the boating season, but there is still quite a lot of traffic going by, around half of which is made up of hire boat holidaymakers. There are three hire companies within a three-mile radius from here which, coupled with the fabulous rural location, means we see a lot of hire boats in this area.

The hire boat clientele seems to be split into three roughly distinct groups. First are the family holidaymakers; usually husband and wife with a nipper or two in tow who make their way quietly along the cut. Next come the retired narrowboating stalwarts who have likely been hiring for years or are ticking off the next line on their bucket-list before proceeding to bungee jumping or a trip to Las Vegas.

But my favourites are the stag and hen party hirers. You can hear them coming from quite a distance. In parties of up to a dozen, they're probably stocked up with alcohol and dressed in pirate gear and singing along to the radio. They'll be laid out on the roof and hanging out on the decks

and they won't have the slightest idea of what they're doing or where they're going or the faintest idea of waterways etiquette or protocol.

And why should they? They're usually young and excited and enjoying their first experience of boating on one of the most beautiful canals in the world. I've been doing this boating thing for a decade and it still excites me every time I slip from my mooring and head off up the cut. I'm well over 40 now and have long since disposed of my youthful exuberance, but if I was still 20, I'd be sipping beers and singing along with them all the way to Five Rise Locks. But I'm not, so I'll wave to and tell them that their costumes look fabulous and offer any advice that I can to keep them safe and happy. They'll interrupt my day for no more than a few minutes at a time, and if that's the extent of the disruption to my day then I have nothing of substance worth complaining about. I'm not quite an old fart yet, but I'm wistful of my youth and there are few things in this world more beautiful and inspiring than watching the next generation doing what they do best – having fun.

Do you know why they're dressed as pirates? Because they AAAARRRRRRR!!!!!

3 BOAT FEATURES AND FIXTURES

Depending on how you intend to use your boat, some boat features will be more useful or attractive than others. In this section we take a look at the most common features and fixtures you will find aboard, while our friendly panel of boaters will share their experiences and preferences. While everyone's circumstances and preferences will differ you might identify with some of the common boater profiles.

GAS

Correct storage of gas bottles is a legal requirement for boat safety test compliance. The lockers will be self-contained and have a drain hole which allows spilled gas to escape outside the boat. In many boats the gas bottles are stored in the very front of the hull inside a locker in the bow and accessed via a hatch and usually on the bow deck. Lockers at the back of the boat are often below the waterline and so these are usually half filled with water as the drain-hole needs to release spilled gas somewhere above the waterline.

Other boats have custom-built lockers in the bow, while some boats store their gas bottles in unusual places. All gas lockers will be self-contained and drain over the side through a hole in the hull, although there is no need for water in this case as the locker sits well above the waterline.

Above: A stock of gas bottles.
Below: Gas bottles securely stored in their locker.

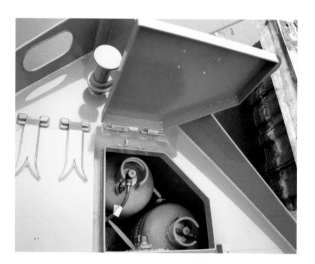

Getting gas bottles out of some lockers can be tricky.

NO EASY ACCESS

Carol: Nb *Caelmiri*

'The gas locker on my boat is in a hatch under the front bow. The bottles are so low down in the locker that I can't reach them, and even if I could I would not be able to lift them. Thankfully the staff at the boatyard are very helpful and always willing to remove and replace the bottles each time I buy a new one, so it is not much of an issue really.'

Gas safety is vitally important aboard your boat. These guidelines will help you to stay safe. (Thanks to www.boatsafetyscheme.org for some content.)

- Boat hulls are watertight and so act as good containers for escaped gas. Liquified petroleum gas (LPG) sinks in air and will spread into low-level, enclosed spaces such as cabins, cockpits, engine and bilge areas. Even small spaces such as cupboards or lockers can contain dangerous amounts of explosive vapour.
- Fit alarms and sensors to detect gas, carbon monoxide and smoke. Optical sensor smoke alarms with hush buttons and 'sealed for life' batteries are best for boats. Check that your carbon monoxide detector is suitable for marine use and meets the EN50291 standard. Test the alarms when you are on board. Never disconnect them or remove working batteries.
- Check that your gas locker drain is not blocked with leaves, spiders' nests or other debris. Be sure not to store items in the gas locker that could block vents, damage gas equipment or cause a spark.
- Check flexible hoses for damage or deterioration. If you're in any doubt about their condition, get them professionally checked and renewed.
- For boat owners the simplest way of having that assurance is to install a bubble tester and use it routinely. The examiner can also use this device to check the system is gas tight too, if it is installed correctly.
- Find a qualified gas specialist to service, refurbish or install gas appliances.
- Never store gas bottles anywhere inside your boat, including in the cratch. Only store gas bottles in the appropriate lockers.

Running out of gas

Changeover valve fittings will switch from one gas bottle to the spare as the first runs out. Whilst this is very convenient it can catch you unawares if you don't keep an eye on your gas supplies, leaving you with two empty bottles. Some find it preferable to manually connect a new bottle when the old one runs out as this acts as a reminder to buy a replacement.

WATER

Whilst some boats store gas bottles in the nose, others use this space as an integral water tank. Others have the water tank fitted slightly further aft, under the bow deck, and some have dual tanks that double as bench seats on either side of the cratch area. Water tanks have to be filled using a hose from the nearest supply.

If you can see into your water tank it is usually not a good idea to look too closely. Inside most water tanks (and especially on older boats) you will find rust, spiders, leaves and other harmless debris. It's no different to the water you get from the tap in your home which will contain both visible and invisible harmless debris. The difference is that on a boat the debris will settle to the bottom of the water storage tank over time. As a result, when your tank is almost empty you might notice the water from your taps becomes rather brown in colour.

There are a handful of ways to address this issue, depending on how much of a problem you perceive it to be. Many boaters carry bottled drinking water on board, using the water tank only for showering and perhaps washing dishes. This is a convenient solution for those who use their boat sporadically, but regular users and liveaboards might find this task rather onerous. Some boaters choose to ignore the issue altogether, assured in the knowledge that a little bit of dirt rarely hurts anyone. Be aware though that water-borne pathogens can make some people ill, particularly the elderly, the very young or the infirm. Installing a filter can improve matters enormously too but eventually you will need to overhaul the water tank and re-apply a protective coating.

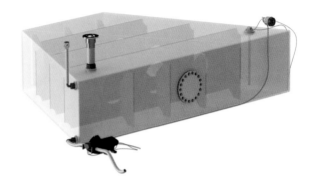

Plastic or catering grade steel are commonly used for water tanks.

Your water supply will be delivered under pressure from a water pump that is fitted somewhere near the water tank and you might also find an accumulator tank in the vicinity too. Often spherical or cylindrical in shape, these accumulator units regulate the pressure in the plumbing system so that a more even flow is achieved. This is particularly useful for boats with instantaneous gas water heaters as these rely upon an even flow to work efficiently.

You should resign yourself to the fact that it is not unusual for boats to spring a leak in the plumbing system. Unlike in a house, this rogue water has nowhere to go and so collects inside the hull, starting in the bilges underneath the floor. With this in mind, it is useful to have some kind of an inspection hatch in the floor somewhere near the stern. As most boats have the engine fitted at the stern this will be the heaviest part of the boat and spilled water will eventually make its way there. If your boat does not have an inspection hatch it is a good idea to get one (or more) fitted.

Prevent burst pipes

Lagging the plumbing pipes on your boat to insulate them from freezing will reduce the amount of leaks caused during cold weather.

HOT WATER

There are a couple of ways to heat your water that are essentially free. While this might seem to be a universally good option, there are reasons you might opt for another means. As with all things boating, you might find that your specific situation means that free hot water is not so great after all.

Calorifiers

These are large copper tanks and will usually be situated somewhere near to the engine. This is because the water that is used to cool the engine while it is running is routed through pipes in the calorifier, thereby heating the water inside. This means that all the time you are running your engine you are heating a tank full of water as a side effect.

Pros
- Free water heating capabilities while engine is running

Cons
- No hot water without running your engine
- Only heats one tank full of water at a time
- Expensive to repair
- Need careful management when winterising; be sure the tank is empty if you leave your boat for any length of time
- Hot water supply is limited to just one tank

Stove with back burner.

Stove with back burner

Multi fuel and wood burning stoves are very common on boats. Stoves that are fitted with a back burner can be used to heat your water too, essentially for free.

Pros
- Free water-heating capabilities when stove is lit
- Can also be used for central heating radiators

Cons
- Stove needs to be lit to produce hot water and so not a good option in summertime
- It's the messiest way to provide hot water – you need to build a fire and dispose of ashes etc.

At first it might seem sensible to assume that free hot water is a no-brainer, but obviously there are circumstances where these systems might not be the best choice. During the summertime it is impractical to rely upon your stove to heat your water. And for those moored in one place for extended periods, running your engine for an hour or two every time you want to shower or to wash up can become rather tiresome. Thankfully there are other options.

Gas boiler

These boilers heat a tank of water and maintain it at a chosen temperature. They can be connected to radiators too. A gas boiler will fire up to maintain the water temperature at a constant, whereas a calorifier will continue to cool after you switch off the engine.

Instantaneous gas boiler

Connected to your gas and water supplies, these units heat the water almost instantaneously as and when you need it, rather than heating a whole tank. They are relatively cheap to buy and easily retro-fitted by those with the requisite expertise.

Diesel heaters

Originally used to heat lorry cabs, these heaters are now frequently seen on boats. They can be used to provide hot water for your taps and for radiators too. However, these units have a bad reputation for poor reliability. Some people swear by them, citing poor maintenance, poor installation and inappropriate usage as the cause for any breakdowns. Experts commonly advise ensuring that the system is run hard to dissipate heat efficiently. Working hard will stop the unit from cycling on and off as this will shorten the life of the unit and waste battery power. If you're happy to keep the unit serviced and use it correctly a diesel heater might be the

Shower can fit in the tightest of spaces.

answer but many boaters believe that there are less troublesome ways to heat your water. That said, there are several hire boat fleets that rely exclusively on these units for all heating needs.

BATHING

The vast majority of boats have a shower, rather than a bath, with a view to maximising space. As well as taking up lots of room baths also use lots of water, meaning you'll be refilling your water tank more regularly. However, the lack of a bath is one of the main things that liveaboard boaters miss and a good soak in the bath is a luxury to savour when using bathrooms elsewhere.

Some boats will feature a bath aboard, particularly wider boats with more space and those that leave their mooring infrequently. When the water tap is next to your boat then refilling is not such an onerous task, but for boaters that cruise regularly a bath is not often a viable option. Narrowboats with a bath usually feature a ¾-length or hip-bath which, for the purposes of a good long soak, are useless. Boat shower facilities are usually surprisingly good, with constant and unvarying heat and enough power to keep all but the fussiest bathroom snob happy. Boat showers are essentially identical to those used in the home, except for the fact that water will not run down the plughole. As the floor of the boat is below water level, the water cannot drain through the plughole by means of gravity. Instead showers use a 'gulper' pump to suck the water from the shower tray, push it uphill through a pipe and out of the side of the boat somewhere above the waterline.

HEATING

The most commonly asked question for those who live on boats is, 'Is it cold in the wintertime?' The answer is largely the same as you would give if you live in a conventional house – of course it is cold if you let the fire go out or switch off the heating, but otherwise no. In fact, given the limited space inside a boat the opposite is more likely the problem. If you don't regulate and manage your stove properly the temperature inside a boat can soon become stiflingly hot. It is not unusual for boaters to fling open all of their doors and windows in the depths of winter in order to release some heat!

Most recreational boaters will limit their time afloat to the warm months of summer, and quite understandably so. However, if you choose to be aboard on colder days you'll need to heat your boat. Again, there are several options and you'll need to choose the one that suits you best. It is a hugely important decision that can make or break your boating pleasure.

Stoves

Multi-fuel or wood-burning stoves are by far the most popular choice for several reasons. In addition to the pleasurable aesthetics and agreeable heat, the stove is the most reliable and maintenance-friendly option. General daily management is quick and easy and most of the routine maintenance can be undertaken by the user. Replacing rope seals around the door, applying a posh new coat of paint and even installing a new flue and collar are all jobs that can be done by boat owners who don't mind getting their hands dirty.

Wood-burning stoves and multi-fuel stoves do differ and if you are fitting (or buying one installed) it is important to know what you are getting. Most boaters would opt for a multi-fuel model as coal makes it easy to keep a fire in over night. Given the limited space inside most stoves it would be difficult to load enough wood inside a wood burner to keep going throughout the night, and even tougher to regulate the speed and temperature at which it burns. Coal and nuggets are easier to regulate, once you and your stove have ironed out your differences.

Multi-fuel stoves complement the boating lifestyle.

Choose your fuel wisely.

Ecofan

Every boat with a stove should have an Ecofan. These amazing units are powered by the heat produced from your stove and push the warm air to the nether regions of your vessel. New boaters are often unconvinced until they have had the chance to borrow a unit from an amiable boating friend, but most graduate to buying their own device. There are other manufacturers now making these devices, but the name has stuck as a generic term, much like the word 'hoover'.

Tony's towpath tales: How to ruin a stove

Like most boaters I have been caught short with dwindling coal supplies and a night too cold to tolerate without a fire. The easy fix, so I thought, was to buy a small but extortionately overpriced bag of coal from the local petrol station. All being well, this would keep me going until I got to the coal merchant. The situation happened several times during the same winter (yes, I was lazy with my coal use and planning), and I got through several bags of 'forecourt coal'. That same winter I got through two replacement grates before finally destroying my stove completely.

According to the man in the stove showroom where I bought my new fire, the coal sold on petrol station forecourts is usually 'petro-coal' which burns far too hot for most makes of stove. By using it I had buckled and broken two grates before finding that my stove unit itself had burst, almost certainly because it was not up to the extremes of temperature caused by the fuel I was using. Needless to say, a new stove was a small price to pay given the level of temperatures the old one must have been producing.

A new code of practice for fitting stoves aboard boats was introduced in 2010. Although stove maintenance is relatively straightforward, it makes lots of sense to recruit a professional when installing a new stove for the first time. Installing a stove that is too large can be dangerous as the unit can be loaded with too much fuel and overheat. Restricting the load will make the unit inefficient as the fuel depth will likely be less than optimum for the design of the stove.

Diesel stoves

If you're not too bothered about watching the flames from your stove (and let's face it, most stove windows are covered in soot anyway!) then you might consider a diesel stove. These units are reliable and cheap to run and a good alternative to coal or wood burners.

Diesel-fuelled heaters

Diesel heaters heat your radiators but they can also provide hot running water too. Depending on whom you speak to, these units can have a bad reputation for being unreliable, but this can often be down to poor fitting, unsuitable usage and lack of maintenance.

CASE STUDY: DIESEL HEATERS

Brett and Jane: Dutch barge *Boadicea*

'We knew that these units have the reputation of being unreliable, but actually when they work well they're brilliant. We did lots of research to find out how to go about making sure our heater did what it was supposed to, this included speaking to a main dealer, downloading a current manual and also ignoring most threads on Internet forums. Essentially it comes down to three things; most importantly, make sure that it is fitted correctly. There are several important details which will stop these heaters from running well, so install the unit as advised by the manufacturer (they designed it after all).

'Next, be aware that these heaters need to be worked hard. This means choosing the smallest unit that will do the job; not the biggest. You can find out which one you need by measuring the pipe runs and radiators etc. then match this information to different heater capabilities (don't exceed what the unit can do). If you run the unit for on-demand hot water it will soon coke up and stop working so heat a full tank then switch off. And last, be sure to service your heater regularly; follow the manufacturer's schedule according to the fuel you are using.

'Ours has worked brilliantly since it was overhauled and installed.'

Installation tips:

1. Fit a seven-day timer; while a little expensive it will allow you to read and clear fault codes. This means that you can see what the onboard computer is doing.

2. If you use a normal-sized fuel filter and housing be sure to prime the heater before trying to use it; it will take around 50 start cycles to get fuel through, by then the small fuel pump will be ruined through dry running. Housings are available with a built-in priming pump.

3. Our unit was out of warranty so I removed the old-style bullet fuses and fitted a blade fuse holder into the top of the control box. This means you can examine and change fuses without taking the cover off.

4. If your unit is used, take it to a dealer before you try to install it; this will save a lot of time as you don't have to overcome any hidden problems such as malfunctioning heater plugs or fault code lock-out.

ELECTRICITY

Shoreline power

Marinas, boatyard and boat club moorings will often have the option to hook up to the on-shore power supply using a shore-line from your boat to a designated socket. Depending on your on-board electrical system you might be able to recharge your batteries and supply power directly to your 240v sockets or any configuration of power your management system allows.

Look after your batteries and they'll work hard in return.

There will usually be a charge administered for electric usage, either via a card meter system or a meter installed in the line from shore to boat. The benefits of shore power are obvious for liveaboards who spend time tied at their home mooring or for those departing or arriving back from a cruise. There is a price to pay for this convenience however, as being on constant charge is not good for your batteries and they will soon require replacement if they are subjected to this treatment for very long. It is very common for boaters who have abused their batteries in this way to find out that their batteries are fried when they reach the end of their first day of cruising. Instead of enjoying a bank of batteries that are well charged from a day of cruising, they run out of power some time after dark. Replacing the whole bank is the only answer.

Battery power

Your batteries will usually be situated near the engine and need to be secured to the hull and have their terminals protected. Typically there will be a series of 110ah 12v leisure batteries and a separate one, usually a standard car battery, to start the engine. Boat batteries are usually dedicated to serve either the engine or the cabin's leisure needs, such as the lighting, water pump and radio. Charging the batteries can be done either by running the engine, from renewable sources such as solar panels and wind turbines or from the shore-line via a battery charger if you have one fitted. It is important to keep the leisure system separate from the engine battery as it would be very inconvenient if you were to flatten them all. If your leisure batteries are running low on power you will need a fully-charged engine battery to start the boat's engine in order to recharge the leisure bank.

There are several ways to keep the engine battery isolated from the leisure bank, the simplest most usual solution being a split charge relay switch. These units favour the engine battery during charging and then isolate it when charging is complete to feed the leisure bank. It also isolates the leisure bank so that the charge in your engine battery is saved for starting the boat.

Inverters

Inverters are used to convert 12v battery power to the 240v power used by standard three-pin plug appliances. Items such as televisions, hair dryers, vacuum cleaners and many others

12v or 24v

The vast majority of boats use 12v power, but a few are wired up for 24v. The reasoning for doing this is unclear and unconvincing for most people. The unequivocal fact though, is that if you're considering a 24v boat then you should not only know why you favour the 24v system but be able to work on the electrics yourself. Few boatyards are geared up to deal with 24 volt systems and few chandlers stock the parts.

Power hungry

Remember that inverters use charge from the batteries in order to do their job, so switch them off when not in use to preserve power.

require 240v and if you're taking your household appliances on board then you'll need an inverter. Power hungry appliances need a powerful inverter so one of the larger, more expensive models around 3200w will be necessary.

A better solution is to use 12v versions of your favoured appliances. Most appliances are available in 12v, although they're usually relatively expensive and sometimes not easy to find. Smaller, less expensive inverters will suffice where boat owners are careful and considerate of their power needs and so a 1800w unit will suffice.

Delicate electronic equipment, such as laptops, apparently require a more advanced inverter called a 'pure-sine', rather than a cruder 'quasi-sine'. However, tech-savvy friends tell me that modern laptops are far more robust than pure-

A shore power pedestal.

sine manufacturers would have us believe and you'd be terribly unfortunate to have a problem with a quasi-sine version. As always, do your own research.

Battery charger

Having a battery charger fitted to your boat means that you don't need to run your engine in order to re-charge your batteries. You'll need a hook-up to land power in order to use it, making them ideal for liveaboards and those who use their boat whilst moored in a marina.

Battery management systems

Sophisticated battery management systems are an excellent solution to most battery charge issues, serving to isolate the engine battery, extend battery efficiency and longevity when using shoreline charging and providing every other service you can imagine short of tucking you into bed at night. However, there is a commonly quoted saying among boaters that reminds us to, 'Keep it simple, stupid!' Battery management systems

Top battery tip

Liveaboards who are hooked up to shore-line power can preserve the life of their leisure batteries by installing only one battery whilst they are moored. Sacrificing one battery to inefficient shore-line charging is much preferable to ruining a bank of three or four when there is no extra benefit. Reattaching more batteries before you cruise is relatively easy and certainly much cheaper than realising you need to replace the whole bank that were fried while you were hooked up at your mooring.

The more the merrier?

Most boats have two, three or four leisure batteries, but surely having more would be better? Actually, the amount of time it would take to fully charge four or more leisure batteries is usually disproportionate to the hours of use you would get from them. Although some boaters do seem to manage with four, most electrics specialists will tell you that three batteries is the ideal number. Of course, this all depends on your set-up and usage, but in most applications, three is the magic number.

are truly wonderful when they are installed and working properly, but should a problem arise it will inevitably be a complicated one and you will need either the expertise to fix it or the funds to pay someone else to do so.

Renewable energies: solar and wind power

The cost of renewable energy supply options has reduced considerably, and at the same time, the efficiency of these units has increased too. Solar panels are becoming a standard installation feature on newly-built boats and even retro-fitting to older vessels is becoming commonplace.

You can generate your own power using solar panels (above) or a wind turbine (below).

The ecological benefits of using solar and wind power are well documented, but it should be remembered that these units must be in service for several years before they have repaid the carbon debt incurred in their manufacture. Similarly, the financial cost of purchase and installation takes a few years to recoup too. The figures for individual units will vary, but after three to five years you can be reasonably confident that your solar panels have earned

Walk-on solar panels

Flexible 'walk-on' solar panels are available but these are less efficient, more expensive and cannot be angled to direct the units to make best use of the sun.

Flexible gel solar panels can be stepped on.

their keep, and free power is not to be sniffed at. The vast majority of solar owners are strong advocates and enthusiastically recommend solar, stating that they get plenty of power even on dull days.

There are some downsides to installing solar panels, however. Apart from the initial cost of purchase and installation there are practical issues to consider too. Most notable of these is the amount of space that the units take up on the roof. For those who regularly walk on the roof of their boat the panels represent a significant trip hazard. Single-handed boaters are most likely to fall (pun intended) into this category as stepping on and off the roof when locking is usually necessary. Also consider that getting a clear line of sight to the sun can be tricky as hedgerows and buildings can block out the sun.

THE ENGINE ROOM

The engine

Despite being the most integral part of any mode of transport, boat engines are often overlooked by purchasers. Most boats are bought with little thought to the engine and rarely with appraisal by someone who knows what to look for. Most engines are bought on trust, and quite understandably so. With so many engines being available and so much detailed knowledge necessary to appraise them, most people will not have the expertise available to make a considered purchase. The big lump of metal in the engine bay, it seems, is often considered to be some kind of voodoo and best left alone.

There are some rudimentary checks that the layman can consider when looking into the engine bay.

* **Is the engine the right size for the boat?**
  Undersized and oversized engines can be a problem, so don't make the mistake of thinking that bigger is necessarily better.

Left: A cruiser stern engine bay.
Above: Andrew hard at work in the engine bay.

- **Is the engine original?** Did it come with the boat or has it been changed recently? A newer engine is usually preferable to an older one as it will be less worn out and usually requires less work. Vintage engines are another matter.

- **Is the hour counter working?** If you can accurately judge the number of hours the engine has been run then this will give you a guide to how worn it will be. This assumes the hour counter is accurate, and many are not.

- **Is the engine bay clean and tidy?** A pristine engine bay will infer a pristine engine, and vice versa.

- **Some engines are easier to work on than others**. Some engines are built in such a way as to make difficult jobs even tougher. If you don't work on your engine yourself then this may not initially appear to be a big issue, but your bill from the boatyard will be more expensive when they spend longer doing the job.

Keel-cooled or raw water-cooled?

There are two ways to cool your boat's engine. Many boats have a skin tank welded on the inside of the hull below the waterline. The skin tank is filled with water that circulates around the engine to keep the system cool. The other option is to use raw water from the canal or river. The water is sucked up into the cooling system and then spit out of the boat when its cooling job is done.

There are pros and cons to both systems. The skin tank is more likely to overheat and cause airlocks as the cooling system is sealed and cannot be replenished if water is lost through overheating. Keeping a keen eye on the temperature gauge is always important, topping up the water and coolant levels when necessary. Raw water-cooled boats are often noisy, sucking and spitting water through the system. There is also the risk of picking up debris from the canal that blocks the filter and reduces the water intake. Again, keep an eye on your temperature gauges.

Some boats have their engines as a feature, housed in the centre of the vessel in a dedicated engine room. Usually these are wonderful vintage, slow-chugging contraptions and often the plaything of the type of boaters who love to tinker. They're usually beautifully maintained with polished brass and hardly a smear of oil to be found.

If you are primarily interested in the leisure aspects of boating then you might find these mid-engine vessels to be somewhat inconvenient, and certainly liveaboard boaters can better use the space that they take up. But for those that appreciate industrial beauty, a new-fangled diesel engine would simply never do.

Gearbox

Again, the proliferation of gearbox types makes it difficult to know enough about them to make a judgement. The general state of the engine bay will be your best guide, and if it is possible to determine that the gearbox is the right size for the boat then this is certainly beneficial.

Quick check

1. Put the engine in forward gear for 3 seconds

2. Put the gearbox in neutral for 3 seconds

3. Put the gearbox in reverse for 3 seconds

4. Put the gearbox back into forward gear

If the engine 'jumps' and clunks when you return to first gear, this is a good indicator that your drive-plate is worn or wearing badly.

No engine?

Believe it or not, not all boats will have an engine. Some permanently moored boats used as liveaboard homes will never move and have no use for an engine, but these are the exception, not the rule.

Stern gland

The boat's engine turns a shaft that is connected to a propeller located outside the boat under the water. The stern gland is the threshold between the inside of your boat and the water outside. The conventional type of stern gland is packed with fibre rope that is fixed around the prop shaft like a collar. There are usually two or three such rope collars in place with the rest of the gland being packed with grease. The gland is kept packed with grease by turning a tap that is located in the engine space, forcing more grease into the gland to maintain a near--watertight pressure.

These types of stern glands are rarely 100 per cent watertight and an occasional drip is usually apparent. This is nothing to worry about and excess water is collected in the engine bilge and can be pumped out using a bilge pump. If the gland begins to drip excessively it is an easy enough job to re-pack the stern gland with new rope and grease. With most it is simply a matter of unscrewing a couple of bolts to remove a collar before removing and replacing the rope and grease with fresh supplies.

Be sure to fit individual rings of rope, rather than spiral coil it around the shaft, otherwise water will inevitably snake its way between the coils. Also, you should mismatch the joins in each ring of rope packing so that there is no clear run for water to

Stern gland.

Conventional stern gland

Pros

- Cheaper to maintain and replace
- User serviceable
- Engine alignment is simple

Cons

- Messier to maintain
- Messier to run (water and grease abound)
- Not as watertight as the alternative
- Need replacing and re-packing at intervals

escape. And finally, be sure not to over-tighten the collar as this will create friction and wear on the prop shaft. The only real problem will likely be that of access in small, confined engine bays. The only other consideration is the potential for spreading grease onto every available nook and cranny of your person and the boat. Very best of luck with that!

The alternative to the conventional stern gland set-up is a system specific to the Vetus brand of engine parts. Known colloquially as a 'water jacket' the gland relies upon a rubber collar with a specific channel to deliver water outside the boat through a hose. Although this type of gland has a great reputation for being almost watertight, the system is far more expensive to fit and maintain and difficult to retro-fit to older boats with imperial measurements.

Water jacket gland

Pros

- Almost watertight
- Rubber collar means less prop shaft wear if engine is misaligned
- Rubber collar is not susceptible to wear and so rarely needs maintenance or replacement

Cons

- Expensive to replace when they do wear out
- Requires dry-docking to replace
- Not a job for the typical boater

BILGE PUMPS

Every boat should have at least two bilge pumps. One should be fitted in the engine bay at the stern of the boat (if that is where your engine is located) to get rid of any water ingress from the stern gland or elsewhere. The other should be included in your emergency tool kit to deal with spills, leaks and other water-pooling problems that will inevitably happen. Make sure that you have enough cable on the spare (or enough spare cable to extend it) so that you can reach from your battery power supply to the heart of the problem puddle.

Bilge pumps can work manually, automatically or both. The automatic types have a float switch that kicks in the pump when the water in the stern bilge rises beyond a certain level. These are great, but tend to make boaters lazy and forget to visually check the bilges for water. Should the automatic float switch fail (and they often do) then the water level will continue to rise until you discover the fault. Manual switches are a more foolproof option. Most boaters simply switch the pump on occasionally to remove any water that has accumulated, and switch it off when the flow stops.

The best option is the dial type bilge pump with a float switch and a manual override switch. This means that if the float switch fails then you still have a pump that works on a regular switch. The clever money also goes on having a float switch that is separate to your pump. This means that you can replace either the pump or the switch, as opposed to having to replace both should one fail.

Weed hatch

Working in the weed hatch is never a joy. If you're in there then you probably have something stuck around your prop, impeding your progress. The weed hatch will be located at the very back of your boat, usually under the stern deck. By removing the lid of the hatch you can reach down into the water to remove anything that is stuck around the prop. That might make it sound easy, but work through the weed hatch rarely is. Access can be a real problem, particularly in trad-style narrowboats.

Right: The weed hatch is held in place by a screw-tightened bar.

Add to that the fact that the water will likely be freezing and the tangled mess around your prop will likely to be a nightmare to get rid of.

You can find almost anything wrapped around your prop. Weeds and other foliage around your prop will impede your progress and can be surprisingly hard work to remove. Worse still is the collection of tightly wound fabric, umbrella frames, mattress springs, rope, wire, bungee cords, webbing straps or, the most frequent menace of all, fishing twine. Gratuitous use of blades, snips and croppers will often get the better of these hitch-hiking materials after some effort, but rarely will it be a quick or

An accessible weed hatch means you can easily clear your prop.

easy task. Watch out for fishing hooks caught in the mess and be wary of the risks of Weil's disease. See page 215 for more details.

Top tip

'The most useful tool for clearing stuff from around your prop is a bread knife. Tape it to a baton if the water is freezing cold and you might be able to keep your hands dry.'

TROY, SNAYGILL BOATS, SKIPTON

What's the worst thing you've found around your prop?

Carol   Nb *Caelmiri*: A tyre and a sari

Tony   Nb *The Watchman*: My own stern rope and a mattress

Brett   Nb *Boadicia*: A tyre and lots of fishing twine

Alan   Nb *Knot Related*: Carpet pieces

Debbie Nb *Dunster*: An umbrella

TOILETS

Where to start with toilets? The littlest room is a big topic and one of the most frequently discussed amongst boaters. Put two boaters in a room and the subject of toilets will usually come up within the hour. The debate is largely split into two camps – in the red corner we have the cassette fans, and in the blue corner are the advocates of the pump-out. Both have their merits and the system that suits you best is entirely down to your own personal circumstances and tastes. Let's look at each in turn.

Cassette toilets

These are the most popular toilet option for several reasons. First, and most importantly for some, disposing of the contents of this type of toilet is free. Elsan disposal facilities can be found at convenient points around the system and so whether you are on the move or moored in one place, there's likely an Elsan near you. Another major consideration is convenience. Pump-out owners have a problem if their boat is iced into its mooring during the winter, or if pump-out facilities are not available nearby. Cassette owners have no such trouble as they can remove their cassette and take it somewhere to be emptied. Putting the full cassette into the boot of the car and driving it to an emptying facility is not an option for pump-out owners.

Cassette toilets are often cheaper to install too with basic units costing around £80. These are rather rudimentary in their design, being largely functional with little in the way of sophistication or aesthetic appeal. They'll be 'gravity fed' with waste being delivered to the holding tank via a lever-pulled trapdoor. The holding tank will be relatively small and the unit flushed with a hand pump.

If you aspire to a throne that is a little more regal then you won't be disappointed as things have come a long way for the modern cassette toilet. Nowadays it is commonplace for cassette toilets to boast a selection of sophisticated features such as electric flushing, swivel seats and vacuum suction. Fixed cassette toilets look much like those you would find in the home, utilising a cassette that can be removed from the base. Larger volume cassettes are usually standard in these upmarket models but most boaters feel it is sensible to have a spare cassette to hand in case they are caught short.

Cleaning cassette toilets is easy and there are several specialist products on the market, although many would argue that everyday household laundry powder does the job just as well. Add solutions to both the top tank and the cassette; shake vigorously and empty into a drain.

And the downsides?

The job of emptying a cassette could never be considered a pleasant experience and, for some, it is just a little too uncivilised. Carrying the unit to the Elsan disposal site is another issue to consider as these can weigh anything up to 20kg. It is usually worth taking some time

Cassette toilet problems

Eroded seals: gaseous build-up can cause an unpleasant spray of discharge if the seals are worn.

Misuse: by unwitting guests. Always make sure a cassette is in place if you have visitors.

Toilet tissue abuse: too much tissue causes blockages. Nobody likes a blocked toilet, so go easy.

Fluid use: most holding tank treatment fluids should not be used in the 'top tank' which holds water for the flush as this can cause erosion of the pump seals. Check the manufacturer's instructions.

Damp: the area around the cassette can become damp, particularly if there is a leak of any kind. Keep an eye out and address the issue with ventilation and repairs.

Oil: smear seals with olive oil or vegetable oil to protect and prevent erosion.

to instruct guests on how to use the toilet when they visit too, as the construction and operation might appear alien to the uninitiated.

Pump-out toilets

For those who prefer a more conventional relationship with their toilet, a pump-out system might be the answer. The biggest benefit of a pump-out toilet system is that, unlike a cassette system, flushing is essentially the last you will see of your waste. Of course, with this convenience comes a cost and most pump-out facilities will charge £10–£20 a time. At commercial boatyards and marinas there might be someone tasked with the job of performing the service for you, but in many cases you will be expected to do the job yourself. Either way, the process is much more agreeable than emptying a full cassette.

Bathrooms are usually small but functional.

I purposely bought a boat with a pump-out toilet because I often have lots of guests aboard. Pump-out toilets look more like the real thing and there is a lot less of the unpleasant messing around to be done when it is full. I'm not sure some of my friends would get along with a cassette, so a pump-out it had to be.

SAM: *Knot Hrd Work*

Pump-out toilets look very much like a conventional home toilet. From basic models such as gravity-fed 'dump through' system to bells and whistles units with vacuum, or compressed air flushes, you can choose from a variety of sophisticated features and add-ons. Vacuum and compressed air flushes are becoming increasingly popular as the contents of the waste tank are sealed off and cannot be seen through the toilet, whereas the basic 'dump through' style allows a view into the tank below. The choice is yours, but as always, there is a pay-off. Should anything go wrong with your pump-out toilet it is usually easier to fix if you have a dump through unit. Like most things concerned with boating, the less complicated system is usually easier to fix.

Holding tanks are a common cause for concern and problems here can be very difficult and extremely unpleasant to fix. If you have the luxury of designing a new toilet system from scratch it is advisable to negate as many problems as possible during the installation. A bottom-draining tank is the best option to ensure a total discharge during pump-out as other suction methods generally leave a few inches in the bottom. During the pump-out it is very useful to have a means to rinse the tank easily as this helps to avoid problems with smell and caking. A good-sized vent (and preferably more than one) will also help to combat smells and you might consider a carbon filter in the vent line too.

Ensure the tank is fixed well and fully supported, as a full tank is extremely heavy. Bumping around in locks could cause the tank to shift and fittings to snap, unloading the

Nature's toilet

Composting toilets aren't common aboard boats given their temperamental nature, but they do exist. It takes a while for the composter to get to grips with the idiosyncrasies of their usage and the system, but once this has been achieved it can work quite well. Ventilation is the key to success and this is often achieved using powered fans and heaters. Guests using the composting toilet might require some supervision.

contents through the broken pipe work. You might also find that plastic tanks will bulge, creating problems for adjacent bulkheads if the tank is not well fixed and restrained.

Problems with your pump-out?

- Blockages can be a frustrating problem with pump out systems, but most can be avoided wi-h proper installation and good toileting protocol.

- Avoid right angles in the pipework

- Have an inspection hatch fitted to allow easy access

- A ventilated holding tank will help to deal with any smell and you'll usually need more ventilation than you thought necessary

- A means to rinse the tank will help to stop any hardened build-up of waste

- Use only the most basic toilet roll, as quilted products can cause blockages. Moist toilet tissue should never be used. Consider anything more substantial than cheap-brand tissue to be a blockage risk

- Watch for leaky valves on the flush mechanism. When eroded these will let water into the bowl, filling your tank quickly. Listen for your water pump kicking in unexpectedly as you'll often not notice the small trickle into the pan

- Macerators go a long way to ensuring that blockages do not occur. However these need to be used carefully as anything more substantial than toilet paper can get trapped and cause breakages

- The build-up of scale in pipework and parts can cause problems. Vigorously massaging the flexible pipework can dislodge the build-up, but often it is better to remove the parts for cleaning

Treatment fluids

There are two types of fluids that are most commonly used aboard boats. The most popular is a formaldehyde-based product and these are usually blue in colour – and often in the name too. These work by essentially 'pickling' the waste to stop odour from being released and are fortified with a fragrance that perhaps some people can get used to. It is worth considering the negative effects of formaldehyde on the environment when deciding on the best toilet treatment fluid and thankfully there are some alternatives.

The other type of fluid is usually green, by name and by nature. Being nitrate- and oxygen-based, this fluid is much kinder to the environment and works by accelerating the decomposition process. Used properly and liberally there is not usually any smell to be discerned (even from gravity-fed toilets) but it is worth ensuring that a breather pipe with an odour filter is fitted to any black-water tank as a precaution.

Switching from a formaldehyde fluid to a nitrate/oxygen-based product is tricky, as the residue from the former will stop your eco-friendly fluid from working. You'll need to flush the tank thoroughly several times to have any chance of success and even then it might be some time before the war is won. In the meantime you would be advised to pump out the tank more regularly than is necessary to stop the waste from caking on the bottom of the tank. Dislodged cakes of waste will cause blockages and so it is best to ensure that this does not occur.

Blockage horrors

In an ideal world, the only thing to go into a boat toilet would be anything that has passed through your digestive system. Although that's not an acceptable option for most people, the rule should only ever be bent enough to accommodate toilet tissue – and even then, only tissue of a particular type. Luxury quilted tissue will block your system in no time and even the cheaper brands will cause problems if used excessively.

> ### The toilet tissue test
>
> The experts at Lee Sanitation recommend a quick test to enable you to select an acceptable brand of tissue. Fill a pint glass with water and add two sheets of toilet tissue. Stir well, and if the tissue breaks up easily then it is OK for boat use. If it stays in a sheet then you're headed for toilet trouble.

Knowing the nightmare of unblocking a toilet will inevitably deter experienced boaters from breaking toilet etiquette, but unwitting visitors are not usually so considerate. Sanitary towels, nappies, condoms, wet wipes, moist toilet tissue, disinfectant blocks are frequently retrieved from blocked toilets and the list of the more unusual items makes interesting reading. Paracetamol blister packs, vegetables, tea bags, keys, dog chews and pages from a magazine have all been retrieved from blocked toilet tanks. One hire boat operator even reported finding 'seven pairs of skimpy ladies' underwear' from a toilet tank that was blocked after a hire period.

Plumbing

Proper installation is vital for pump-out toilets, particularly those where the tank is situated remotely from the pan. In these cases, the waste must travel through pipework until it reached the tank and it is here that blockages can be an issue. Michael Punter, from Lee Sanitation, recommends a 'rise and fall' method to routing

waste plumbing. 'The waste hose should rise steeply as it leaves the pan before falling gradually into the top of your black water tank. A vacuum or compressed air flush will easily push waste over the apex of the pipe. It can then travel downhill at its leisure into the waste tank, thus avoiding it being stored in the pipework for any period of time. It's also a good idea to keep waste pipes away from hot water plumbing in order to avoid drying and blockages.'

Other types of toilet

Despite the generally eco-friendly nature of boating and boaters it is rare to find a composting toilet aboard a boat. This is because the composting process needs to be kept mostly dry which means you would need to dispose of your urine by another method. With this being the case, most simply plump for a cassette system on board rather than accommodate two different types of toilet and disposal systems. That said, composting toilets might be an option for those with permission to have one on land nearby their mooring.

Self pump-out kits do exactly what you would expect, enabling boaters to empty their pump-out black-water tanks into the same disposal sites used by cassette owners, thereby avoiding the associated cost. The kits often work by pumping a hand lever, but newer models have an electric motor to do the job. While this might seem like a good idea the reality is not usually so straightforward. The process is inherently more hands-on than a conventional pump-out process, both in terms of the effort required and the unsavoury nature of using the equipment. Also, navigation authorities deem their use to be largely unfavourable. Many Elsan disposal points disallow self pump-out from black-water tanks due to the volumes of waste involved, particularly those sites which discharge into a septic tank.

CANVAS COVERS

There are three main reasons to fit a boat cover; to protect an area from weather, to enclose an area to deter unwanted attention and to make use of the extra space.

CHRIS SAILSBURY, OWNER AND DIRECTOR OF CANVAS MAN COVERS IN OTLEY, WEST YORKSHIRE

Types of covers

Cratch

Cratch covers are the most popular type of cover. In addition to protecting the contents of the bow from opportunist theft, bird droppings and leaf litter, cratch covers also provide a service in leaking locks by deflecting water off the bow deck.

Most are fitted around a traditional 'A frame' cratch board but boaters starting from scratch without an A frame in place might consider a hood supported by a collapsible stainless steel frame. These are quickly gaining ground over the traditional type, not only for their modern aesthetic appeal, but because these often cost less to install. Storing non-valuable items in the cratch area is very tempting but, as most boats allow access through the cratch, keeping it as clear as possible is sensible.

Stern covers

Cruiser stern hoods have stormed the boating scene, becoming almost a standard feature on semi-trad and cruiser stern boats. 'Extra covered space aboard a boat has enormous value, particularly for liveaboards,' says Chris Sailsbury at Canvas Man. 'The deck above the engine on semi-trads and cruisers is just dead space, but with a canvas cover it becomes a useful and practical area.'

A cruiser stern hood on a wide-beam boat, complete with stitched lettering.

Most people use the space as a dual-function utility room and porch area with a view to having a cleaner, tidier boat. Keeping coal and wood and ash buckets out there greatly reduces the mess from your stove, and there is something civilised about having somewhere to remove muddy footwear and wet coats.

Cruising with a stern cover

Although it is possible to use the covers to cruise in comfort in the rain, in reality, few boaters ever do so. Visibility is greatly reduced under a rain-splattered cover and the front-facing window will invariably need to be unzipped and rolled away. Even in good weather, cruising with a tall stern hood requires expert tiller-work to avoid smashing the hood on low bridges. Most people will sensibly negate these stresses by collapsing the hood when cruising.

> *Having a stern hood means I can keep my back doors open to let some fresh air in without letting the bad weather in with it.*
>
> CAROLINE, NB *NAMASTE*

Tonneau

This type of cover is most frequently fitted on semi-trad boats but is also seen on cruiser stern vessels. Tonneaus are most suited to leisure boaters wishing to seal their boat for extended periods of time. Those requiring regular access will find crawling under a tonneau to be a frustrating challenge. In addition to discouraging unwanted attention from opportunist thieves, the tonneau cover will stop rain water leaking into the engine hole, given that even the best self-draining decks are rarely 100 per cent effective.

If you need to buy a canvas cover for your boat then understanding the processes involved in the design and manufacture will help you to make the right choice. Chris Sailsbury from Canvas Man takes us through the process.

THE STORY OF A BOAT COVER

Stage 1: *Consultation*

'The best way to choose a design is to look at other hoods to see what you like and what you don't like. We usually show photographs to illustrate the design choices and discuss the options,' says Chris.

Details such as size, fabrics, colours, window placement and access zip configurations are all decided at this stage. Optional extras include storage bags to use when the cover is removed, window privacy curtains and even lettering options if you want to display your boat name.

Once those details are finalised, a pattern maker then visits the boat to measure up and design the frame for manufacture. Frame design is crucial as it is the foundation of the whole structure. A good designer will use their experience and craftsmanship to produce a frame that will withstand all weathers, collapse conveniently and complement the lines of the boat.

Stage 2: *Patterning*

A second visit to the boat is required to construct a pattern by covering the frame with patterning vinyl and tape. This precision work is dependent on good weather as high winds or rain makes the job impossible. Once the pattern is in place the plan for windows and zip access is finalised.

Again, the craftsmanship and experience of the pattern maker will ensure that the pattern is practical and efficient and complements the idiosyncrasies of each individual vessel. 'You need to consider every inch of the boat, from the paintwork coach-lines to the position of mooring ropes and fenders. One tiny oversight can make the cover very clumsy to use or can spoil the look when it is fitted; then the whole cover needs to go back to the workshop and be reworked. Thankfully that hardly ever happens.' says James Ineson, pattern maker at the Canvas Man.

Aftercare

- Leave a newly fitted hood in place for at least two months to allow the canvas to 'settle'.
- Clean the canvas at least once a year using a non-detergent product. Detergents damage the fabric proofing. Soap flakes or a specialist canvas cleaning product are preferable.
- Do not jet wash the canvas as this damages the fabric and proofing.
- Try not to fold the window sections of your cover as these can cause your window to discolour, crease and possibly crack over time.

Tonneau cover on a semi-trad stern.

Stage 3: *Workshop*

The workshop process is more high-tech than you might expect. Here the pattern template is digitally transferred to a CAD (computer-aided design) programme where design details such as storm flap covers for zips are added to the pattern. This digital pattern is then fed to the computerised cutting machine that cuts the fabric to the exact size.

'Like all computers, the cutting machine will only do what it is told and you only have one chance to get it right. A mistake here can be costly so it is important to double-check everything before we press the start button.' says Joanna Koziolek, seamstress supervisor at Canvas Man HQ. 'You develop a kind of sixth sense to notice when something isn't right.'

Once the fabric is cut, it is then stitched in sequence by the team of seamstress machine operators and, after a final quality control check, it is ready to be fitted.

Stage 4: *Fitting*

Fitting a new boat cover is a tough job in many ways. The canvas must be stretched extremely tightly if the cover is to retain its shape after it is bedded in. The positioning of each fitting is crucial, and if their placement means hanging off the boat with a drill in one hand over a freezing cold canal then that's just another day at work for the fitting boys. Unlike the patterning stage, the fitters can (and do) work in all weathers.

'The best thing a customer can do at this stage is to keep these guys supplied with tea and biscuits,' says Chris. 'Fitting a hood is an endurance event but you should end up with a tight, smooth and almost ripple free hood.'

Although the covers are made to a precise pattern, there is still some considerable art and skill involved in fitting a new cover well. A good fitter will not only make sure the cover is fitted securely and tightly, but they will also pay attention to the lines of the boat and the positioning of seams, hems, zips and fastenings to ensure the end result is practical and good looking.

New cover checklist

Materials

- Most modern covers are made from a Teflon-coated acrylic canvas. This fabric is ideally suited to boat covers as it is hardwearing, weatherproof, and breathable and is also resistant against shrinking, stretching and fading.
- Some boaters prefer covers made from PVC, as it is easier to clean. On the downside PVC will shrink when cold making it difficult to fit and it does not age as well as acrylic canvas, causing the surface layers to peel and the cover to contract.
- Marine-grade stainless steel is the gold standard for frames. Lesser-grade stainless steel frames and nickel fittings are cheaper but do not stand the test of time. Aluminium frames are cheap, but rarely withstand hard weather conditions.
- Rot-resistant thread should always be used.

Functionality

- The cover needs to fit tightly to make an efficient run off for rainwater.
- Using the correct fittings will simplify the removal and re-fitting of the cover and will ensure it does not get caught when cruising or manoeuvring around the boat.
- Large, fat, spiral-type zips are the most practical, hardwearing and smooth to operate.
- Covers should accommodate movement of the tiller, the hatch and any mooring ropes.
- The frame should collapse and stow in a position that does not hamper the helmsman.

Aesthetics

- Boxy, angular framework is cheaper to produce but results in a cover that is less pleasing to the eye.
- Seams, hems and frame alignment should complement the lines of the boat and its paintwork.

LIGHTING

Fluorescent tubes are almost obsolete nowadays as more efficient and attractive units are cheaply and readily available. Attractive brass fittings with integral switches are the most common type you will find aboard, but you might be surprised to find something unique. Incandescent bulbs are fast losing favour too. LEDs are much less power hungry, last much longer and the difference in purchase price is not significant enough to be an issue for most people. Add to that the on-going improvements in light quality and you can see why incandescent bulbs have almost had their day.

If you're fitting out a new boat, or even choosing a pre-loved vessel, it is worth considering where you are likely to need lighting most as retro-fitting is either costly or impossible. Think about places such as the galley, above the bed and above chairs where you will be reading or working. If you do have a lack of lighting headache, you might consider stick-on or magnetic LED lights that are battery operated. These are cheap and easy to fit and very effective, the only downside being that they might not be in keeping with the rest of the boat's fittings.

Naked flame

Candlelight and gas lamps are always beautiful aboard a boat, but please please please be careful with them. Unlike houses, boats are unstable surfaces on which to balance naked flames. Coupled with the proliferation of highly flammable fittings and features there is plenty of reason to be extremely cautious.

BEDS AND BUNKS

The sleeping arrangements aboard a boat are a huge consideration. You'll need to consider your usage needs and temperament quite deeply in order to ensure you make the right decisions. There are basically four different choices:

Standard bed layout

Most boats will have a bed that is positioned against either one of the boat sides. It will usually be around six feet long and four feet wide, allowing enough space to walk down the side of it. They'll usually have some very useful storage space beneath, but be sure to only store items here that are rarely used as access to them is cumbersome. However, if you can install pull-out boxes or drawers beneath then some of this space becomes rather more accessible.

Pros
- This layout does not restrict access to other areas of the boat and offers useful storage space beneath

Cons
- While many couples do comfortably sleep in these types of bed, they may be too narrow for some. Sleepless nights can quickly dull your enthusiasm for boating

Cross bed layout

This type of bed runs its length between the two side walls of the boat. While this offers the opportunity to have a much wider bed, the length of it is restricted to approximately six feet. This type of set-up will mean that you must climb over the bed to get to whatever is on the other side. This layout is invariably found positioned at the furthest ends of the cabin –

that is near the stern (restricting access to the tiller), or near the bow (restricting access to the cratch). There are a couple of workarounds for the problem, the most practical using a pull-down door to create a 'bridge' over the bed when it is opened for access, so keeping dirty boots off the bed. Otherwise you'll need to bridge the bed with covers or some other walkway option if you want to keep your bedding clean. If you are considering a cross bed layout it would be wise to ensure that your routine access to the boat does not involve climbing across the bed as this will quickly become a chore.

Pros
- Wider bed option

Cons
- Restricted to six feet in length
- Restricted access to other parts of the boat

Transformer bed

These are similar to the cross bed layout, but can be folded to make access to the walkway. The mattress is in two pieces that are stitched together. The piece blocking the walkway is folded on top of the fixed piece. These offer a bigger bed without permanently blocking the walkway, although having to faff about with them regularly might be too fussy for some boaters.

Sofabed

On smaller boats there is much to be said for the sofabed option. The ability to convert living quarters into bedroom space can vastly reduce the cost of boating as you can get away with a much smaller boat. This option might not suit liveaboards as the constant conversion from

A transformer bed.

Sofa beds are an excellent option on smaller boats.

sofa to bed and back becomes tiresome. The temptation to leave it out as a bed becomes overwhelming, but this simply impairs your enjoyment of your boat as the living space is taken up. However for leisure boaters, it can be a viable option.

Pros
- Adaptable use of space can make boating cheaper
- Can offer additional sleeping arrangements when several people are aboard

Cons
- Can be too cumbersome and tiresome for regular use
- Usually less storage space below

Dinette/pullout/other

Many boats have a dinette-type set-up that can be pulled out and converted into bunks. By removing the table and re-arranging the seating configuration the bench and tables layout becomes a very useable bed. Similarly there are various other seating arrangements that can be transformed into a sleeping station of some variety and some boats even have beds that can be pulled down from a vertical position against the wall. Most of these are featured as a supplemental sleeping option in addition to a regular bed, but some boats have these as the sole place to sleep. The benefits and pitfalls are much the same as with the sofabed option above.

Pros
- Adaptable use of space can make boating cheaper
- Can offer additional sleeping arrangements when several people are aboard

The extra width of a Dutch barge allows for a more conventional bedroom.

Cons

- Can be too cumbersome and tiresome for regular use
- Usually less storage space below
- Usually much smaller than other bed options

Bunk beds

Lots of boats feature bunk beds in different configurations and some are so versatile that they can be converted from singles to doubles. These are often found in hire boats where the usage is very variable, but they're also popular with boaters who have intermittent guests.

'Given the type of use my boat gets it needs to be able to sleep as many people as possible. I have fixed beds, convertible pull-outs and a sofabed on board and they all get used. Having so many bunks does mean there has been a compromise in the amount of storage space available aboard, but it's not a big issue at the moment.'

SAM, Nb *KNOT HRD WORK*

WINDOWS AND PORTHOLES

Originally hijacked from the caravan world, these caravan-style windows are still the most common installation. However, the boating world has more than caught up and is becoming increasingly sophisticated, with double-glazed units, emergency exits, and various configurations of openings, with most being available in a range of colours. Some even allow you to remove the glass completely so that it can be replaced with fly screens so that you can enjoy the fine weather without the annoyance of intruding insects.

The windows of a narrowboat are arguably the weakest link in terms of security. Newer varieties are more secure, having fittings on the inside rather than the outside, but always consider the security risk of sliding glass and louvre window types.

Portholes are more secure as they are generally too small to allow entry if smashed or removed. That said, some boats now have portholes so large that a small person could easily fit through. Although most will concede that portholes generally allow less light aboard, there are several means to redress the issue.

Houdini hatches, pigeon boxes

There are ways to let more light into your boat besides windows. Houdini hatches are essentially a window in the roof and are indeed large enough to fit a person through. A pigeon hatch is a more secure option which, although they don't let in quite as much light as a Houdini hatch, is arguably a more interesting design. Be sure that both are well fitted and maintained as they are commonly known to leak.

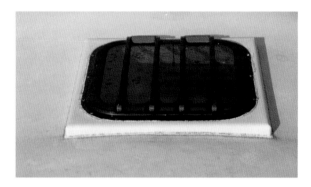

Houdini hatch.

Pigeon hatch open.

Drip, drip, drip

Condensation can be a problem for single-skin roof fittings such as Houdini hatches and pigeon boxes. This can be minimised by employing a padded foam 'bung' – but you might not want to have one installed over your bed, just in case.

Prism

These clever little devices are installed into the roof and provide a surprising amount of light. The wonders of science in action!

FRIDGES

Most boats will have a fridge aboard which can be 12v, 240v, or gas powered. A 'three-way' unit gives you the choice of using whichever of the three power options you prefer.

A 12v fridge is quite power hungry, but they can be ideal for those boaters who are happy to cruise or run their engine every day or so. A 240v fridge is often the choice of the liveaboard boater with intermittent cruising habits. Being cheaper to purchase than a 12v or three-way unit, the 240v fridge will be fine for the most part while the boat is hooked up to the mains at the mooring, and doing without a fridge for the occasional cruise is not too much of a hardship.

The best of all three worlds is the three-way fridge as these give you the versatility to choose whichever suits your current boating circumstances, although they are more expensive to purchase.

Gas-powered refrigeration

Running a fridge using gas negates any battery charging problems and is the cheapest way to keep your cucumber cool. It is unclear why more boaters don't choose this option.

FLOORING
Carpet

Almost all boats have a floor made from marine plywood which is then covered with more aesthetic flooring. In most cases this will be carpet, and frequently this will be carpet tiles. In addition to looking and feeling nice, carpet also does a great job of insulating the floor.

As the floor of your boat is below the water line, anything that provides insulation is worth having. The downside of carpet is that it gets dirty easily, particularly in the muddy winter months. Muddy towpaths are unavoidable and it is almost impossible to avoid bringing the towpath into your boat with your boots. Using carpet tiles can help here, but replacing dirty tiles with spares can create an ugly mismatch of new and faded colours. A rug can go some way to solving the problem too, but carpets of all types will likely need replacing regularly. Boating goes hand in hand with the British weather and all of the accompanying benefits and pitfalls. Muddy boots and dirty floors seem to be one of the unavoidable pitfalls.

Vinyl flooring and lino

As boat floorings go, lino has plenty of advantages. It is easy to clean, relatively cheap to install and replace and it has at least a modicum of insulating quality. Today's lino comes in a fabulous array of styles and designs and so there's very likely to be one to suit your taste. Lino and vinyl can be easily damaged by high heels, but then, high heels are hardly the best footwear for boating anyway.

Laminate flooring

This is becoming an increasingly popular option, especially for newer boaters aspiring for a more modern look. Easily cleaned and easy on the eye, the only downside of a laminate floor is the comparative lack of insulating qualities that can leave you with cold feet when the water temperature drops. Rugs can largely solve this problem and they also give some relief to dog owners who might be annoyed by the constant sound of paws and claws clicking on the floor.

CABIN WALLS

There is an almost clear division between older boats with tongue-and-groove covered cabin walls and newer boats with veneer panelling. Veneer panelling is much cheaper and easier for boat builders to install and it looks very smart and modern, so it's no wonder that this has become the norm for today's boat builders. For some though, real wood tongue and groove cabins are the only thing to have, for no other reason than the fact that it is a more traditional finish.

Boats with veneer panels are usually fitted out with the same both above and below the

A light, bright interior on a modern boat.

gunwales and on the cabin ceiling too, whereas tongue and groove fit outs are usually only present above the gunwales and on the ceiling. Below the gunwales is usually fitted out with marine ply and finished with a different covering entirely. Sometimes the ply is simply painted, sometimes papered, but often it is finished with carpet to enhance insulation.

You'll often see tongue and groove interiors that have been painted, usually a light colour, to make the cabin brighter. This works a treat and gives even the darkest, oldest boat a new lease of life. However, beware that painted interiors can be off-putting for some purchasers should you ever come to sell your boat. Real wood finishes are sacred to some and removing the paint to reveal the wood beneath is a massive task. Many are of the opinion that painting over good wood is tantamount to vandalism.

INTERIOR LAYOUT

The layout of a boat is one of the most important considerations when planning a new purchase or build commission. In such a limited space, getting it wrong can make boating so bothersome as to dampen one's enthusiasm irreparably. Liveaboards particularly must give great consideration to interior layout as they will need to live with any imperfections 24/7, but leisure boaters should still pay heed as there is not really any need to own a boat that you are not happy with.

Despite having such a limited space to work in, boat builders and fitters manage to install an amazing degree of variety. The positioning of doors and bulkhead walls (or the absence of them) is one of the most fundamental defining features of a boat interior. You might prefer open-plan style boating, allowing easy access and a sense of space. It is also easier to heat the nether-regions of your boat when there are no doors or walls in the way too. Others might prefer to have a bedroom section that can be closed off for privacy, or have the galley kept separate and out of view from the cabin seating area to cultivate a more relaxing and homely atmosphere.

Having a corridor that runs along one side of the boat is great for access and manoeuvring, but bear in mind that having all of the fittings and features on just one side of the boat can mean that it will naturally list to one side. This can be remedied with strategically placed ballast but it is something to consider when planning or purchasing. Alternating the load so that it is evenly balanced can produce some very interesting and innovative fit outs and storage solutions, and it can make the boat seem very cosy. The downside is that this can make it cumbersome to get from one end of the boat to the other; particularly if you are carrying something.

Most boats will have a bedroom near the stern, but this is not always the case. Bedrooms at mid-ship are to be found, particularly on boats with more than two berths. Beds positioned near the bow are becoming increasingly popular too. With this style of layout you can accommodate a decent-sized bed by sacrificing the ease of access to the bow, giving you the option of opening up the rest of the boat for an open plan-style layout.

The position of the toilet should be seriously considered too. It should be easily accessible from every berth for ease of morning ablutions, but ideally not too close to the galley or eating areas on the boat.

STORAGE SOLUTIONS

One of the greatest attributes any boat can have is an abundance of good storage solutions. Despite the best of intentions, there will always be 'stuff' that needs to be kept aboard, and that stuff all needs to be stored somewhere. The most useful storage solutions are the places that can be accessed easily, so the more of these you can have on your boat the better. Under beds and in tucked away compartments is useful space for items that are not used regularly such as tools and similar items.

Be sure to ask your boat vendor (whether new or second-hand) to explain the storage features of your boat. If you're having a new vessel built, spend some time appraising the storage options that other boaters have installed and show your builder the ones you covet. Compromises will always be necessary, but it is impossible to emphasise the importance of having adequate storage on board a boat.

OPTIONAL EXTRAS
Bow thrusters
A bow thruster is an electrically powered device that is installed in the hull at the bow of the boat to assist with steering. Handling is vastly improved using small propellers at the bow of the boat. There's no question that bow thrusters make handling easier, but purists will argue that boat folk have managed without them for centuries and so they are largely unnecessary now. Like all things, good handling boat technique comes with lots of practice and there is a risk that those reliant on using a bow thruster will run into trouble when it breaks down or if they use a boat that does not have one. Most boats will not have a bow thruster fitted. Consider too that this extra kit will inevitably

enforce extra maintenance and having a bow thruster means you have something else that will eventually go wrong. There have been examples of boats that have sunk because rust in the bow thrusters has caused a leak. Their location and structure makes bow thrusters almost impossible to maintain and check.

It comes down to whether you're looking for boating luxury and you're happy to pay for it, or if you prefer keeping it simple and stress free.

Generators

You'll often see boats with generators running aside them on the towpath. Often they are used as the primary means of charging the boat's leisure batteries instead of using the engine. Sometimes this can be to save money as a decent modern generator is cheaper to run than an old boat's engine. At other times it is an attempt to negate the noise that running the engine causes, despite the fact that the noise of a generator on the towpath can be an annoyance to everyone else in the vicinity.

There are a couple of important safety points to consider if you end up with a generator on board. Most generators are petrol driven and storing petrol aboard is inherently hazardous, as are the exhaust fumes that are produced when the generator is running. And secondly, any generator that is on display has the potential to become a target for opportunist thieves.

Anchor

If you are likely to cruise on a river then you need an anchor. It is important to make sure that your anchor is in good order, particularly the connections, chain and rope. The day you need your anchor is not the day to find out that it is faulty. Be sure to check too that your anchor size, chain length and rope length are adequate for your specific boat and cruising plans.

White goods and other electrical items

Whilst most boats will have a fridge on board very few will feature a freezer. Freezers are so power hungry that very few boats have anything more than an ice box in the refrigerator. Dedicated freezer units are rare given that boats will usually only have one or two people on board for most of the time and therefore the power required to run one is disproportionate to the amount of benefit it would provide. Liveaboards who are plugged into the mains and who rarely cruise will be an occasional exception.

Washing machines and dishwashers are similarly rare, not only due to their power usage but also because of the amount of water they use. Again, liveaboards with mains hook up and easy access to water will be an exception to this rule, but most boaters who cruise regularly will forego these luxuries.

Televisions are very popular aboard, but you might be surprised by the amount of boaters who decide to ditch the gogglebox completely. Many feel that they detract from the relaxing and stress-free boating experience. That said, it is not unusual to find an enormous wide-screen installed aboard, particularly on a wide beam boat, but many feel that these look rather ridiculous and incongruous and are not in keeping with the boating ethos. It's your call.

Bath

One of the main downsides of boating for many is the lack of a bath. Most boats have a shower unit installed, and most of those that do feature a bath will usually have a smaller than standard sized tub. Again, it is the wide beam and Dutch barge owners who revel in the space they have by installing a full-sized bath, but for most narrowboat owners a bath takes up too much space and uses too much water.

Additional items of boating kit

Although these items won't be fixed to the boat, they're important bits of kit to have on board. Use these bullet points as a checklist to make sure you're not caught short.

- Fenders – front back and sides
- BWB/BW/CRT key
- Handcuff key
- Windlass
- Mooring pins and mallet
- Piling/mooring hooks
- Sea magnet
- Canal map guides
- Head torch
- Sensor lights and magnetic LED lights
- Gas spanner
- Shore line electrical cable
- Water hose
- Hose adapters and connectors
- Coal scuttle and companion set
- Ecofan
- Fire extinguishers
- Chimney
- Life rings and life jackets

A variety of boats moored up.

4 THE COST OF OWNING A NARROWBOAT

If the best things in life are free, then narrowboating must be the exception that proves the rule. Narrowboating costs money. From the initial purchase and legal documentation to running costs and maintenance, it all comes at a cost. Indeed it can seem as if using the word 'narrowboat' before the name of a product can add another 50 per cent to the price. The spending starts the moment you buy your boat but, despite the costs, most boaters would say that it is worth every penny.

PURCHASE COST

Less than £10,000

Cheap narrowboats aren't often good and good narrowboats aren't often cheap. You can occasionally find unloved used boats on sale for as little as a few thousand pounds, but these will invariably be small boats with a good few years on the clock and in a very poor state of repair. Bringing one of these narrowboats back to life is a labour of love and will often end up costing more than the boat is worth. If you have the time, skills and money to invest it can be a rewarding endeavour, but if you're looking for a cheap way to get boating then boats at this end of the price range are rarely a good choice.

£10,000 to £25,000

If you want to get started straight away without taking on major renovation work then you'll likely be looking at used boats nearer the £10,000 to £20,000 mark. These boats will still probably be at the smaller and older end of the boat market but diligent searching and a little bit of luck will find you a boat that is ready to go. You'll almost certainly have to spend money on upgrading and refurbishing parts of the boat so you'll need to take that into consideration when comparing the market. A price list of common necessary works can be found on page 174. It is very unlikely that you'll find a used wide-beam at this price, but if you do it'll be in need of a lot of TLC.

£25,000 to £40,000

In this price bracket you'll usually find slightly larger used boats. You start to see boats that are 40 feet long or more, with the longer boats being predictably more expensive. However, there's plenty of crossover and by playing around with the length, price and age you can find really great boats in this price range. They'll usually be in a reasonably good state of repair commensurate with their age but you should expect some maintenance and refurbishment

Can you put a price on fun and relaxation?

costs. Repairs to worn-out running gear and utilities are likely and might not be immediately obvious at the point of purchase, but you should expect them nonetheless. You'll find 'value' wide beams available at this point in the market, usually at the upper ranges of the price scale.

£40,000 to £70,000

Now you'll be looking at some very smart used boats that will largely have been well cared for and be in good shape. This is the quality end of the used market and the boats you'll see will be less worn from age and showing considerably less defects and damage. You'll find nearly new smaller boats or well cared for larger boats with a few more years on the clock. There is no guarantee that they won't need repairs but the likelihood of serious defects diminishes as you move up to the top end of this price range. Decent used wide beams can be found at these prices too.

£70,000 to £100,000

At this point you get to choose from excellent quality used narrowboats and wide beams and a range of new boats too. Used boats will be in excellent condition and likely to include any features you covet. A new boat at this price might not have every feature your heart desires, but if you're not too picky you might find just what you're looking for.

£100,000+

At this price, the world is your oyster. A boat built to your specific requirements with exactly the features and fittings you would like is easily attainable if you're willing to pay the price. The most important consideration at this end of the market is to know exactly what you're looking for. Getting the boat of your dreams requires an experienced and discerning eye to determine the right mix of features for your specific needs.

CASE STUDY: THE COST OF BOATING

Tony: Nb *The Watchman* 50FT
LIVEABOARD

'I live and work on my boat, so my power usage is comparatively high.'

Gas: (gas boiler & cooker)12 x 13kg canisters @ £27.50 = £330.00 per annum.

Electricity: (240v appliances: fridge, laptop, CD player, mobile phone charger) = £245 per annum.

Coal: one bag per week in the winter months, using around 30 bags per year. £7.25 x 30 = £217.50 per annum.

Pump-out: About one per month = £300 per annum.

Repairs:
- New vinyl flooring: £200.
- New horn: £30.
- New paint job: £5,000.
- New galley hob plus fitting: £350.
- New engine room hatch and repairs: £200.

TRANSPORTATION COSTS

In addition to the purchase price and estimated repairs, there are other costs that you should consider when buying a boat. Most significant of these is the cost of getting the boat from its current location to your preferred mooring which could run into several hundred pounds or more. If you're going to move the boat yourself you'll need to factor in both diesel costs and your time. You may need to take time off work or even hire someone to move the boat for you.

Depending on the distances involved, it may be cheaper, quicker and easier to have the boat craned out and transported by road. The cost of this method is dependent on the available access at both ends of the journey, the weight of the boat, the size of the boat and the miles it needs to travel. It's also important to know exactly what type of hull you have as this can affect the type of vehicle that is needed, or at least the type of equipment the truck driver needs to lift and secure the boat safely.

Most narrowboats can be moved to anywhere in the country for under £1000. Wide beams and barges will usually cost more as the increased weight brings extra overheads, costs and administration issues. For instance, vehicles with a combined weight over 44 tons need to notify several authorities if they are to use bridges on their journey. The transport company will be able to advise you regarding costs, admin and regulations. All the owner needs to do is make sure that everything on the boat is stowed away safely, removing everything from the roof and from surfaces inside the boat.

PETER HIGGINS BOAT TRANSPORT,
BINGLEY, WEST YORKSHIRE

FUNDING YOUR PURCHASE

If your bank balance is large enough to purchase your boat outright then you can probably skip this section. For the rest of us, raising the capital to buy a boat is usually the biggest hurdle we face. Whether you're new to the water or already boating and looking to upgrade; it's not just a case of finding the asking price. You'll likely need a slush fund for repairs, licencing and hidden initial costs, so make sure you have enough capital to cover these expenses too.

Boat finance or 'marine mortgage'

Very few companies offer finance specifically for inland waterways boats. Some banks will create finance based on the equity you have in your home, but the provision of straight-up finance for narrowboats and wide beams is severely limited. If you can find a finance provider, the deal usually works in much the same way as a traditional house mortgage finance deal, where an initial deposit is required before the remainder is loaned with interest to be repaid monthly. The loan is secured against your boat which means that if you default for any reason and don't pay, the boat is reclaimed by the lender. Details vary, but most will lend around 80 per cent of the value of the boat and so expect you to have a cash deposit to pay the remainder. Most will also restrict lending to the middle and upper ends of the market with loans for boats valued at around £40,000.

No liveaboards

Note that many companies will not lend money if you intend to live aboard.

Personal loan

If you're able to secure a personal loan for the amount you need then you might find the interest rate to be comparable to that of a marine mortgage. These loans are not secured against your boat however, and so your boat cannot be repossessed if you default. Your credit rating will determine if your bank will offer a loan for this purpose. It seems the old adage that banks will only lend to people who can prove that they do not need the money might be particularly true here.

Housing equity

In the years before 2007 when house prices were rising quickly, releasing equity from your home to fund other purchases was a real option. Many people did exactly this, but since the start of the recession it has been a less viable springboard into boat ownership. Some prospective boaters, and particularly those who intend to live aboard, will use the proceeds from a house sale to fund their purchase. Your circumstances will determine if this is a viable option for you.

THE ADMIN

Every boat using the inland waterways must be licenced, insured and certified as safe. These requirements are akin to the tax, insurance and MOT for road vehicles and similarly, your licence will not be issued without insurance cover and Boat Safety Scheme certificate. Let's look at each of these in turn.

Licence

The kind of licence you will need depends on the type of boat you have, how you use it and the waterways you wish to cruise. Historic boat owners and those who run a business from their boats will need a specific type of licence, but most leisure and liveaboard boaters will require one of the licences listed below. In most cases length of your boat is used to calculate the cost of the licence. The beam width is not a factor except for some of the less popular types of licence. Discounts are applied for prompt payment but a surcharge is charged if payment is received late.

CASE STUDY: THE COST OF BOATING

Tim: Widebeam *Ascension* 60FT X 12FT
LIVEABOARD

'The boat has diesel central heating (five radiators and a towel rail) and a wood burner. In one year my diesel expenses were around £1400. That's with the heating running for an hour in the morning and about four hours at night. I am a continuous cruiser but during the winter I am moored in one place for five months with the winter mooring licence. I work during the day five days a week. I have a diesel generator which I use to charge the batteries during the winter months as well as solar panels (420w in total) which almost covers the summer months without the generator although the generator is used when the washing machine, tumble dryer are on. I have nine leisure batteries at 110a each. I have used four 13kg bottles of gas in a year because, although I'm no Nigella Lawson, I still have to eat. I'm afraid I have no definitive costs for coal or logs but I'd say a bag of each a week would be about right during the winter months. I've had no major expenses as far as repairs are concerned but servicing the generator and engine amounts to around £250 per year.'

All boats using the waterways need a licence of some description.

Gold Licence: go almost anywhere

Most of the UK's inland waterways are managed by the Canal and River Trust (formerly British Waterways), with the vast majority of the remaining navigable rivers being under the control of the Environment Agency. A Gold Licence will enable you to use all of the waterways controlled by these two main organisations and is therefore the most versatile licence for those who cruise extensively. Here's a list of the waterways you can cruise with a Gold Licence.

Canal and River Trust Waterways covered by Gold Licence	
Aire and Calder Navigation	Montgomery Canal
Ashby Canal	New Junction Canal
Ashton Canal	Oxford Canal
Birmingham and Fazeley Canal	Peak Forest Canal
Birmingham Canal Navigations	Regent's Canal
Bow Back Rivers	Ripon Canal
Bridgwater and Taunton Canal	River Avon (Hanham Lock to Bath)
Calder and Hebble Navigation	River Ouse (Yorkshire)
Chesterfield Canal	River Severn
Coventry Canal	River Soar Navigation
Erewash Canal	River Ure
Fossdyke Navigation	Rochdale Canal
Gloucester and Sharpness Canal	Stort Navigation
Grand Union Canal	Sheffield and South Yorkshire Navigations
Hertford Union Canal	Shropshire Union Canal
Huddersfield Broad Canal	Staffordshire and Worcestershire Canal
Huddersfield Narrow Canal	Stainforth and Keadby Canal
Kennet and Avon	Stourbridge Canal
Lancaster Canal	Stratford-on-Avon Canal
Lee Navigation	Tees Navigation
Leeds and Liverpool Canal	Trent and Mersey Canal
Limehouse Cut	Trent Navigation
Llangollen Canal	Upper Trent Navigation (incl. the Nottingham and Beeston Canal)
London Docklands (a fee is charged for short-term moorings)	Weaver Navigation
	Witham Navigation
Monmouthshire and Brecon Canal	Worcester and Birmingham

Environment Agency waterways covered by Gold Licence
River Thames
River Medway
River Nene
River Great Ouse System
River Ancholme
River Glen above Surfleet Sluice
River Welland above Spalding Lock
River Stour

Most rivers in the UK are administered by the Environment Agency.

Canal and River Trust Standard Long-Term Licence: for CRT canals and rivers only

If you're going to stay within the boundaries of waterways managed by the Canal and River Trust then you'll need a Long-Term Licence. These start on the 1st of any month and can be purchased for three, six or twelve months in advance. Obviously the twelve-month licence works out at the best value per month, but you can pay for your licence (of any duration) by direct debit in instalments at no extra cost.

Why buy a three-month licence?

Short duration licences are great for boats that are not in the water for the whole year, such as plastic cabin cruisers that are often kept on hard standing during the colder months. Your boat does not need a licence if it is not in the water.

Waterways covered by the Canal and River Trust Standard Long-Term Licence	
Aire and Calder Navigation	Leeds and Liverpool Canal
Ashby Canal	Limehouse Cut
Ashton Canal	Llangollen Canal
Birmingham and Fazeley Canal	London Docklands (a fee is charged for short-term moorings)
Birmingham Canal Navigations	
Bow Back Rivers	Monmouthshire and Brecon Canal
Bridgwater and Taunton Canal	Montgomery Canal
Calder and Hebble Navigation	New Junction Canal
Chesterfield Canal	Oxford Canal
Coventry Canal	Peak Forest Canal
Erewash Canal	Regent's Canal
Fossdyke Navigation	Ripon Canal
Gloucester and Sharpness Canal	River Avon (Hanham Lock to Bath)
Grand Union Canal	River Ouse (Yorkshire)
Hertford Union Canal	River Severn
Huddersfield Broad Canal	River Soar Navigation
Huddersfield Narrow Canal	River Ure
Kennet and Avon	Rochdale Canal
Lancaster Canal	Stort Navigation
Lee Navigation	Sheffield and South Yorkshire Navigations

Now that licence evasion has been almost eradicated, CRT now seem to be focused on catching those boats that overstay on visitor moorings.

CRT Rivers only licence: for Canal and River Trust-managed rivers only

If you intend to stay within the boundaries of CRT-managed rivers then there's a specific licence for you. These licences are rarely used and only remain as a quirk of legislation specific to some older rivers. If you intend to use this type of licence, but want to travel on waterways not covered by your licence to reach another river, then you can get 50 per cent off a 'short-term licence' to cover your journey. Or, you could just buy a more inclusive licence and do away with the administrative headache.

Too short

Some rivers covered by this type of licence are very short so compliance with continuous cruising rules is essentially impossible.

Waterways covered by the CRT Rivers only licence
Avon between Hanham Lock to Bath – East Bristol to Bath
Fossdyke to Withham
Lee Navigation Hertford to Limehouse (inc Limehouse Cut)
Bow Back Rivers
Kennet and Avon
London Docklands (a fee is charged for short-term moorings)
River Avon (Hanham Lock to Bath)
River Ouse (Yorkshire)
River Severn
River Soar Navigation
River Ure
Rochdale Canal

Mooring costs and licence fees are the most significant overheads for most boaters.

How CRT licences work in practice

For more information about CRT licences visit http://canalrivertrust.org.uk/boating/licensing. You'll find information on how much the licence for your boat will cost and how each type of licence works. In the meantime, here are a few examples.

Nb *The Watchman*

Length: 50 feet (15.2m)

Licence type: 12-month England and Wales standard 'canals and rivers' licence

Cost: £848.57 (Or £763.72 for prompt payment)

Nb *Aldebaran*

Length: 60 feet (18.3m)

Licence type: 12-month Gold Licence

Cost: £1181.00 (or £1275 when paying in installments by direct debit)

Environment Agency 'registration'

If you don't have a Gold Licence and wish to use any of the waterways managed by the Environment Agency then you'll need to 'register' your boat with them. Registering your boat is much the same as buying a licence as it entitles you to cruise and moor on those waterways. Only the Gold Licence entitles you to use your boat on all EA rivers, otherwise registration for the specific river (or rivers) you wish to use is required. The EA annual registrations run from 1 January each year and do not roll or work pro-rata. If you register in March, you'll pay the same price as you would if you'd registered in January. There is a 50 per cent discount if you register after September, although some conditions apply. The EA do intend to introduce a rolling pro-rata tariff, but there is no indication of when this might happen as yet.

Visitor's licence or long-term licence?

If you have a boat that will stay on a Canal and River Trust-managed waterway, you will need a long-term boat licence. If your boat is based on a navigation managed by a different organisation (e.g. the Environment Agency, Broads Authority), or if your boat is very small and you only put it into the waterway for the occasional trip, a short-term visitor licence will suffice. The definition of 'waterway' includes most long-term mooring sites and marinas, so your boat needs a licence whether or not you actually take it out to cruise.

Examples of visitor's licence fees (50-ft narrowboat)

1 week on the Thames £51 (Note: length and beam are considered.)

1 month on the Basingstoke Canal – £40

21 days on the River Wey £112 (lock tolls included.)

The EA has three licencing areas, the Thames, the Medway and the Anglian, which incorporates EA rivers in that area including the Great Ouse and the River Nene. Short-term licences are available for those boats that are visiting the area, and boats that are based there for longer periods can buy an annual registration.

The cost for the different licences varies with the region and the size of your boat. On the Thames and the Medway the licence cost is calculated using both the length and the beam width, whereas the licence for the Anglian rivers is based on the length only. This is likely to change as the EA standardise the process, but there is no set date for this change at present.

CASE STUDY: THE COST OF BOATING

Kit: Nb *Here Be Dragons* 57FT
LIVEABOARD

'We spend about £40 a month on diesel. In the summer months we move the boat every day and in the dark quarter of winter we run the engine for half an hour a day for charging purposes, supplementing our 220w of solar production.

'We buy 13kg of gas per quarter for cooking purposes. We hunt for cheap gas and at the moment pay £19 per bottle. We run a twin tub whilst the engine is running massively saving on launderette bills. We use about three bags of coal a week when necessary, running a small stove which also has a back boiler providing winter hot water. We spend £24 per week on supplies from the coal boat who we like to support as we value their service to the communities we travel through. Solar panels supply our electricity requirements for well over nine months of the year, which is outstanding; however we use very little power. We use LED lights, charge phones and play the radio and suchlike. We are ridiculously frugal because we value freedom over income so I suspect my figures may be highly under representative.'

Thames registration examples
Length: 50 foot
Beam: 6 foot 10 inches
1-year registration: £547.80

Anglian registration examples
Length: 60 foot
1-year registration: £864.87

Environment Agency registered visitor privileges

If you have a licence for any of the rivers under EA management, you are also entitled to visit any of the other EA managed rivers for up to 14 days. These visitor licences are available in seven-day chunks. You can split the 14 days across two separate visits on different rivers, or you can spend the whole 14 days on one river in one visit.

Boat Safety Scheme certification

The Boat Safety Scheme certificate is akin to the MOT test for a car, except that the examination is required every four years. The scheme aims to protect the safety of waterways users by minimising the risk of fires, explosions and pollution that could be caused by your boat. Unless your boat is less than four years old, it needs to pass the BSS examination before you will be issued with a licence or insurance cover and before you cruise the waterways. The examination focuses on points such as fire hazards, carbon monoxide risks, electrical issues and gas safety.

The test points are identical for all boats, irrespective of size or type, and so these variables will not affect the cost to any great degree. Although the cost of the test is not fixed, most inspectors will charge around £150 which covers the examination and the issue of the certificate. Most fail points can be remedied with minimal financial cost and a couple of man hours, although non-compliant gas cookers are sometimes more easily replaced than repaired. Some examiners may make an additional charge if a second visit is required following a fail, particularly if they have any distance to travel.

Insurance

Like all insurance the price of cover is dependent on risk and the amount of cover required. Rod Daniel of Craftinsure sheds a little light on the dark art of boat insurance: 'The value and age of the boat are key premium pricing factors rather than the length or beam width. Other factors to consider include where the boat is based and any additional cover you might require for boat contents. High-value items such as jewellery, cash, credit cards and electronic goods over £250 will be excluded from many policies. If you'd like items such as these included in the premium it is important to let the insurer know when the policy is being calculated. By that token, if you live aboard you can expect to pay a little more. Although liveaboard boats are less likely to be left unattended for long periods, increased use and the value of items on board do tend to add to the risk.'

Some insurers will make separate provisions for liveaboards and some even ask about your cruising profile. Continuous cruisers will obviously present a bigger risk than those moored permanently on a marina. Also be aware that most insurers will not cover craft used as rented accommodation, or will at least need to be informed that this is the case in order to provide cover. Standard cover will usually specifically exclude this type of arrangement.

Avoiding tidal waterways and opting for a higher excess can reduce your insurance costs but price is not the only consideration. Boaters might want to cut costs, but it is important to ensure your insurance provides adequate cover. Remember that for some tidal waterways your insurance policy may stipulate that you use a qualified pilot. Some insurers will also ask for a hull survey if your boat is over 20 years old. This can add up to £500 to your insurance expenditure once crane/dry dock costs are included, although this survey will usually be valid for insurance purposes for five years.

CASE STUDY: THE COST OF BOATING

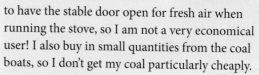

Polly Parrott: Nb *Springy*
30FT LIVEABOARD

'**Coal**: around £400 a year. Kindling/firelighters £20. I like to be warm, and I also like to have the stable door open for fresh air when running the stove, so I am not a very economical user! I also buy in small quantities from the coal boats, so I don't get my coal particularly cheaply.

Diesel: £300–£400 a year.

Gas: one 13kg bottle of gas lasts me almost dead on three months if used for my cooking and hot water via a Paloma. If I am also running the fridge on gas, each bottle lasts nearer six weeks.

Electricity: I have moored at two places that had shoreline electricity hook-up: Braunston Marina was 14.8p per unit including their service charge. My offside online mooring for winter charges an eye-watering 25p per unit (service charge of 10p a unit which is almost certainly illegal!). These are fed via a plug-in meter. Some places make you buy or pay a deposit for the meter, for example Braunston charged £95. It's worth noting that I have 360w of solar panels and am not a heavy electric user, so in the summer months I literally get totally free electric and, in winter, it still covers around 50 per cent of my usage. I am a liveaboard with a mooring. I don't move in the winter and in the summer I go out for short trips/weekenders/a couple of longer journeys.'

CASE STUDY: THE COST OF BOATING

Carol: Nb *Caelmiri* 55FT
RETIRED FAIR-WEATHER BOATER

'I used to cruise extensively when my husband, Tony, was alive but nowadays it's usually only for a few days at a time for a few outings each year. My boat is a nostalgic luxury.

Licence: I have a standard canal and river licence that costs £840 per year.

Insurance: £123 per year.

Mooring: I pay £1268 per year for a very nice mooring in a beautiful location. It's more than I used to pay at a different spot but it has many extra benefits. All of the usual facilities are there and more; from the easy access and car parking to the on-site boatyard facilities, it's ideal for my needs. The biggest benefit is that the boatyard staff are really helpful. My late husband, Tony, used to maintain the boat but I don't really want the hassle. The staff at the boatyard do all of that for me now. It's well worth paying for the service.

BSS: Every four years, but this year was the year: £125.

Pump-outs: 5 x £15 = £75.

Diesel: £100–120 per year. I normally fill up at the end of the cruising season so that my tank is full during the wintertime. With no space for condensation to build up there is less risk of suffering with the diesel bug nightmare.

Coal: £145 per year. I can easily use 20 bags a year and sometimes more. I don't like to be cold so I build a fire whenever I want. I don't mess around being a martyr in cold weather.

Gas: £56 per year. I'll use two bottles a year usually. I only use it for cooking and we often eat out when we're aboard.

Electricity: £50 per year. The boat is shut down when it is not in use, turning off the fridge and the lights etc.

Hot water: This is from my calorifier by running the engine, so see diesel costs above.

Repairs and maintenance: I don't do any repairs or maintenance myself. I leave it all to the boatyard staff and pay for the pleasure of not having to worry. Thankfully my boat is in good shape having been maintained well, and I keep on top of things so big bills are very rare. This year's maintenance bill includes a couple of larger expenses, but it is otherwise pretty average.'

- Fix leaky plumbing under sink: £24
- Re-pack and grease stern gland: £12
- Repair to side hatch: £72
- New chimney: £30
- New ropes: £40
- Electrics repair: £48
- Winterising: £48
- New stove and fitting: £800
- New batteries and fitting: £400

Insurance cost examples (courtesy of Craftinsure.com)			
Boat	60' x 12' wide-beam	57' semi-trad narrowboat	30' cruiser stern narrowboat	25' GRP river cruiser
Value	£130,000	£50,000	£15,000	£10,000
Age	Two years	20 years	45 years	15 years
Approximate quote	£443.00 pa	£192.61 pa	£153.00 pa	£105.00 pa*

(All quotes assume no previous claims, zero no claims bonus and £150.00 excess.)

(*Cruiser quote assumes no previous claims bonus and £100.00 excess.)

Not a survey

A hull survey is not the same thing as a Boat Safety Scheme certificate. Owners of older boats will need to provide a hull survey to confirm the integrity of the steel. A BSS pass certificate does not include this information.

Marinas often have a thriving community spirit but some people prefer their neighbours to be at more than arm's length away.

MOORINGS

The cost of mooring is likely to be the biggest regular annual expense for most boat owners and the price you pay will be largely dependent on geography, available facilities and the length of your boat. Most moorings will also charge different fees if moored alone or abreast another boat and some also differentiate between frequent and infrequent usage. If you have a wide-beamed vessel then most mooring providers will also consider the width of your boat when pricing too.

Living next to the canal has become extremely desirable.

Moorings with the best range of facilities in the most popular areas will, of course, cost more. As with most things in the UK, moorings in London will cost more than a comparable site elsewhere. However, city-centre locations in other parts of the country don't always command a premium over rural locations. Many boaters value tranquillity and therefore a quiet mooring away from nightlife and road noise is a perfect choice.

There are lots of different types of mooring and providers too, from large commercial marinas and boat clubs to 'end of garden' and 'online' moorings. Commercial moorings tend to be the best equipped and most costly, but some boat club moorings have facilities to rival the big marinas and are usually priced very competitively indeed. End of garden spots are exactly that and can represent good value, particularly if the

facilities you need are available locally. If you're lucky to have enough navigable water at the end of your garden then you're onto a winner. CRT usually charges half of the local going rate for a comparable CRT mooring in these circumstances, providing the boat is for leisure use and you are the owner of both the property and the boat.

Mooring tenders

The Canal and River Trust operates around 3600 long-term moorings at over 330 sites nationwide. As would be expected, boats do come and go, vacating moorings that then need a new boat to fill them. In 2013 there were approximately 900 vacancies across the regions in England and Wales, so there'll usually be something to consider in your chosen area. The prices for these moorings are not set and so can vary wildly depending on location, facilities,

Online moorings will often cost less than a place in a marina.

convenience and pot luck. The moorings can be online, or in marinas of all types and sizes in all sorts of places.

The sales of these moorings are conducted in much the same fashion as online auction sites such as eBay, with a chance to grab a deal by bidding against other boaters, or you can Buy It Now and pay the advertised price. You can pay as little as a few hundred pounds for an online mooring with no facilities in a secluded part of the system, or you can shell out £10,000 for a residential berth in the centre of London. Are you feeling lucky?

Free moorings

It is possible to moor your boat for free at visitor moorings that can be found at thousands of places on the waterways network. It is also possible to moor for free at the water's edge where this is practicable and where the land is not privately owned.

Whilst these 'free' moorings bear no financial cost, there are strict rules that govern how these visitor moorings are used, which some boaters will find inconvenient or impractical depending on their lifestyle. The amount of time you are allowed to stay ranges from a maximum of 14 days to as little as a few hours. Boaters who don't have a home mooring are called 'continuous cruisers' and usually live aboard their boat. They are subject to specific rules that govern how long they can spend in any one area, so before you consider this option it is important that you familiarise yourself with what the lifestyle entails. For more information on moorings and continuous cruising, see Chapter 5 starting on page 113.

CONSUMABLES

Heating, lighting, cooking, water usage and waste disposal will all cost money one way or another. The cheapest of these are water usage and waste disposal as these are essentially free for boaters. Water taps and bin facilities are provided as part of your mooring agreement if you're based at a well-equipped marina with facilities on site, so while the price of these can't be quantified easily there is a cost incurred. If you're out and about there are intermittent bins and water taps provided at random points along the waterways network and the cost of these is included in your licence fee. It's not unusual to see boats carrying bags of rubbish on the roof in search of somewhere to dispose of it properly.

Heat

On most boats heating is provided by a solid-fuel or wood-burning stove. Kindling, logs and coal costs depend on how much you use your boat during the colder months. Low usage boaters might use just a couple of bags of coal during the whole year, whilst liveaboards can easily get through two or three bags each week. Most use coal 'briquettes' such as Excel or Burnwell, but there are plenty of other products and brands to choose from too. Costs for a 25kg bag seem to range from £7–£10 each. Household coal is cheaper but few people seem to find a use for it. Debate about which type of coal nugget offers the best value and performance rages every winter, so you'll need to experiment for yourself.

Kindling can often be found for free by foraging, but care should be taken to avoid depleting the local area of dead wood. Dead wood is an extremely valuable source of shelter, food and nutrients for plants and animals and

Be prepared

Beware of 'petrol station' coals. These are usually not suitable for the types of multi-fuel stoves you find on boats as they get too hot and can cause damage. Tempting as it may be, when needs must, you run a serious risk of having to shell out to replace your damaged stove.

CASE STUDY: THE COST OF BOATING

Dave: Nb *Clay Hamer* 45FT
CONTINUOUS CRUISER

Coal: 18 bags.

Gas: three bottles @ 13.5kg each.

Fuel: 234 litres (and spent 273 engine hours).

Total spend for the year = £465.

over-enthusiastic collection is detrimental to the local ecosystem. Many boaters manage the balance by laying claim to any wood that is within arm's length of the towpath and leaving the rest for Mother Nature. Boaters are usually canny enough to find a source of free wood to avoid having to forage or spend money. Any business that uses wood will usually have off-cuts that they are pleased to dispose of and it makes sense to keep an eye out for trees being trimmed and felled.

There are other ways to heat a boat that do not rely on coal or wood. Diesel heaters (such as those found in lorry cabs) are the most popular alternative choice. There are several types to choose from. Most are fed from the same diesel tank as the boat's engine, making accurate running costs difficult to obtain. Calculations vary, but rough estimates level out at 0.4–0.6 litres an hour. Once installed, most diesel stoves have very low maintenance costs, but some types of diesel-fuelled heaters will require regular servicing. Indeed many boaters complain that these heaters break down and need servicing far too regularly. Jason Kay of BK Marine Systems specialises in servicing Eberspacher and Webasto diesel-fuelled heaters and was keen to address the reliability issue. 'The units have a two-year warranty from new and I wouldn't expect them to need any attention at all in this time. After a few years of use I advise that people get a routine service done every couple of years at least, and possibly yearly in high usage applications such as liveaboard boats. More frequent problems are likely due to poor installation or poor quality fuels. A standard service kit plus labour will usually not break the £200 mark.'

Diesel-fed stoves are another popular option and are reputed to be much more economical than their solid fuel and wood-burning cousins, but the premium for a pleasing flame is one most boaters are prepared to pay.

Gas

Gas can be used to heat your water, cook your meals and even keep your food refrigerated. Costs here are almost impossible to predict.

CASE STUDY: THE COST OF BOATING

Sam: Nb *Knot Hrd Work* 57FT
REGULAR WEEKEND BOATER

'My boat is essentially a party boat for friends and family that gets used every weekend in all but the worst weather. We cruise to the local gastro-pubs or meet up on the boat and stay on the mooring. My consumable costs are quite low compared with liveaboards and those who go on extensive cruises.

Fuel: Filled the tank up once in two-and-a-half years, approximately £100 per year.

Gas: Two 13.5kg bottles per annum. Used for cooking and occasional gas central heating.

Coal: Less than £10 per year. We rarely buy coal, preferring to use wood from the felled trees in my garden. I guess we've used a couple of bags in the whole time we've had the boat.

Electricity: We don't plug in to the mains and so have no electricity costs. We're frugal with the electricity usage and we don't have a TV on board.'

It will vary depending on how many units on your boat use gas, the amount of time you use them and even the size of gas bottle you can fit into your locker. The best means to predict or estimate your usage costs is to look at a case study with a similar profile as yours.

Electricity

Electric usage is similarly dependent on your specific circumstances and the means of producing it varies even more. Shoreline provision from your mooring spot is usually

CASE STUDY: THE COST OF BOATING

Brett and Jane: Dutch barge *Boadicea*
LIVEABOARD BOATERS

'We've lived aboard for almost two years and we live and work locally. Until now we haven't moved much but we intend to cruise much more in the coming year.

Licence: Our Dutch barge is 60' x 10.5' and was built in 2003. We pay for our licence in monthly installments of £84.18 pcm, making a total cost of £925.97 per year including VAT.

Insurance: £440 per year. We got a one-year no claims discount this year of £21.38 which I thought would be better. We stuck with our current insurer, Haven Knox-Johnston, this year. I admit that we didn't shop around but we will probably consider other insurers next time to compare prices. One of the reasons we stayed was because of the option to include £14.25 for legal expenses. It didn't seem too much to add on for something that I imagine is more niche than car legal expenses cover.

Mooring: £235 per month. Our mooring has pontoon mooring with cleats, electrical hook up, water points and a facilities block with a basic shower and toilet in an unheated building. There's also a coin-operated washer and dryer, but we have our own on board so don't use it. The mooring is well contained with locked gated access during the evening. During the day the businesses around the mooring are open so the place is theoretically accessible, but in practice there are never any problems.

Gas usage: one 13kg bottle lasts five weeks. We use gas only for cooking. We both enjoy cooking and so will be using oven and gas rings for around two hours every day.

Electricity: £40 per month. We heat our water through an electrical immersion heater in a tank.

I think this is why we have a fairly large electricity bill. We have changed the timer a little to get best economy; it's currently on for 45 minutes twice a day. That does enough for two showers and two big washing-up pots per day. Plus we have two laptops, a TV, two mobile chargers and stereo CD player.

Coal and kindling: winter usage last year worked out at £90 pcm January to April, and 2013 it was a particularly hard winter. We were using a mix of solid fuel coal and wood. This year so far we have purchased wood in bulk one tonne deliveries and have sourced a cheaper coal supplier. So total for winter this year is approx £70/month. Our summer usage is next to nothing.

Diesel: we use diesel for cruising and for our generator at the moment, but we're about to fit a diesel heater, so the usage will increase. Our massive engine uses a lot more diesel than a regular narrowboat engine so we try to avoid using it if possible as it uses a lot of fuel per hour. Fuel cost depends on whether we use red or white but averages around 95p per litre. See below.

Pump-outs: none. We use a cassette toilet.

Repairs and upgrades:

1. Fitted a generator: Total cost including additional parts, materials £2000. This will cut our running costs because it means we can fill up with red diesel and benefit from lower battery charging costs as opposed to using engine. We did this for more flexibility to move around.

2. Sourced, reconditioned and installed Eberspacher diesel heater which will (eventually) run our central heating and heat our water. Total cost to date approximately £500.

3. Fitted a washing machine. After doing the sums we found that it would actually save us money over the year as opposed to using service washes. It's more convenient too.

Heating: We have every option under the sun now including solar! We bought the boat with under-floor heating fitted. This is a big luxury and is fine if you want to use this method of heating occasionally but this proved to be an expensive option to use as the main source of heating the boat. We tried it for a few weeks and the electricity cost £25 per week cost to heat the boat to around 12 degrees in winter. The stove is much better; with gravity feed radiators coming off the back boiler to the back cabin and wheelhouse.

Hot water: We struggled with hot water to start with. The plumber worked out the heating element in the water tank wasn't working very well and it was replaced at a cost of £190.

We decided that making sure the boat was fully insulated was the best way to go. We spray-foamed the front cabin just where the chine starts to the floor as this area hadn't been very well insulated. We spray-foamed an estimated area of 15m square at a cost of around £500 and we have definitely noticed the difference. Probably the best money we have spent on the boat.

Emergencies and unforeseen costs: Repair to raw water sump = £150. Cost included materials, labour and dry dock cost for one day in a wide beam dock.

Boating saved us money: By not buying more food than we can use at any one time because we have a smaller fridge and freezer. It was a big surprise as it actually really encourages us to use food up and you can see exactly what you have. We're also much more conscious of the power and water that we use and we're very careful not to waste either.'

Battery charger pros and cons

If you're plugged in to a land-based mains point you'll need a battery charger to convert the 240v supply to the 12v required by your batteries. Beware of frying your batteries with constant charging as this will mean you have to replace them regularly. At over £100 each, it's a cost that is worth avoiding.

a cheap option. This is because marinas buy electricity in bulk and cannot charge a premium as they are not registered energy suppliers. If you're out and about then your batteries will be charged by running your engine. This, of course, uses diesel, and despite the energy generation being a pleasing by-product of cruising, the cost can be quantified. As a rough guide it is estimated that each hour of engine use will use around a litre of diesel. From four hours of engine use you'll generate enough battery power to last between 24–72 hours, depending on your usage and the efficiency of your system.

Solar and wind generators are increasingly popular on boats. Comparing the cost of purchase with the benefits thereafter is becoming more favourable each year and so soon it might be foolish to do without.

Fuel usage

Almost every boat on the inland waterways is fuelled by diesel and the amount that you use will depend on how far you cruise and how you charge your batteries. Again, the case studies highlighted here will offer the best comparison for your diesel usage. However, although many kept a log of the fuel they purchased, few keep records of engine running hours.

A ball-park figure

Cost of owning a boat for a whole year = £6826.

(A small survey of annual boating costs across 13 respondents of differing boating profiles.)

Recent legislation taxes fuel for boats differently depending on how it is used. Fuel for propulsion is taxed at a higher rate than that used to charge batteries for domestic use and heating. For those with a single fuel tank it is impossible to accurately measure the proportions of fuel used for each and so a sensible approximation is usually implemented. 'After much discussion within the industry it has become almost standard practice to implement a 60/40 split when selling red diesel for boats,' says Troy of Snaygill Boats. 'Customers sign a declaration of usage which we keep on file for HMRC to view if requested.'

It is the responsibility of the boat owner to accurately declare their usage proportions for tax purposes and it is entirely legal to purchase diesel at domestic tax rates if the boat will use the fuel whilst moored, during the winter for example. It is also worth noting that HMRC does not require fuel suppliers to record fuel sold in volumes of less than 100 litres, although many keep records of all sales, regardless of volume sold.

PUMP-OUTS

The main factors governing pump-out costs are frequency (of boat use) and volume (of your black water tank). The cost to pump out is usually between £10 and £15 and very few places charge more. Many boaters negate the cost completely by utilising cassette toilets as these are free to empty at Elsan sanitary disposal points. It would be an easy decision to opt for cassettes if cost were the only issue, but there are many factors to consider besides. Be sure to read the section on boat toilets on page 68 before you decide which type of toilet you want. It is one of the most important decisions you'll face and getting it wrong can be a real pain.

Both pump-out and cassette owners will use solutions to neutralise odours and 'treat' the sewage. The cost of these fluids is negligible at around £30 per annum. Replacements, spares and repairs are listed in the maintenance section of this article and are thankfully rarely needed.

REPAIRS AND MAINTENANCE

It would be impossible to list every cost associated with boat repair and maintenance here, but maintaining your boat will cost money regardless of age or condition. It's important to budget for this as some problems can stop you dead in the water, or worse still, sink your boat. Often you won't see the problem until something stops working, but other maintenance costs can be predicted. Replacing your batteries, re-packing your stern gland and replacing your water pump are standard maintenance costs that will occur intermittently. You'll see the signs that these need addressing long before any emergency repairs are necessary. Other jobs, such as blacking your boat's hull and servicing your engine, should be in your diary to tackle as a matter of course.

Boating is often cited as a contact sport and boats can take a beating. So, inevitably, sometimes you'll face a repair bill. The hull structure is almost indestructible, but not quite. Despite being made from thick steel, damage and deterioration can still occur. The most vulnerable parts of the hull are the bends at bow and stern as these are the areas that are bumped most frequently. Most bumps are nothing to worry about but gashes can happen if you hit something that is sharp or pointy. Rust is a more usual culprit for causing hull breaches. A regular hull survey schedule will let you know well in advance if your hull is rusting away. Over-plating is the remedy for both of these issues and you'll often hear of older boats having this work done.

BOAT PAINTING

For the purposes of this section I have concentrated on information from professional boat painters as DIY jobs vary widely in their costs and finish quality.

St Mary's Marina in Rufford near Preston has an excellent reputation for boat painting. They say: 'In boat painting as with many things, you usually get what you pay for. Our standard service will usually take the boat back to the metalwork so that we can deal with any rust issues below the surface of the current paintwork. We take out all of the windows and remove all roof fittings to be sure that there is no rusty metal beneath, as this can easily spread and ruin a new paint job.'

Prices for paintwork vary widely dependent on which painter you use and how much work is involved in the preparation for the job. At St Mary's for a routine, well-prepared, multi-coat job you can expect to pay anything from £2500 for a 40-foot boat up to around £5000 for a 57 footer. 'The amount of prep will define the exact price,' says St Mary's.

CASE STUDY: THE COST OF BOATING

Phil Shackleton: Nb *Felicitas* 57FT
LEISURE BOATER

'We use the boat around four times per year, for at least two weeks at a time when I am not in Germany. Sometimes we're here for a couple of months during the summer.

Diesel: 75 litres all for propulsion.

Gas: Up to two to three 13kg bottles. The Aldi boiler runs small radiators. Plus cooking and occasionally for warm water. I also use an immersion heater or the calorifier when engine is running.

Coal: Five 25kg bags of Burnwell coal.

Maintenance: Not a lot of maintenance this year. Planning a paint job but I've spent about £20 this year in maintaining the outside, undercoating and rubbing down. I am a big believer in engine maintenance and I regularly change the oil. I have some contacts in the motor trade and so I've spent around £40 on fan belts, oil and filters.

Mooring = £1400 per year.'

Resale value

The difference a good-quality paint job can make to an old or tired-looking tub is remarkable and it can have an enormous influence on the value of a boat, something worth thinking about if you intend to sell your boat at any point.

BOAT MAINTENANCE AND REPAIR COSTS

An interview with Jo Dortona from Snaygill Boats

It is impossible to list all of the repair and maintenance jobs you might face on a narrowboat. However, Jo Dortona who wields the spanners at Snaygill Boats on the Leeds and Liverpool Canal in Skipton, North Yorkshire gives us the lowdown and some rough prices for common boating repairs and maintenance issues.

Tony Jones: *Having run the workshop here for so many years you must have seen it all?*

Jo Dortona: Yes, that would be an understatement. No two days are alike and I'm often surprised by the jobs that come in.

TJ: *But surely there are jobs that you see time and time again?*

Jo: Yes, but even then they'll be different somehow because it seems that no two boats are the same. That's why it's difficult to give prices for jobs over the phone. You never know how much work is involved until you've finished the job.

TJ: *How about if I ask you for a rough estimate for some of the jobs you see quite often.*

Jo: Rough price estimates are always very vague for exactly the reason I've said, but I can give you an indication. Just don't hold me to it.

TJ: *OK, can you give me a very rough indication on how much it would cost for you to:*

Replace a broken window. I hit a swing bridge as I was going through it and smashed the glass.

A new window costs around £180 and it will cost around £60 to fit, but as with all things, if there are any complications this hourly fitting cost could be more.

Q My water tank has sprung a leak. Can you fix it or will I need a new one?

A Tanks can be repaired, but if it has failed in one place then it is likely to fail again somewhere else soon. For that reason we will recommend a new unit which will cost around £500. Fitting it will take half a day at £40 per hour plus VAT.

Q I need a new paint job. How much?

A Depending on the design a new paint job will likely cost around £80–110 per foot. Coach-lines, harlequin, door design and sign-writing are the things that will push up the price.

Q I badly scratched my new paintwork on some overhanging branches. Please can you touch up the damage?

A This one really is dependent on so many variables, such as the age of the paintjob, the severity of the damage and the ease of matching colours. You can sometimes polish out the damage, otherwise you'll need to match the colours. This is easier on newer paint jobs, but if the paint has faded it will be much harder to do. I don't even want to estimate a price for this job until I see it.

Q I let my stove get too hot and it has been so badly damaged that it is leaking smoke from the joints. What can be done?

A Repairs are possible, but sometimes these can be costly to attempt and not always solve the problem. A new Morco Squirrel-branded stove, including fitting, will be around £800.

Q My propeller came off! What can I do?

A You'll need a day in the dry dock at £115 per day. Depending on the type a new propeller will be between £250 and £600. Fitting it will cost around £100

Q I think my gearbox is broken. Is it going to be expensive?

A It's rare for a gearbox to break. It's more likely an oil or linkage problem that can usually be fixed in half a day or less. If we need to remove and strip down your gearbox you can expect a bill around £500. If you need a new one the cost is around £900 plus half a day of work to fit it.

Q My batteries don't hold their charge and I run out of power after just a couple of hours. I think I need new ones fitted.

A They'll cost around £100 each including fitting.

Q I'd like a newly-fitted bathroom please.

A If you use good-quality fixtures this job will be around £1500 inclusive of fitting, but it really depends on the quality of the kit you want installed.

Q One of my window frames leaks when it rains. How much to fix it?

A round £65, as long as the frame isn't damaged.

Q Can you winterise my boat so that it doesn't burst its plumbing when the weather turns cold?

A A boat with easy to reach fittings that hasn't much water left in the tank can be done quickly, but you should budget for around £120, just in case your boat is a pain to sort.

Q My water tank is a bit yucky.

A To clean and repaint with the appropriate paint will cost around £500.

Q I don't fancy re-packing my stern gland. What will it cost for you to do it?

A About £40.

If a full assault on your boat paintwork is out of your price range, most places will offer an 'economy paint service' that can be considerably cheaper. Either by not removing the windows and fittings or by being less particular about going back to metal, you might be able to get away with less prep and still end up with a great paint job. This breathes new life into an old paint job and costs considerably less – usually just a grand or two.

BREAKDOWN COVER

Boating breakdown cover is usually a sensible precaution particularly for those new to boating and so it is a cost I always quote to the uninitiated when the question of expenditure arises. The cost will depend on the level of cover required and can range from £55 to £140 a year with the ever popular River Canal Rescue. The types of cover available aim to cater for all kinds of boat user profiles, so make sure that you check the details before you buy. For example, some levels of cover will look after the boat and the whole crew, whereas others will cover only the boat and the owner.

Entertainment and technology

Surfing the net from your boat is easy nowadays. Contract deals which include the cost of the USB mobile dongle start at around £10 per month, or if you don't mind paying for the dongle then a pay-as-you-go deal may suit you better. Top-up vouchers start at around £10 for 1GB of data and are valid for 30 days. If you sign up for a contract you can often get more data for your money, particularly if you are already a customer. Some marinas offer a wireless Internet service at hugely varying costs; I've paid as little as £5 per month and as much as £15 per month.

When choosing between a dongle or marina-based Internet service, it is worth remembering that both have their downsides. Mobile Internet dongles rely on the strength of a signal which is variable in different parts of the waterways network. Marina-based wireless services only work whilst you are moored in your marina.

TV licence

If you have a TV licence for your home then you do not need to have another licence for the TV on your boat. Otherwise you will need a licence for your on-board TV. Continuous cruisers without an address may have difficulty obtaining a licence.

Sundries: a rough price guide	
Windlass	£15–£30
Mooring pins	£8–£15
Chimney	£30–£75
Fire extinguisher	£15–£40
Waterways guide map	£12
Pump-out key	£5
Brass gas spanner	£6
Water hose reel	£30
CRT facilities key	£6
Anti-vandal (handcuff) key	£5
Key float	£3
Sea magnet	£30
Tiller pin	£10
Ecofan	£100

5 MOORINGS

Finding the right mooring is a crucial part of owning a narrowboat. Whether it's a designated spot that you pay for or a temporary mooring at the end of a day's cruising, it is important to choose wisely. There are many different types of mooring and each will have its own idiosyncrasies and specific culture. Mooring places are often in high demand and so it helps to consider the options that others might disregard, as these may be cheaper and more available due to the laws of supply and demand.

OBTAINING A MOORING

Your choice of mooring will be determined to a greater or lesser degree by the constraints of your lifestyle. Those who need stick to a specific region will have fewer options than the boater who is free to cruise the network. But regardless, there are usually options and choices to be made. New boaters are often advised to secure a mooring before getting a boat. This is indeed sensible, particularly if you need a mooring in a very specific area. However, if you're prepared to be flexible then an acceptable mooring can usually be found. There are so many factors to consider that it is inevitable that you will need to compromise somewhere, but by being flexible and objective a suitable mooring solution is usually available. In an ideal world you would find a friendly, perfectly-located and well-managed mooring with great security in a beautiful location with great facilities and lots of accessible local resources. And it would be inexpensive too. In

Finding a mooring space can be hard work.

reality you will probably need to compromise and your personal circumstances will dictate which of these areas you can be most flexible in. It will come as no surprise that you will usually get what you pay for.

Facilities, features and services

The kind of mooring you need depends entirely on the type of boating you want to do. Some people hope for a quiet spot in the middle of nowhere, whilst others want a full service marina with all the bells and whistles. Here's a list to help you to decide what's important to you.

- Fixed mooring rings, pins or cleats
- Full-length or part-length pontoons
- Single moored or moored abreast
- Secure or gated mooring
- Children allowed
- Stove fires allowed
- Easy access close to road or parking
- Private parking available
- Electric hook up
- Water point
- Pump-out facility
- Elsan/cassette disposal facility
- Gas, coal and other fuel for sale
- Canal shop for basic boating supplies
- Chandlery supplies

- Local grocery shop for pre-cruise stocking up
- Boatyard facilities on site – for those inevitable maintenance jobs
- Dry-dock or crane out facilities
- Poly tunnel – for boat painting
- Laundry
- Club house
- Bar, café or restaurant
- Social events calendar
- Community
- Wi-fi access
- Postal address provision
- Pets allowed
- Good access to local roads
- Local train service
- Access to local town or shopping
- Overhanging trees can soil boat roof or cause damage in bad weather
- Towpath or offside access
- River mooring pontoons that rise and fall with tides and river levels

A typical pontoon mooring.

Your new mooring

It is often said that finding a suitable mooring is the most difficult part of buying a new boat. In reality this depends on how flexible you are with regards to the location, and how accommodating your mooring provider can be regarding the space that is available. If you need to be located at a specific mooring spot then reserving that place as soon as possible makes good sense. Reserving a mooring before you get a boat requires some thought. The boat-buying process can take a while and so you'll need to budget for the time it will take to find a boat and the inevitable delays. Reserve too early and you could end up wasting money. Reserve too late and you might miss your spot.

Remember that most mooring providers rent space by the foot, so you'll need to let them know how big your boat will be. This is not always an easy question to answer as you could easily end up with a boat that is longer or shorter than you planned. Reserving a space that is too long is not usually a problem, so long as you are prepared to pay for the space you're not using. If you end up buying a boat that is slightly longer than you planned then you might find that the extra mooring space isn't available.

If you do buy the boat before finding a mooring you will need to move quickly to secure a spot as soon as possible after purchase. This might mean that you need to compromise on location in order to get sorted quickly, or you might fall lucky and secure a good spot straight away. There is always the risk that no convenient moorings are available, leaving you mooring on the towpath until space becomes free. This can take months or even years in popular locations. Lingering on visitor moorings and 'bridge hopping' will soon attract the attention of the waterways licencing agents and so the prospect of this being your only option should not be taken lightly.

With all of that said, many people seem to find entirely suitable moorings with little fuss or compromise. Besides, one of the good things about owning a boat is that it can be easily relocated to another spot if you change your mind or your circumstances change. Your choice of mooring is an important decision, but whatever happens there is usually an entirely agreeable option if you're flexible and resourceful.

Pontoon moorings at a marina.

The options

Commercial marina moorings are usually the easiest and most available mooring option. These will usually be well equipped, have convenient access and be at the upper end of the luxury scale. Of course, you'll pay for these privileges through your mooring fees, but for most people a commercial marina will tick all of the boxes.

Right: Boats moored at Pyrford Marina.
Below: Braunston Marina.

MARINA CASE STUDY: BRAUNSTON MARINA

Heralded by broadcaster and journalist John Sergeant as 'the best looking marina in Britain', Braunston Marina is ideally located for the canal enthusiast. It lies at the crossroads of the Grand Union and Oxford canals, and indeed of the whole waterways. The marina is located alongside the A45 between Daventry and Rugby. It is only 20 minutes from junction 16 on the M1, under an hour from Birmingham.

Price

£150.00 per metre per year by direct debit.

£135.50 per metre per year payment in advance.

Facilities

Facilities	
Fixed mooring rings, pins or cleats	Y
Full-length or part-length pontoons	Y
Single or moored abreast	Both
Secure or gated mooring	N
Children allowed?	Y
Pets allowed?	Y
Stove fires allowed?	Y
Easy access – close to road or parking	Y
Private parking available	Y
Electric hook up	Y
Water point	Y
Pump-out facility	Y
Elsan/cassette disposal facility	Y
Gas, coal and other fuel for sale	Y
Canal shop for basic boating supplies	Y
Chandlery supplies	Y
Boatyard facilities on site	Y
Dry-dock or crane out facilities	Y
Poly tunnel for boat painting	N/A
Laundry	Y
Club house	N
Bar, café or restaurant	N
Social events calendar	Y
Wi-fi access	Y
Postal address provision	Y
Good access to major roads	Y
Local train service	N
Access to local town or shopping	Y

Boatyard moorings are usually less salubrious but often provide maintenance services that are not available at commercial marinas. Be aware that working boatyards can be noisy and often untidy places that aren't attempting to be conventionally pretty. Some boaters actually like the busy industrial setting so it is a case of horses for courses.

Above: Boatyard moorings on the Leeds and Liverpool Canal.
Below: Hainsworth's boatyard in Bingley, Yorkshire.

BOATYARD CASE STUDY: HAINSWORTH'S

Hainsworth's is a typical boatyard location that has a handful of online moorings alongside the premises in a beautiful, but accessible rural location. As a fully operational boatyard there is a full range of services available, and occasionally, a little accompanying noise.

Price
Narrowboats: £36.40 per foot per year.
Wide beams: £41.60 per foot per year.

Facilities	
Fixed mooring rings, pins or cleats	Y
Full-length or part-length pontoons	N
Single or moored abreast	Both
Secure or gated mooring	N
Children allowed?	Y
Pets allowed?	Y
Stove fires allowed?	Y
Easy access – close to road or parking	Y
Private parking available	N
Electric hook up	Y
Water point	Y
Pump- out facility	Y
Elsan/cassette disposal facility	N
Gas, coal and other fuel for sale	Y
Canal shop for basic boating supplies	Y
Chandlery supplies	N
Boatyard facilities on site	Y
Dry-dock or crane out facilities	N
Poly tunnel for boat painting	N
Laundry	N
Club house	N
Bar, café or restaurant	N
Social events calendar	N
Wi-fi access	N
Postal address provision	N
Good access to major roads	N
Local train service	Y
Access to local town or shopping	Y

Boat club moorings often have a very sociable culture with an emphasis on leisure and community. There's often a clubhouse with a bar where members will socialise and there is usually a calendar of social events and club cruises. Some clubs have facilities to rival top-end marinas and most are adequately equipped with the essentials. Fees are usually very agreeable because the clubs are often run by a committee of volunteers as a not-for-profit organisation. The only downsides are those that often plague committee-led organisations and there is usually a long waiting list to join.

BOAT CLUB CASE STUDY: AIREDALE BOAT CLUB

Airedale Boat Club is located directly next door to Hainsworth's boatyard and so gives a good comparison between these two moorings. It has limited facilities but enjoys a broad community events catalogue and a close community spirit.

Price
Moored abreast: £20 per foot per year.
Single mooring: £25 per foot per year.

Airedale Boat Club in Bingley, Yorkshire.

Facilities	
Fixed mooring rings, pins or cleats	Y
Full-length or part-length pontoons	N
Single or moored abreast	Both
Secure or gated mooring	Y
Children allowed?	Y
Pets allowed?	Y
Stove fires allowed?	Y
Easy access – close to road or parking	Y
Private parking available	N
Electric hook up	Y
Water point	N
Pump-out facility	N
Elsan/cassette disposal facility	N
Gas, coal and other fuel for sale	N
Canal shop for basic boating supplies	N
Chandlery supplies	N
Boatyard facilities on site	N
Dry-dock or crane out facilities	N
Poly tunnel – for boat painting	N
Laundry	N
Club house	Y
Bar, café or restaurant	Y
Social events calendar	Y
Wi-fi access	N
Postal address provision	N
Good access to major roads	N
Local train service	Y
Access to local town or shopping	Y

End of garden moorings: In order to secure licencing for an end of garden mooring you will need to own both the boat and the land. Not only that but you must not use the boat for residential purposes. CRT charge approximately half the price of a comparable local mooring if you want to keep a boat in the canal at the end of your garden. For those in the fortunate position of having a canal at the end of their garden, this type of mooring is usually perfect.

Online moorings are those located on the main navigation. These can be towpath or offside and are often owned by the agency that looks after the waterway. These are often a low-cost option and facilities are usually few. While that might not seem like a good mooring choice, online moorings are widely available in a huge range of locations and settings. You can often

Online moorings at Stanley Ferry near Wakefield.

find something that's just right for you. Other boats moored locally will provide a measure of community, making some online moorings an ideal spot that's great value for money.

River moorings

Canal water levels rarely change enough to cause concern, but river levels can fluctuate quickly and wildly. River moorings need special consideration to avoid the risk of sinking and flooding. It seems to be becoming increasingly common for rivers to burst their banks and a handful of boats each year are left on dry land as the water levels recede. Mooring with ropes is not a good option. Hard moorings made with scaffold or other metal lines are necessary in most cases. You'll also need a hinged gangplank that rises and falls with your boat. Beware of canals near river openings as the levels here can rise and fall significantly.

Tony's towpath tales: A mooring lesson learned the hard way

I arrived at Castleford just in time to have a quick chat with the lock keeper before setting off for a meeting 70 miles away in Derby, and was almost there when my phone rang. On the other end of the line was a CRT member of staff giving me the news that every boater dreads. 'Your boat is listing badly. It is taking on water and looks like it may sink.' I span the car around and set off back to my boat, being sure to observe the speed limits.

When I arrived back at the mooring my boat looked fine showing no signs of trouble, and I wondered if the CRT operator had made a mistake. It was then that a head appeared from inside the next boat along. Apparently my boat *had* been listing badly up until just a few minutes before, but the problem hadn't been caused by water ingress. Instead my boat hull had caught on a small lip below the waterline as the water level dropped, tipping the boat to a steep angle. The problem had been cured by slackening my mooring ropes and waiting for the next gravel barge to cause enough waves to sweep me off the lip. Inside the boat there was no water to be found and the only evidence of tipping was the former contents of my desk that were now strewn across the floor.

The lesson learned through this experience was to be wary of changing water levels when mooring near a river junction. The water levels on the canal side of the lock can change drastically, so slack mooring ropes are recommended.

BOATING COMMUNITIES

One of best things about boating is the sense of community that can be found on the waterways and each mooring location will have a different community culture. You may find that your preferred mooring is hierarchical, some have an eco-friendly focus, some are purely business-orientated, others are big on social events and some are simply somewhere to park a boat with little interaction between boaters at all. Each mooring is different to some degree.

Recreation, entertainment and boating events feature strongly at some sites, particularly at boat clubs where there is often a committee to organise such get-togethers. Other sites are less sociable, but that's not a bad thing. Not everyone wants to be the life and soul of the party and some boaters like to keep themselves to themselves. It makes sense to visit your potential mooring options several times to see what kind of community culture they have and if that suits you. Meet as many boat owners as you can and ask about the site's social functions. You may or may not want to attend the barbecues, cruises and karaoke nights and the choice is entirely yours.

Strong boating communities are very much like close-knit villages where people are often eager to look out for their neighbours. The flip-side is that everyone in the village will often know your business and have a view about how you live your life. It's all part of boating culture and how much you wish to engage in the community is something you will need to consider.

Residential mooring options for liveaboard boaters

Official residential liveaboard moorings with the appropriate planning permission are costly and extremely rare. Many areas where boats moor do not have residential planning permission to stop the area being developed for housing – and rightly so. Unfortunately, the marinas and mooring providers based in these locations are subject to the same rules that disallow residential status, thereby technically outlawing anyone being able to live on their boat. It is not clear how much boat usage would legally constitute living aboard. As most boats leave the marina for some weeks or months during the course of any given year they cannot be accurately described as permanent residents. In reality, many mooring providers disregard the issue and turn a blind eye and local councils and waterways agencies seem to be similarly unconcerned so long as the situation isn't causing any problems for them. Even some marinas owned by CRT offer a 'Class A' or 'Class 1' mooring which entitles boaters to stay on their boat all year. Clearly, the law is ambiguous and largely unsuitable when applied to boaters and a revision is well overdue.

Marinas wishing to offer residential moorings need to apply for and be awarded proper planning permission and in many areas this type of planning status for 'dwellings' is prohibited. Even when planning permission is granted, it is often applied specifically to a single boat or a specific mooring spot and is not transferable – just because a marina has planning permission for residential mooring in one spot, they usually need to reapply should there be a need to change either the boat or the specific mooring spot. Those boaters who do secure a residential spot potentially have all of the amenities of a land-based home including a postcode and postal service, a telephone landline and sometimes the opportunity to pay council tax too. However, liability for council tax is ambiguous where liveaboard boaters are concerned and the Residential Boat Owners Association has defended several cases where liveaboards have been faced with a bill. The general rule is that if the terms of your mooring stipulate that your boat is likely to be moved to a different mooring spot, then you are not liable for council tax.

If you're planning to live aboard at a mooring it is wise to do some research before meeting with the owner or manager of the site. Look for signs that people live aboard and ask other boaters about the local liveaboard options. It is rarely fruitful to enquire about moorings by phone or email as mooring providers often want to check out a potential liveaboard before agreeing the deal. When speaking to the manager or owner of the mooring be careful before asking, 'Can I live aboard here.' The answer is often an official 'no', but there is often a way to achieve an unspoken understanding. Some will ask outright if you live aboard and explain that living on site is not allowed and that you must vacate your boat for a set number of days per year, whilst others have a higher tariff for 'high-use' boats. Answering questions honestly and complying with the rules laid down by the site is always the best policy to avoid issues further down the line.

A typical liveaboard with wood, coal and well-tended plants.

It is worth bearing in mind that moorings providers are not obliged to give you a mooring and so you should make your application as attractive as possible. Some places, clubs and private marinas especially, will discriminate against untidy-looking boats with the view that these will 'lower the tone' of the establishment. A boat roof lined with piles of firewood, pushbikes, loud unruly dogs, a TV aerial and bags of rubbish can hint that not only are you likely a liveaboard, but likely a messy one at that. Presenting a good image and reading between the lines when discussing moorings can make the difference between their site being full and them being able to squeeze your boat in somewhere.

We do not have planning permission to offer residential moorings and so cannot accommodate liveaboards, but every now and again it becomes evident that someone is living aboard on site. Of course we understand that boaters will occasionally overnight here, but we are always clear when we welcome new boaters that we cannot accommodate liveaboards. It is awful when you realise that a new customer has been less than honest when claiming they do not live on their boat.

JO, SNAYGILL BOATS

MOORING FOR FREE

It is possible to moor your boat for free, but there are very strict rules to govern how this is done. Those boats without a permanent home mooring are called 'continuous cruisers' and, as the name suggests, these boats will move around the waterways system to undertake an ongoing journey. There are thousands of dedicated visitor moorings at convenient and popular locations all around the waterways system and boats can stop here for free whenever they like. It is also possible to moor anywhere on the towpath where this is possible and courteous. (Shallow water may prevent mooring and you should not moor next to locks, bridges, winding holes or facilities.)

This might sound like an obvious way to avoid the expense of paying for a mooring; however there are rules and restrictions to which continuous cruisers must comply. Continuous cruising is not for everyone. A continuous cruise is a slightly ambiguous activity, but it is defined by CRT as a 'boat [that] travels widely around the waterway network without staying in any one place for more than fourteen days (or less where local CRT signs indicate a shorter period)'. The specifics are not set in stone and while CRT have done their best to define the rules for continuous cruisers, there are many boaters who endeavour to inhabit a grey area within the regulations.

Most CCers are liveaboard boaters and so, in a bid to ensure that popular visitor mooring sites are not clogged up with boats, most places have a maximum stay of 14 days. Some popular spots might allow even less time, some restricting the stay to just 24 hours. Even if you are moored in a quiet rural location on the towpath, the maximum stay is still only 14 days, after which you must move on or face the attention of CRT.

The rules state that the boat must move to a new location at least every 14 days, with a new location being defined as a new district rather than a different mooring spot in the same area. The guidance states, 'The necessary movement from one neighbourhood to another can be done in one step or by short gradual steps. What the law requires is that, if 14 days ago the boat was in neighbourhood X, by day 15 it must be in neighbourhood Y. Thereafter, the next movement must normally be to neighbourhood Z, and not back to neighbourhood X (with obvious exceptions such as reaching the end of a terminal waterway or reversing the direction of travel in the course of a genuine progressive journey).

STRESSFUL BOATING

Continuous cruisers needing to be in a particular area (usually for work) will often resort to what is known as 'bridge hopping', moving short distances in a given area before returning to the original location at some future point. This is rarely a successful strategy and will soon attract close attention from CRT enforcement staff, the resultant stress being a veritable coffin nail in the carefree boating lifestyle most of us aspire to. The only way to avoid the hassle is to abide by the rules and move to a new neighbourhood every 14 days. The definition of a neighbourhood varies with geography and not by mileage. In urban areas a new neighbourhood might be the next town a short distance away, whereas in rural areas the distance could be far greater, and this is where some boaters feel there is a grey area. 'A sensible and pragmatic judgement' is required according to the CRT's guidelines.

The mooring rules are overseen by enforcement staff whose interpretation of the regulations seems to vary enormously according to reports from boaters from across the country.

Specifically-allocated visitors' moorings are more strictly enforced, as are the stopping places on all of the busy parts of the network. Patrols are less frequent on quieter and less desirable stretches of water but consistently stubborn over-stayers will soon attract attention.

More information about mooring regulations can be found online at: http://canalrivertrust.org.uk/boating/licensing

Despite (or rather because of) the rules, continuous cruising can be a splendid option for those boaters who have the lifestyle that allows you to do it properly. It's hard to argue against the fact that boats are made to be mobile and you're missing much of the fun that could be had if you always see the same view from your mooring. Continuous cruising is an ideal way to have it all; experiencing all of the variety and freedom that boating has to offer.

Continuous cruising can give you the best of boating, but make sure you know the rules.

Continuous cruising for non-liveaboards

It is possible for non-liveaboards to continuously cruise. In addition to making strategic mooring choices, many marinas and other mooring providers offer temporary places for those who wish to leave their boat for short periods of time. Often these are more secure, convenient and compliant with the rules than if you were to leave your boat for any length of time on the towpath. Of course, there will be a charge for the service, but it's another option to help you to enjoy the continuous cruising lifestyle.

When is bridge hopping not bridge hopping?

These boats with a home mooring will usually get less attention from CRT staff than those with a continuous cruiser licence. Overstaying is always addressed, but boaters with a permanent local mooring will be more inclined to visit their favoured local spot, and so are less likely to be accused of bridge hopping.'

6 THE ART OF BOATING: OUT AND ABOUT

Basic boating isn't difficult. Each year thousands of hire boaters manage just fine after a quick 'crash course' from the hire company. With just a little practice and a dollop of common sense, most people can enjoy boating without any major headaches. Barring a couple of golden rules about locks and weirs, there's not much else to go badly wrong. Most mishaps are minor bumps, inconveniences or poor boating etiquette, not much of a problem at all in the grand scheme of things.

For those of us who aspire to be better than just 'OK' there's plenty to learn. Experienced boaters collate a vast collection of clever tricks to save time, effort and headaches. First-hand experience is the best way to learn, and sometimes it is the only way to learn; but there are plenty of ways to prepare for the trials and tribulations of boating. This chapter looks at common boating scenarios and offers a series of hints, tips and tricks to help you to deal with them.

PREPARING PEOPLE AND PETS

From grocery provisions to weather-proofed gear, it is important to have the right kit if you want to stay safe and happy. Narrowboating is a typically British outdoor pursuit and you should be sure to take all of the kit you might need, despite the weather reports. A set of waterproof clothing for everyone who will be outside the boat is vital. The skipper and each lock-monkey should have waterproof tops, bottoms and boots on standby. A pair of waterproof gloves is a godsend in the cold months, as locks, bridges, ropes and tillers are distressingly cold without them. Waterproof boots are important, but avoid Wellingtons as these are a slip hazard waiting to happen.

However rare it may be, you should be prepared for warm weather too. Sun block is worth keeping near the tiller, ready to grab when necessary, as it's easy to not bother if it means mooring up and/ or walking into the boat to find it. Bug repellant and bug bite ointment are sensible precautions to include in your boating kit list. Sunglasses are a godsend. I also strongly recommend wearing life-vests, especially if you have children aboard or if you're venturing onto a river.

Think carefully about protecting your valuables. Find a way to protect your keys, phone, camera, wallet, purse, handbag, iPod, tablet and other trinkets; not only from theft but from being

A glorious and busy day on the canals.

dropped in the water. My rule is never to have anything of value outdoors on the roof, deck or cratch area.

Lastly, make sure you have enough supplies. Provisions for the journey need careful planning. On most waterways there are usually plenty of convenient local shops, but you can guarantee that you will run out of milk, tea, wine or other necessities on a stretch when you're in the middle of nowhere. Many boaters keep an emergency kit of provisions ready for these situations. If you're taking a pet on board you'll need to be prepared for their dinner needs. Dogs are the most frequently seen pets aboard moving boats and so it is important to ensure you have enough food for the journey between shops.

PPPP: Prior planning prevents pitifully poor performance

Your boating expertise will be evident long before you start the engine and untie your ropes. Being prepared for the journey ahead will prevent many of the problems that might impair your enjoyment later in the trip and proficient boaters will have their pre-boating routine nailed down tightly.

PLANNING YOUR TRIP

Even the most carefree boater should plan their journey at the beginning of each cruise. Knowing where you can find the facilities can stop you getting caught short for things like water, gas, diesel, winding holes and provisions. There are several map sources, both printed and online, that can help you to plan your trip. These maps show the locations of the most important canal features and facilities and will show mileage for your journey too. Although canal features rarely change, it is still worth using an up-to-date map as boatyards and other canalside businesses will come and go. If all else fails, it is generally accepted that the best source of canal info can be obtained from the local boating community. Speaking in person or posting in one of the online discussion forums will usually give you all of the information you will find in a map, and more.

Above: Like most dogs, Puck loves boating.

Below: Ready to depart?

Don't be late

It is particularly important for hire boaters to know where they're going. In addition to likely being unfamiliar with the area, you'll need to know when to head back to base in order to be back on time. Late returns will usually incur heavy fines.

Handy tip

When planning your cruise you can use the following formula to work out how long it will take you to get somewhere. The timings are approximate; you must slow down for moored boats and some boaters may tackle locks and bridges quicker than others.

4 miles = 1 hour
Lock = 15 mins
Swing/lift bridge = 15 mins

Preparing your boat

Now that all of the people and pets aboard are shipshape and ready to go, it's time to ensure your boat is ready too. You'll have already checked that you have enough fuel in the tank and that your engine oil, water and gearbox oil are topped up. It's worth taking a look into the engine bay to check for anything unusual and a quick peek into the bilges to look for unexpected water.

Next, check you have enough gas and fill up your drinking water. Indeed, it is worth filling up with water whenever possible along your journey as there can be long stretches of waterway without a convenient tap. You might also want to empty your toilet cassette or pump out your toilet tank before you set off, even if it is not completely full. Unless you know where the next convenient facility is, the full tank can creep up on you and you'll be in deep do-do.

Next, go inside the boat to stow or secure anything that might fall if the boat gets bumped. Check shelves and surfaces for anything that isn't screwed down and move it somewhere safe if it has any worth. A common item to forget is

the Ecofan on top of the stove, as these tend to develop a very annoying rattle in use when they have been dropped. Be particularly vigilant of anything that might start a fire if it is dislodged. Candles, incense, tea-lights, gas lamps and anything that is near the stove or your cooker that might fall and be set alight – move all of these things and be extra cautious as a matter of routine.

Remembering all of the kit you might need for a trip is difficult, particularly in the excitement of preparing to set off, so it is worth making a list of the kit you will need to navigate the route you are planning to take. A utilities key from the Canal and River Trust (formerly known as a BW key) is necessary for most boaters on most routes, but remember that other, non-CRT waterways have their own specialist equipment. Some even require a different type of windlass, so it is worth checking.

Other things on your list might include:
- Handcuff key
- Pump-out key
- Binoculars
- Hoses and fittings
- Mooring pins

Keep the roof clear so it's safe to walk on.

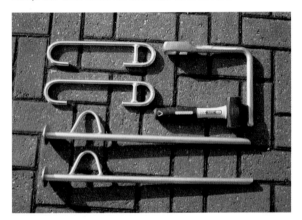

A selection of cruising hardware.

- Mooring hooks
- Lump hammer
- Firelighters
- Coal
- Kindling
- Axe
- Saw

Poles, planks and hooks will often come in handy.

Last minute checks

Clear the roof

There's a good chance that you'll need to walk on your roof at some point during your journey, so it's a good idea to remove as many trip hazards as possible.

Remove your chimney

Low bridges and branches can easily knock the chimney off. If you don't want to remove it, at least tie it to the boat using a fine chain.

Remove your side fenders

These are something of a hazard when boating as they can get caught up in locks or when passing other obstacles. Not lifting them will probably cost you money too. They can become detached and lost when bumping the side and they cause drag in the water which increases your fuel usage.

Disconnect electric cables

It is surprising how many boats set off while their landline electric cable is still plugged in. The damage caused is usually minimal, but worth avoiding nonetheless.

Check horn and light

Horns and lights don't get used much, so it is easy to forget about them. You won't notice they're broken until you need them.

Check bilge pump

Water ingress from your previously drippy stern gland will get worse when you're underway, so it is worth checking that it still works before you set off.

Pole and hook to hand

Most boats have a specific place to stash their hook and pole. You might choose to leave them there, or you might choose to move them so they're handy near the tiller. It is often true that when you need them, you *really* need them.

Midline rope to hand

Your midline looks very neat coiled in the centre of your boat, but it is better to have this handy rope at your fingertips, near the tiller, while you are underway. Otherwise, you'll be speeding down the gunwales to retrieve it at the first lock or swing-bridge.

A well-prepared boater.

131

Check for boats before you untie

Setting off on a cruise is usually exciting. In the excitement of the moment you might forget to check for oncoming traffic before you pull out into the cut. Have a look around before you untie.

When you're underway

To my knowledge, there isn't a word that describes what you are doing when you're out on a narrowboat. As there are no sails it is impossible to be 'sailing' and most boaters would object to the idea of 'driving' a narrowboat. Nevertheless, your time at the tiller will be much more fun if you know what you're doing.

Most boaters will know that we 'drive on the right' on the UK's inland waterways, but there are often circumstances where it is easier to pass on the other side. When negotiating around other boats at locks, bridges and other obstacles you might ignore the rule to make an easier manoeuvre for both boats. Indicate your intention by holding out your arm in the direction you intend to travel and look out for an acknowledgement or wave from the other boat.

Generally, though, you must drive on the right. While you're underway it is advisable to stick to the centre of the channel as the edges of many canals and rivers are silted up or fouled by obstacles such as rocks or other debris. Make enough room to let boats pass without having to risk running aground at the edge of the water. In some places it is impossible for two boats to pass, so be ready to stop and wait for a clear run if necessary.

It is also wise to slow down as you approach blind corners and bridges, just in case you meet someone coming the other way. Sound your horn to signal your presence, but be sure to use a long note. A short 'pip pip' could be mistaken for a car horn and so ignored by other boaters.

Inside story

The inside of a corner on any waterway will likely attract the most silt. Avoid the inside of the corner if you don't want to run aground.

Tiller skills

It is surprisingly easy to veer off course at such low speeds and all boaters have come a cropper at one time or another – some of us, more than others! Taking your eye of the ball for just a few seconds is often all it takes to send you on a collision course.

For such a slow moving vehicle as a narrowboat, it is surprisingly easy to veer off course. The best skippers have a rod-straight wake that doesn't weave about. What does your wake look like?

GO SLOW

One of the main causes of bad blood on the waterways is speed. When passing moored boats it is safer and more courteous to slow down, but every day the speed of passing boats is blamed for ruining peace on the waterways. But why is it such a big problem?

Speeding boats can cause disruption aboard a boat moored at the water's edge. The amount of water that is shifted by a fast-moving boat can make waves that rock moored boats to the point where plates fall from worktops and books fall from shelves. It's frustrating and potentially dangerous. I've even seen boaters fall onto their hot stove. Slowing down for moored boats is important for so many reasons.

However, the disruption is not always the fault of the moving boat. Many boats are moored so badly that even the slowest boat will cause them to rock. If you find yourself annoyed by speeding boaters, you might want to check out your mooring ropes. Try using 'springs' to stop forward and backward motion, and use decent fenders to buffer the bumps.

How fast is too fast?

Now that the practical stuff has been addressed, it is important to look at the most frequent major causes of boat speed altercations. The biggest factors that contribute to the frustrations of speeding boats are actually perception and attitude, and this is true of both sides. Moored boaters are, by definition, stationary and so have a much different perception of speed than someone who is underway. The often-advised 2mph for passing boats is difficult to estimate and so it makes little sense to guess how fast they're moving.

Go slow to keep the peace.

Similarly, for boats that have been chugging along at 4mph (and we all stick to that speed limit, do we not?) it is difficult to gauge how much we have slowed down. Engine revs are little indication of speed given the amount of time it takes for a boat to slow down. More to the point, it is not the actual speed of your boat that causes the problem; it's the amount of water that is being pushed ahead of you that causes the moored boats to rock. It's a point worth noting, especially for large, deep-drafted or wide-beamed boats as these can push significant amounts of water.

So, what's the solution? In truth, there are several answers to the speeding boat problem. First, if you're underway it makes sense to remove all doubt and estimation from the equation by slowing down to the slowest speed your boat can do. If you're passing boats with just enough revs to make your prop move, then you can go no slower. This way there is no room for error of perception or estimation. Make sure you start your slowing down procedure well in advance. It's no good hammering along at ramming speed until you're level with the bow of the moored boat before taking all the revs off. You're still moving too fast and you're still pushing a lot of water ahead of you. Slow down early and incrementally so that, by the time you reach the moored boats, your engine has reached neutral. Then, nudge your revs up until your prop just about kicks in. That's a speed that no-one can complain about.

If you're in a moored boat, make sure that it is well moored and has plenty of well-positioned fenders. You might need to adjust the ropes at intervals to ensure you stay well moored, particularly if you are on or near a river. But finally, and most importantly, make a resolution that you won't complain about fast-moving boats. Believe it or not, it's the easy option, because otherwise you have to use your brain to decide which boats you will moan at and which you won't. Does it depend on their speed and how much faster they are going than your (rough) estimate of what is allowed? Does it depend on the time of day or how tough your day has been? Does it depend on the cycles of the moon? Or do you shout at every boat that passes? Either way, shouting at boats is never a good thing. It's juvenile. It's just not worth it and shouting at your fellow boaters achieves nothing except bad feeling and high blood pressure. Let it pass, it will calm. Remember, we're all here for the peace and tranquillity.

SMOOTH MANOEUVRES

Boating is pretty easy when you are underway, cruising along and watching the world go slowly by. It gets trickier when you need to make a manoeuvre such as mooring up, turning around (winding), locking or negotiating a swing bridge.

Take it easy and you'll appreciate the beauty of your surroundings all the more.

A little tuition from a seasoned boater is worth its weight in gold and will likely equip you with enough skill to complete these manoeuvres well enough. After that it is a case of 'practice makes perfect', or at least as close to perfect as boating will ever be. The notes below will give you some basic knowledge of what to expect, but really, you're going to need to have a tiller in your hand if you want to be proficient.

Proper locking

Negotiating a lock is probably the biggest worry for new boaters, and rightly so. While accidents are rare, locks present one of the greatest risks for boaters and so knowledge and careful consideration are vital. It would be of little use to attempt any lock safety training here in this book, but there are a handful of points that are worth considering. Knowing the dangers and how to avoid them will, hopefully, enable you to approach lock training with fore-warned preparation.

If you're steering the boat
Do …
Approach the lock slowly In fact, do the whole locking manoeuvre slowly as most accidents are caused by high speeds and rushing.

Moor up loosely until the lock is ready Lingering in the cut, using fuel and constantly tillering to maintain your position is unnecessary. For the few seconds you will save, you might as well throw a rope round a bollard and wait until the lock is set. It's less stressful, less likely to go wrong and less likely to be an inconvenience to other boaters arriving, leaving or moored nearby.

Enter the lock slowly This helps to avoid damaging the lock gates should you accidentally bump them. We all hate leaky lock gates as they make locking slower, wetter and potentially dangerous; not to mention the costs involved

My pet peeve

'My pet peeve is boats that go too fast when negotiating swing bridges and locks. It seems they're in a rush to clear the obstacle and so race through at unnecessarily high speeds. It's a problem for several reasons, not least because every boat that is moored near a swing bridge will be regularly plagued by speeding boats. Worse still, speeding boats leaving locks can cause problems for those boaters awaiting their turn. It's tough to hold onto a rope in readiness to set off when a speeding boat is pushing so much water that you're struggling to keep your footing.'

CAROL: NB CAELMIRI

in repairing them that are passed on to boaters as increased licence costs. Entering slowly also cuts down on the engine revving that is necessary to slow the boat once inside the lock. You're not in a hurry, are you?

Take care if using the lock ladder These ladders were not installed as an aid to boating, but as a safety escape option should a person fall into the lock. However, the ladder is certainly useful for those using the locks, particularly when boating single-handed. It's common sense, but watch out for slippery, cold, wet and muddy rungs. Have three points of contact at all times. When descending, turn and climb down the ladder facing the lock wall – not facing the water.

Watch out for the cill This is the big one. A boat becoming caught on the cill is the biggest and most dangerous hazard when locking. The cill position is marked on the brickwork, so stay forward of the mark and keep your eye on your boat position as the water level drops.

Above and left: Beware of gongoozlers – they can be more of a hindrance than a help.

Agree a signal with your crew to alert for danger Sounding the horn is usually the best way to signal to your crew that their attention is urgently needed. Problems in the lock, man overboard, imminent bumps and instances where their assistance is required; they all need a fast response from your crew.

Keep an eye on your button fenders Be careful to avoid wedging these fenders in the woodwork of the gates as, when the water level changes, you could sink your boat. It happens.

Consider using ropes around bollards when using locks At many manned locks the keeper will insist that you pass a rope or two around a bollard when inside the lock. This helps to keep your boat steady when the water level is changing, avoiding you bouncing your boat off the walls inside. It's not strictly necessary and those who understand the flow of water inside the lock can use it to their clever advantage instead. But for those of us who never did or have yet to learn that skill, a rope can cut down on the bump and grind that is often inherent with locking. Beware, though, and take care not to hang your boat from the rope as the water level drops.

Don't ...

Jump down from the lock onto your boat The roof may, or may not, be slippery. Regardless, a lock is one of the last places you want to slip and fall in.

Throw windlasses For obvious reasons.

Rev your engine excessively Use a rope around a bollard to steady your boat and insist that those operating paddles do so slowly to create less turbulence.

Disappear into your boat or become otherwise distracted Things can go wrong very quickly in a lock, so pay attention at all times. Chatting with your crew or with other boaters sharing the lock is fine, but pay attention.

Allow anyone on the roof of your boat unless it is absolutely necessary Again, this is a precaution against the increased danger inherent with slips that occur inside a lock.

Attempt to force open the gate with your boat If the gate won't open there is likely a problem with the paddles and water levels. Remedy this and push the lock beams manually. Ramming with boats will usually cause more serious problems and could put your boat at risk.

Always keep a watchful eye when locking.

If you're working the locks
Do ...
Look out for other boats. Save water by sharing the lock with another boat, if possible. Also, look out for boats coming the other way and let them use the lock first if it is set better for them.

Take keys and windlasses with you. It's a pain to pick them up after the boat has entered the lock as it will often mean throwing them ashore or using lock ladders.

Take care Walking on lock beams, lock ladders and wooden walkways is a significant hazard, particularly in wet or cold weather. If you must do it, take care; lots of care.

Wield your windlass with care.

Go slow Opening paddles quickly can cause fast-moving water flows in the lock which will throw the boat around against the lock walls. It can be dangerous too, especially if the turbulence causes the boat to become snagged or the stern catches on the cill or causes someone to lose their footing.

Open gate paddles last When locking uphill, opening gate paddles too early can release torrents of water into the front of the boat below. Use the ground paddles first and wait until the gate paddles are covered before opening them.

Hold onto your windlass firmly If you lose grip on the windlass it can spin wildly on the spindle. If you're lucky you'll not be close enough to get hit, but every year people are injured by spinning windlasses. Usually they're hit on the hand or arm, but occasionally the victim is hit in the face. Injuries can be very painful and often require hospital treatment. The best means to avoid this is to pay attention to what you're doing, take your time, stay in control and don't lose grip on the windlass.

Keep your eye on the boat Look out for problems and pay attention to instructions from the person at the tiller. Be ready to drop the paddles and stop all water movement as this is the best response to most locking problems.

Listen to other boaters If you're sharing the lock then safety is the responsibility of both boat crews. Bear in mind that the other boat may be more (or less) experienced than you and have a different way of doing things. Be courteous and work as a team, but err on the side of caution and make safety a priority. Locking is not a race or a competition.

Be nice to single-handed boaters. Yes, they can do the locks alone, probably as quickly as with your help, but it is much easier and safer for them to stay on the boat. Give them a break and leave them to look after their vessel while you do the lock for both boats. You'll often be rewarded with biscuits, or some friendly banter at the very least!

Don't …
Jump on or off the boat Always step aboard or ashore safely. There's no rush and it's not worth the risk.

Be lazy If you're sharing a lock, do your fair share of the work. Expecting the other crew to work the locks while you sit around drinking tea is very bad form indeed.

Trust gongoozlers Spectators at locks will often want to help, sometimes with disastrous results. By all means, accept their help to push beams or keep watch, but be very wary of eager amateurs wanting to wind paddles or handle ropes. They might be ok. They might know what they're doing. But they might not. Whether they help or not is your call, but always be very

Some locks are wide enough for two narrowboats, but others will only take a single boat.

wary of unsolicited help. Some lock flights have 'unofficial friendly help', particularly on long flights of multiple gates. Sometimes these can be very helpful indeed, but be aware that they'll often expect remuneration.

Get distracted Entertaining as it is, do not be distracted by chit chat, putting rubbish in the bin, collecting kindling, herons, clouds or any other form of entertainment. By all means, partake, but always keep an eye on the job too.

Leave your coffee mug behind If you do, you can guarantee it will be one of your favourites and it will be lost and gone for ever.

Swing bridges

To the untrained eye, swing bridges can appear to be a real nuisance. They can be extremely tough to move, come in many different varieties and, worst of all, open on the opposite side from the towpath; making life very difficult for single-handed boaters. However, it is important to appreciate the necessity and beauty of swing bridges as, without them, boat and road traffic could not happily co-exist.

Boating through a swing bridge when you have a crew to help is relatively easy, particularly if you have enough muscle aboard. Some swing bridges can be extraordinarily tough to push, creating a problem for the elderly or less able.

Swing-bridge top tips

- A swing bridge that is stuck can often be freed if you add weight to one side. By using the bridge as a lever you can sometimes tilt the bridge off the obstruction. It might mean you bouncing the bridge a little, and it doesn't always work, but it can work wonders.

- If it won't move by bouncing it, don't strain yourself; recruit some help. Get more help from anyone who is on board, including the person on the tiller. Usually the bridge only needs a little help getting started, so the help can get back aboard once the bridge gets going. Sometimes you can enlist friendly passers-by to push, but if there are several bridges in the same stretch you might want to wait for another boat to turn up. It'll be easier and more sociable with more hands and you'll be helping each other.

- Sometimes pushing the other side of the bridge will get it moving. Walk across and give it a nudge, but be sure to get back over the bridge before it gets away from you. Alternatively, get someone else to push the other end of the bridge and you stay where you are.

- Using the power of your boat to move the bridge is not recommended as this could damage the bridge and possibly your boat too. Nudging from the front or using ropes to pull the bridge are both risky and require almost expert precision to execute safely.

- Be careful of wooden bridges in wet or cold weather as they can become ridiculously slippery. Many bridges are covered with a non-slip coating, but many still resemble an ice rink. You have been warned.

- Look out for other boats approaching the bridge as you use it and hold it open for them to pass through. They'll probably do the same for you at the next one.

- If using the swing-bridge requires a handcuff key, then it is good etiquette to avoid over-tightening it when locking it back up after use. Changes in the weather and even your brute strength can cause the lock to stick. It's a real pain for the boat that comes through after you. Securing a couple of thread turns is ample and much easier to unlock.

You'll need an anti-vandal 'handcuff' for many locks and swing bridges.

Winding holes

Winding holes are the wide areas of canals that are made especially for turning boats. There is an ongoing debate as to how the word is pronounced. Some say it is pronounced the same as winding a watch whilst others insist it is pronounced like windy weather. Either way, there is etiquette and method to consider when using them.

On canals, proper winding holes will be big enough to turn the longest boat the canal can accommodate. On most canals this will be a boat 72 feet long, but on waterways such as the Leeds and Liverpool Canal boats are restricted by the length of the locks. Winding holes there need only be 62 feet long. Of course, shorter boats can utilise areas of the canal that are not strictly designated winding holes, but care should be taken. Often the edges of canals are silted up or fouled with rocks and other debris. An area, at first, might look like a viable place to turn, but it can sometimes turn into a headache. Choose your turning place carefully.

141

Winding holes are a rare delight on some waterways and it is important to plan your cruise to take account of where you can turn, if necessary. The next winding hole might be some distance away, causing disruption to your cruising plans and, for hire boaters, causing you to miss your return deadline.

Executing the turn itself is not particularly difficult, although practice helps to improve the manoeuvre. Try to execute the turn slowly as boats can sometimes run aground on the mud and silt in the mouth of the winding hole, and watch out for overhanging branches too as these could tear canvas and scratch paintwork. Finally, try not to bump your rudder on the towpath edge behind you.

Tunnels

Although it might seem sensible to build a tunnel straight and true, few, in fact, are. Despite the curves and corners, tunnels are surprisingly easy to navigate if you are reasonably proficient with the tiller. Some tunnels allow two-way traffic so be sure to stick to your side of the water. Others run a traffic light system to allow boats in from either end alternatively, meaning you shouldn't encounter any boats coming towards you. Either way, it's a test of your skill to avoid pin-balling your boat off the side walls.

Few, if any, tunnels have light enough to navigate easily and so it is useful to have a working headlamp on the bow of your boat. Be sure to test your light before you set off into the darkness as sod's law says it will have developed a fault since you last flicked the switch. You should also adjust your lamp so that it aims the light slightly up and to the right as this will give you the best visibility without blinding any boat coming in the other direction. It's also a good idea to turn on all of your cabin lights and open your curtains too, as this will offer an amount of illumination off the tunnel walls alongside.

Navigating a tunnel is never as simple as it first appears.

MOORING UP

Also often called 'tying up', this manoeuvre is one of the first real tests you will encounter when you begin boating. Having mastered the art of steering the boat, safely approaching a mooring and tying up will require some practice. The best advice is to do everything very slowly as this will reduce the amount of corrective engine revving that is otherwise necessary. Slow down early and plan your approach path in advance.

Bring your boat near enough to the towpath (or pontoon) to step off; jumping ashore is not recommended in the vast majority of cases. Take your boat's midline ashore with you and use it to hold your boat in to the side. If you have crew, ask them to use the ropes at bow and stern to hold the boat while you find the most appropriate mooring option. If you don't have crew then you'll need to tie your midline to something (perhaps a mooring pin) while you find fore and aft moorings.

Tying up tight?

Generally, on non-tidal inland waterways, tying up tightly to the land is recommended. However, care should be taken when mooring on any

Right: Mooring like this is not recommended. Ropes will eventually fray and snap.

Good mooring	Better	Best
Drive in mooring pins at a point that will allow you to tie up your boat with ropes at 45°. Tying ropes at 90° allows your boat to move with the water and as boats go past.	If the waterway has sidings then you can use your mooring hooks. Unlike mooring pins, these cannot be dislodged and so provide a more secure mooring. Tying on with ropes at 45° is still a good idea.	Mooring rings and cleats can often be found at marinas and designated visitor moorings. They can be the best option as they're the most secure. It helps if your boat is a convenient size to fit in the space between the mooring points, but there is usually some way to make a secure mooring if you're clever with the configuration of ropes.

waterway with water levels that rise and fall. Tidal rivers are an obvious example, but even those described as non-tidal can vary enough to cause problems if boats are moored too tightly. Canal moorings near river junctions and even those near locks can catch boaters unawares, and so it is certainly worth checking the situation with the locals to ensure your boat doesn't get hung up or tipped. Flood situations are an obvious risk that all boaters should be wary of. Be sure to check on your boat regularly if you are moored in an area that is at risk of flooding.

Using fenders is recommended, as even the best mooring will allow movement. There are so many types of fenders it would be impossible to discuss the benefits of each type, and

Knots

There are several different knots that are considered useful depending on the type of mooring and the length of time you intend staying there. So long as the knot you tie is secure for the purpose then there's little to worry about. I'm of the opinion that just enough is enough. Too many knots and elaborate configurations of rope are unnecessary, time-consuming and a pain in the backside to untie when you need to set off.

besides, there's little difference to be had and so the choice is often down to the preferences of the boater. One important consideration is to ensure that you remove the fenders when you're underway. Dragging fenders wastes fuel and they can be a hazard if they get caught up, particularly when navigating through locks.

Tidal moorings

Mooring on tidal rivers requires serious consideration. The rise and fall of the water level can sink boats that are moored badly. Your boat can become hung from its ropes if the level drops. Should the level rise flood onto what is usually land, your boat can be stranded aground or ashore when the level drops again.

Many designated moorings on tidal rivers have floating pontoons that rise and fall with the water levels, thus solving the problem and providing a safe, hard mooring. The only downside to these is the noise that is often made as the pontoon slides up and down on the securing structure. Another solution is to use hard mooring bars instead of ropes. These work by holding the boat at a fixed length from the bank as the water rises and falls. During flood the boat can rise safely at the end of the bar and be held at that length as the water drops to ensure the boat does not come onto the land. A walkway from the land to the boat will usually have wheels affixed to move the ramp accordingly, whatever the water level is doing.

Mooring etiquette

The rules and regulations that govern the mooring of your boat are easy enough to comply with in most cases, so problems rarely occur. Once you're clear about overstaying and know not to moor inconsiderately near waterways features, the rest of the waterways are yours to tie up and enjoy. Beyond that, it is simply a case of being polite and considerate to your neighbours and, in the vast majority of cases, that's something that boaters are very good at.

Bad places to moor up

- Lock landing areas
- Swing bridge landing areas
- Near bridges
- Near winding holes
- At water taps
- On private property (without permission)
- In narrow waterways impeding other boats' progress

Cleaning up after your dog and keeping a lid on loud music is something we would do as a matter of course. Generators and engines should not be running between the hours of 8pm and 8am, except in very exceptional circumstances. If you must run your engine outside these times then it is polite to keep it to a minimum and apologise to your boating neighbours as soon as possible. Cake or a bottle of wine will usually smooth the creases in a strained neighbour relationship, but don't make it a habit.

Some people gravitate to boating as a means to enjoy peace and seclusion away from the hustle and bustle. These people will usually moor their boats on quiet parts of the network, out of town and away from the facilities that might attract heavy footfall. While there is no rule to say that you can't moor nearby, I like to leave these boaters in peace and moor elsewhere. After all, if they desperately wanted to be sociable they would likely choose a more popular place to tie up.

In busy mooring locations you might have trouble finding a space, particularly if boats are moored with significant spaces in between. It makes sense to optimise the area and leave space to accommodate as many boats as possible in these popular places. As a boat leaves it is sensible to move boats closer together to leave a decent gap for new boats turning up. If you arrive at such a place with haphazardly-moored boats, most owners will be quite happy to shuffle along if you need to fit into a gap that isn't quite big enough. Many boaters are also happy for you to moor abreast next to them if necessary, although it is polite to always ask first and use this option only as a last resort.

River boating is lots of fun, but be sure to stay safe.

RIVER BOATING

River boating, particularly on tidal rivers, is inherently more difficult and risky than canal boating. Tides, currents and flooding will significantly affect your boating, not least how you decide to moor your boat. New boaters are often advised to avoid river boating until they are a little more experienced, but there are certainly some rivers that are easier than others. The friendly River Nene is a much better place to get started than the mean old Trent, Thames or Severn.

If you're thinking about river boating it is a very good idea to get advice and guidance from someone who has plenty of experience on the waterway you're aiming for. Find out about the specific hazards you might experience there and how to avoid them and be sure to ask about the best places to moor. Pay attention to any lock

River locks are often much larger than canal locks and can accommodate much bigger boats.

keepers you might encounter and be sure to ask their advice. The lock keepers on any given river will usually be in contact with each other and will ring ahead to tell their colleagues that you are on the way. If you're going to moor up for any length of time, be sure to let them know so that they're not wondering where you got to when you don't turn up at the next lock.

Make sure that you have the right safety equipment on board and that your crew know what to do and how to use it should the need arise. In a deep and fast-flowing river, even the strongest swimmer is in danger if they fall overboard. Life jackets must always be worn and the boat should be equipped with throwing ropes and life-rings kept in easy reach. A VHS radio is

River insurance

Make sure that you and your boat are insured to travel on tidal waterways. Some policies specifically exclude this.

invaluable for communication with lock keepers and large commercial vessels that are commonly found on rivers. Coming across one of these large craft laden with cargo is daunting to say the least, so best to be prepared for them and ensure that they are prepared to meet you.

River locks

Beware of tides when using locks on rivers. Leaving the river via a lock is a bit of an art.

A fast-flowing current can make the manoeuvre quite tricky, bouncing your boat against the lock wall as you enter or causing you to overshoot the entrance to the lock. Follow the advice of the lock keeper closely, as they know their lock and the river flow well and will have done the manoeuvre many times before.

- When approaching *with* the tide you should begin your approach turn into the lock very early and be ready to use your engine in short sharp bursts as you enter the lock.
- When entering a lock *against* the tide you should advance slightly past the lock entrance before turning in as the current will drag you back the way you came as your boat turns broadside.

It may seem that river cruising is a risky business and perhaps well avoided, but like most risky endeavours, there are significant rewards to be had in return. Access to many sections of the waterways network is only possible via a river stretch and besides, river cruising is exciting and awe-inspiring with its grand scale and new experiences. It might be worth hiring an experienced skipper to coach you as you navigate a river cruise or perhaps join another experienced boater on their next river jaunt. There is much to learn and safety should be your first consideration, but river boating is a fantastic experience if it is done correctly.

River boating tips
- Travelling with another boat will help to safeguard against many of the problems that can occur on tidal waterways. The availability of another boat to tow you to safety is a valuable backup plan should things go wrong.
- Listen to the advice of lock keepers regarding currents when planning your cruise. If you think your engine might struggle against a current, try to plan your trip so that the current assists.
- Make sure you have a suitable anchor, rope and chain for any journey on tidal rivers and be ready to use it if you get into trouble. Mooring at the bank is usually a bad idea, so using your anchor to keep you afloat on the river is preferable to risking your boat on steep muddy banks when the tide goes out.
- If you do use your anchor, it is better to secure it to the bow of your boat rather than throw it off the back. This will ensure that your bow faces the approaching tide as the bow is designed with a better angle to cut into the moving water. There are also fewer holes in the bow so water is less likely to breach your exhaust, engine vents, bilge pump drains etc.

HIRE BOATERS

Hirers are not pirates but many private boat owners have a holier-than-thou attitude towards hire boaters. Whilst it is true that most hirers will not have the experience and expertise a seasoned boater does, it is worth remembering that we were in exactly the same position once upon a time and many of us were bitten by the boating bug through hiring. 'If it wasn't for hire boats then the waterways as we know them would not exist,' reminds Steve Vaughn of www.considerateboater.com.

Hire companies work hard to ensure that their customers have enough tuition to manage the boat, but an hour of coaching cannot make an expert boater. Few hirers will be purposefully discourteous but novices are going to make mistakes. Often a hirer will welcome some considered and friendly advice, but don't be put out if they don't want it. Few of us enjoy our errors being highlighted.

It is worth remembering that, with only a few hours of experience under their belt, hire boaters are bound to be still learning the ways of the water. Any inconsiderate or dubious boating is more likely to be a mistake than done with malicious intent, so try to react accordingly if you must react at all. Be friendly and helpful. After all, you were a rubbish boater once! Indeed, if you're one of the boaters who only ventures out for a week or two each year, chances are your skills are a bit rusty for a few days until you get back into the swing of things. It's nice to be nice, so let's try not to be too judgemental.

SINGLE-HANDED BOATING

Although boating is marginally easier if you have a crew, some people prefer cruising alone. There is something supremely peaceful about travelling the serene waterways without the distractions or interruptions of other people. Of course, it's not for everyone, but if you're someone who is happy in their own company then single-handed boating might be the ultimate meditative experience.

Single-handing during the summertime is marginally easier as there are usually enough boats out and about to share the work at locks and swing bridges. Oftentimes the boat with crew will be happy to do the donkey-work and leave the single-handed skipper aboard. It is important not to take their help for granted. If there is anyway to reciprocate then you should be inclined to do so, whether it is with witty banter, biscuits or a beer at the end of the day's cruise. At the very least you should be polite and very thankful for the assistance, but I'm sure that goes without saying.

If you're truly alone and need to do locks and bridges yourself, the principles are much the same as when you have crew. Extra care and safety is required, but the methods and processes are much the same.

Mike the Boilerman single-handing.

Single-handed locking

There are a couple of ways to negotiate a lock single-handedly, but slow and steady is the key in both cases. The main difference lies in how you take your boat into and out of the lock. You can either drive your boat into the lock, using the lock ladder to get back onto the land, or you can stay on the land and use your ropes to pull your boat to where you need it to be. Your main consideration is always your own safety. After that, it's a case of executing the procedure slowly and carefully to ensure your boat stays afloat. If you can minimise the amount of bumping and grinding your boat endures as the water level changes then you're doing a great job. Here's a run-down of how it is done, but really, you need to practice with someone who knows how it's done to ensure you're doing it safely.

1. Moor your boat before the lock and jump ashore with windlass and keys, if necessary.

2. Check around for approaching boats. They'll usually help if they're going your way or if the lock is set against them.

3. Prepare the lock for your boat to enter, then open the gates and either drive your boat in or pull your boat into the lock using the bow and/or centre rope.

4. If you've driven into an empty lock then you'll need to use the lock ladder to climb back onto the land. Walk along the roof of your boat to the ladder, taking your centre rope with you. The ladder will be cold or slippery or, more usually, both.

5. Use your ropes to secure your boat to one side of the lock, staying away from the gates as far as is possible. Keep a close lookout for any part of your boat snagging on the lock.

> ### Top tip: beware the revs
>
> If you leave your boat in the lock without someone at the tiller, ensure your engine is in neutral when single-handing through locks and bridges. The usual flick at the lever or speed-wheel might appear to have selected neutral, but check again, just to be sure. Even a few revs above tick-over can create a disaster when you're not aboard to notice. It's a surprisingly common clanger.

Fenders at the side, bow and stern are the usual suspects of snagging problems.

6. Open the paddles slowly, a couple of turns at a time, constantly checking progress and the position of your boat.

7. Be ready to close all paddles and stop the flow of water. It is often possible to correct the boat's position by pulling on the ropes and retying to the bollard.

8. Locking down, or emptying the lock with your boat inside, entails the most risk, so be very vigilant. Make sure you have control of the ropes and let your boat descend slowly, paying out rope as it drops. It's easier to do this with one loop of rope around a bollard as the friction affords you more strength than your muscle power alone.

9. Locking down also poses the risk of being hung up on the cill, so be watchful that your boat does not creep too close to the back of the lock.

10. Once the lock is ready, open the gates and take your boat out using either the ropes or the engine.

Single-handed swing-bridge skills

Swing bridges are probably the most troublesome waterways feature for single-handed boaters. The problem arises as most bridges can only be operated from the bank opposite where your boat is moored. If you can, picture your boat being moored on the towpath side, crossing the bridge to the opposite side in order to open it, thus leaving you with an open bridge and no means to get back to your boat to bring it through.

There are ways to get around this, but none are easy or practical. The best ways include recruiting assistance, either from passers by or from other boats passing through the bridge. If that's not a practical or available option, then you could try one of these methods listed here.

The convenient bridge method

Although most bridges open to leave you on the wrong side of the water from your boat, some bridges have convenient mooring places on the same side as the mechanism. This allows you to moor up, step ashore and use the bridge all on the same side. Check if this is an option before attempting other solutions.

Risks: Virtually none.

The chain method

Some swing bridges have a chain attached that you can use to pull the open bridge back into place from the towpath side. The sequence allows you to moor up and use your pole to push the bridge open from the towpath side. From there you get back aboard your boat and bring it through the bridge, mooring up on the other side. Once that is done you can go back to the bridge and use the chain to pull the bridge back to its closed position.

Risks: Bridges that swing loosely can close on your boat as you pass through. To avoid

Why oh why?

I've often heard boaters bemoan the construction of bridges and the fact that bridge and boat are often left on opposite sides of the canal. 'Why can't they change the bridges so that they open on the other side?' they ask.

There are a handful of reasons why the bridges open the way that they do. The bridges were originally constructed that way so that the horses pulling the boat would not be impeded by the open bridge.

Now that horse-drawn boating is rarely seen on the canals, why can't bridges be changed to be more user-friendly? One of the main reasons is because doing so would be damaging to the heritage of the canal system. However, I think one of the most compelling reasons to leave the bridges as they are is because it means boaters *must* close them in order to get back to their boat. If it were possible for boaters to leave the bridge open and continue on their journey then some would do so, despite the inconvenience this would cause for others.

smashing windows and bashing paintwork you might want to observe the bridge for a while before you take your boat through, just to check how likely it is to swing shut. Other than that, cold, wet hands are the only thing you need to concern yourself with.

The nifty footwork method

If you can find just a small piece of bank on the offside that is suitable, you can position the bow or stern of your boat there and step ashore. Take a long rope with you and tie it securely so that you can retrieve your boat when the bridge is open. Take your boat through and repeat the process on the other side.

Risks: Try not to fall in and avoid trespassing on private property. Consider what the wind and current will do to your boat while it is moored so loosely when you are away working the bridge. Also, make sure your boat will not foul the bridge as you open it.

The rope haul method

Moor your boat on the towpath side and take a long rope across the bridge with you. Move the bridge, and then haul your boat through by hand. Some find this process easier using two ropes secured to different parts of their boat, either the bow, mid or stern.

Risks: If you're lucky to have enough rope for this method, then your only worry is bumping the boat on the way through the bridge. Take your time and keep the boat moving very slowly. This should allow you enough time to fend off should a window or canvas cover be at risk.

Go slow and steady when tackling a lock single-handed.

The joys of single-handed boating.

Tony's towpath tales: The joys of single-handed boating

It was still pleasantly warm as I rocked gently in my hammock after a long day on the cut. The claret red backdrop of sky was gate crashed by occasional swooping bats as they hunted for their supper, whilst fat silver carp jumped and flipped in the water. The sun was finally dipping below the horizon of hills and I grinned again as I looked around, pleased with myself for finding such a beautiful and serene mooring. My journey would begin again tomorrow and this place would become another memory of a great day on the cut. But for a few hours it was mine to enjoy selfishly, all to myself.

I've lived aboard my 50ft narrowboat for more than ten years and I've explored a fair chunk of the network in that time. I'll often have at least one crew on board to help with locks and tea-making duties and the like, but I always look forward to those days when I can cruise alone. Perhaps it is because our modern world is so full of continual catter and communication that we don't often get a chance to enjoy being by ourselves. Whatever the reason, I look forward to for those long stretches of canal when I can cruise along in my own little world of quiet, uninterrupted solitude.

Summertime

During the summer months there are plenty of other boaters, fishermen and pedestrians around to punctuate my day and for the most part these are a welcome distraction. Whilst I am perfectly able to negotiate locks and moving bridges single-handed, the opportunity to shoot the breeze with other boaters is one of the greatest pleasures of life on the cut, despite our conversations being executed in series and cut short when the lock gates open to let us out for the next round of tillering.

I always make a point of hopping ashore with a windlass so that I can do my fair share of the work, but more often than not there are enough hands and I'm encouraged to stay aboard. I must admit I do feel quite lazy, perched at the tiller, chatting with the other skipper whilst the industrious crew scurries across the locks. I always keep a supply of biscuits handy to share by means of a thank you.

Locks and moving bridges

Locks and moving bridges can be wearisome when cruising alone. As a remedy I have found the best approach is to dispense with the idea of speed and efficiency, and instead embrace the slow and methodical nature of the process. Indeed I find that almost every part of boat life is more pleasurable if one adopts this philosophy. At locks I use my binoculars on the approach to select a suitable mooring point before sauntering up to the towpath

Solo boating in the wintertime.

at a slow tick-over. I'll moor loosely, take a leisurely look around and perhaps collect some unsightly litter before preparing the lock and bringing the boat in at a crawling pace.

It seems that the deeper the lock, the more nervous I become, particularly if using the lock ladder to board and alight. My boat always seems a little forlorn and vulnerable when left on its own at the bottom of a lock and I'm always eager to get back aboard. Despite this impatience, I feel entirely more comfortable and confident if I use only the paddles on my side of the lock, dispensing entirely with the need to rush across the gate. Admittedly this is a time-consuming option, but I'm happy to compromise speed for serenity. As I step aboard and pull away I say a little thank you to the Waterways Gods for allowing me safe passage through another lock, single-handed.

Executing swing bridges is an exercise in science, skill and luck in equal proportion. There are many variables to consider and even a moment of distraction can prove troublesome. I am always wary of windows and cratch covers becoming impaled on the corner of the bridge, which always seems to swing closed a little no matter how stiff it was to open. The wind is no friend of mine either and seems to conspire against me consistently when negotiating a tricky swing bridge. Again, I find that the answer to swing-bridge stress is a slow, considered approach where I resign myself to the fact that it will never go perfectly according to plan and that life would be boring if everything did. The tribulations of single-handed swing bridging are part of the ever present trials of boat life and one must either get on with it, or give up. I do always feel a little smug and accomplished when I'm safely back on board and the sight of the bridge is fading into the distance behind me.

Safety

Sir Francis Younghusband once said, 'Experience teaches much, and teaches it sharply,' and thankfully my experiences of mishaps have been few and the consequences minor. Relishing the carefree, idyllic life on the waterways alone must be contrasted with a strict and concentrated approach to safety; particularly one's own. It is foolish to risk personal injury in an attempt to save a window or cilled stern gear, particularly as incidents involving single-handed boaters may go un-noticed for hours. Despite my own cautiously focused approach there have been occasional near misses where only my strong grip on the boat or lock ladder has saved me after a slip. I'm convinced enough of the risks to always wear a self-inflating life jacket when locking single-handed. Despite having not yet fallen into a lock I can't help calculating the increasing odds of doing so each time I repeat the process. Perhaps one day my luck will fail and my number will come up. On that day I'll be wearing a life jacket with a waterproof mobile phone and a whistle in the pocket.

Wintertime

If pushed to make a choice I would grudgingly admit that I prefer boating in the warm summer months, but winter cruising has its own magical charm. I love frosty mornings when the branches are sleeved with a silver sheen, smoke unfolding from my chimney and not a soul in the world to be seen. True connoisseurs of solitude will relish these cold, crisp months when one can cruise for days without passing another moving boat, enjoying the fantasy that the waterways are yours to own.

During the winter, boating comes into sharp focus as every activity and manoeuvre becomes more acute. My fingers are crossed with prayers and curses each morning as I attempt to start my decrepit old engine that really should have been serviced during the comfortable summer months. I cling to the hope of finding a coal merchant to replenish my dwindling supplies, and another bottle of gas would stop me fretting too. Icy lock beams and ladders concentrate my attention, as do the freezing cold handrails of my boat.

I'm always amused when my wet ropes from yesterday are frozen in coils or straight like dowelling rods by last night's freeze. All of these musings trip through my mind repeatedly during the day and without a crew to confer with, the responsibility for dealing with them is all mine. Some may consider such tribulations to be a bind, but for me they are tests that give me a sense of pride once each is safely overcome.

Single-handed cruising is not easy and usually requires adaptations in both technique and attitude. But for those with sufficient supplies of brains and brawn, cruising the waterways alone can be a rewarding and often meditative enterprise, despite the logistical conundrums presented by the various designs of locks and bridges.

Repetition is the mother of all skill and many single-handed boaters will claim to be at least as efficient as crewed vessels. But the real joy of single-handed cruising lies not in the speed at which one can negotiate a lock or ease with which one masters a swing bridge, but in the uninterrupted and serene enjoyment of the waterways and one's boat. I love spending time alone and aboard and I would highly recommend the experience. But I don't think I can sincerely say that I have ever truly cruised alone.

The centre rope is a single-handed boater's best friend.

Single-handed cruising tips

1. Safety is the most important consideration for single-handed boaters. With nobody on hand to help in case of an accident you need to legislate for the worst and have a plan in place of what to do should something go wrong. In business it is called a risk assessment, but really it amounts to simple common sense. A self-inflating life jacket is a no-brainer. A fall that incorporates a bang to the head becomes a life or death situation depending on whether you're wearing one. Have your mobile phone in a waterproof bag to use if you're hurt and far from help. A whistle can attract attention too, so be sure to have these about your person at all times. Don't jump, slip, trip or take risks when boating alone. Waste a few seconds walking around the lock or bringing your boat nearer to the bank, rather than take a risk.

2. Ladders are a relatively recent addition to the historic structures of locks and were introduced as a safety escape feature, rather than as an aid to boating. Although many single-handers find the ladders useful some consider them unnecessary, preferring instead to haul their boat in and out of the lock using ropes. This bow-hauling method works fine in most cases although those locks with bridges at their entrance or exit can prove problematic. For boaters with the necessary co-ordination, one answer is to stand atop the bridge and nimbly flick the rope beneath before catching the end at the other side. For those of us lacking in the skill, using the lock ladder is arguably a more efficient method so long as one is conscious of the ever-present slip hazard.

3. One of the greatest dangers when negotiating a lock alone comes in the form of friendly help. Despite the best intentions, enthusiastic assistance from inexperienced or distracted windlass wielders can create problems and things can go wrong surprisingly quickly. Don't be afraid to decline help as most boaters will understand that everyone has their own way of doing things. Explain that you have a 'system' and that it is hard to break the habit. Of course, if you are sharing a lock with another boat and their crew then it is everyone's responsibility to stay alert to danger. By all means enjoy the company while you can, but keep a watchful eye on proceedings to ensure everyone stays safe and stays afloat.

4. A centre rope is your greatest friend when boating alone. Ensure the end of the rope is within reach of your position at the tiller ready for when you need to step ashore. In most situations one can use the centre rope alone to moor to the bank whilst preparing a lock before using a bow rope to haul the boat in when the lock is ready. Use the centre rope again to maintain a good position in the lock, taking in or letting out slack when necessary. Be especially careful when locking down as boats can easily be hung up if a rope is tied to a bollard. It does also help to have a centre rope on each side of the boat if possible as this avoids the need to flick the rope over chimneys and other roof clutter when the need arises.

5. 'Thumb-lining' is an intricate method by which a lock gate is opened and closed without disembarking by using ropes and was routinely used by working boats towing a cargo butty.

The process is unfortunately now almost extinct and indeed modern lock-restoration work has often disposed of a mandatory small pin that protruded near the top lock, making thumb-lining impossible.

6. Lift bridges and swing bridges rely on the use of long ropes, convenient landing points and accurate boat manoeuvring, often supplemented with a ration of agility and climbing skill. It should always be approached slowly and methodically and it is useful to practice the process when you have a crew to step in with help should motorists become impatient. Be aware that some electrically-operated bridges have a timer to delay over-frequent usage or a locking period to prohibit usage at peak road traffic times.

NARROWBOATING PERILS AND HOW TO DEAL WITH THEM

Fouled prop

Your engine is revving but your boat isn't going anywhere fast. Chances are, you have something around your propeller or prop shaft. The first thing to try is putting your boat into reverse for a few short bursts. This can often dislodge whatever is fouling the prop, particularly during autumn when leaves will pack tightly around the blades. Dropping into reverse and revving sharply will usually clear autumn foliage.

If the problem is more persistent then you'll need to get into your weed hatch. Depending on the type of material you find there, you might need wire cutters, sharp blades, scissors, hacksaws or bolt croppers. During the winter months when the water is painfully cold, it may be worth taping your cutting implements to a wooden handle of some kind to keep your hands out of the freezing cold water. Beware of fishing twine with hooks attached too.

A key float is an essential item.

Run aground

It happens a lot, particularly near the edges of the waterways and on the inside of a bend. The best redress is to stop forward motion as soon as you realise you're aground. Then, reverse off the way you came and navigate around the obstacle. It may be necessary to redistribute weight aboard the boat. This can be done by sending your crewmates ashore or to another part of the boat. Gentle rocking can also help but, if you're stuck fast, you might need a tow from a passing friendly boat.

Chimney loss

Sometimes it is impossible to avoid low branches and anything on the roof of the boat is at risk of being swept into the water. Chimneys are especially vulnerable, and they're expensive to replace. Ideally you would remove them when you're underway, stashing them somewhere safe inside. If you're prone to forget or can't be bothered to remove your chimney then it is worth securing it to the boat somehow using chain or rope. That way, if it does get knocked it won't fall into the water and be lost.

Items dropped overboard

Keys should ideally be furnished with a float that is big enough to hold the bunch. However, even if the bunch is heavy enough to sink the float, it is still more easily retrieved with a rake or similar. The float is easier to find and hook out than keys that sink to the bottom into the mud.

Other ferrous metals can be retrieved with a 'sea magnet', if you're lucky and persistent. Windlasses are the usual suspects here. While aluminium windlasses are lighter and less wieldy, they can't be found with a sea magnet and therefore many boaters stick with the steel ones, just in case.

Ten boating etiquette tips

1. Cruising a frozen canal is possible but be aware that fragile GRP and wooden boats can be damaged by large sheets of moving ice.

2. When setting off, be sure to check for approaching boats. It is easy to get caught up in the pre-cruise concentrated excitement and not notice that you are about to cast off into the path of an oncoming vessel.

3. Give a long toot of your horn when approaching bridges and blind bends. Short toots can be mistaken for car horns. Using your horn to signal to an oncoming boater in plain view is not ideal as it could be misinterpreted. It is much better to flash your headlight and use clear hand signals.

4. Cyclists, anglers, walkers and other boaters will all appreciate a smile and a wave as you pass and as this is one of the most pleasurable aspects of boating, not doing so is almost unforgiveable.

5. Always knock and ask before boarding someone else's boat. Stepping aboard uninvited is usually considered impolite.

6. Use hi-vis tape or white plastic bags to highlight mooring pins and keep the towpath next to your boat clear of other trip hazards.

7. Be ready to help at locks and bridges, even if you are cruising single-handed. Be considerate that the skipper of the boat might want to do things differently or more slowly than you might be accustomed to. Not everyone is an expert boater.

8. Try to leave space for other boats to moor at popular visitor moorings. This may mean shuffling along a few feet as boats arrive and leave.

9. Be aware that fallen dead wood is a valuable ecological commodity, being home or food for a wealth of flora and fauna. Localised collecting near marinas or popular mooring points can desecrate an area in a very short time. Most boaters consider it acceptable to collect dead wood that can be reached from the towpath. Everything else belongs to Mother Nature.

10. Moorings with facilities for the disabled are rare so stay off these unless you are entitled to use them. There is usually only a small sign to highlight this type of mooring so keep a keen eye when mooring up.

Anglers

Anglers and boaters invariably get in each other's way and the only way to avoid conflict is to be as courteous as possible. Slow down as you approach them and do not increase your revs until you are well past their position.

Look out for anglers and be nice to them.

159

Be polite and you'll enjoy your boating all the more.

Stick to the centre of the navigation and, if the angler is landing a big fish, stop your boat and watch the proceedings. Look out for fishing competition notices when mooring up or you could get an early wake-up call. Remember, the canals are still in use because they're popular with many different groups of people. Let's be nice to one another and enjoy the cut together.

7 THE ART OF BOATING: THE GREAT INDOORS

Good boating comes with experience. Seasoned boaters build a virtual toolkit of hints, tips and tricks to make boating easier, safer, more efficient and more fun. Predictably, the learning never stops, and the acquisition of a new skill or method is one of the many joys of boat ownership. A comprehensive list of boating know-how is impossible to compile, but the list of skills below will help you to grasp the basics more quickly than if you relied on experience alone.

ELECTRICKERY – A POWER MANAGEMENT FAQ

It could be said that happy boating depends on the ability to plan ahead and willingness to forgo convenience. This is never truer than when discussing power usage. Unlike in a house, the power available aboard your boat is finite and will require topping up at intervals. How close together those intervals are will depend on the type of system you have in place and how much power you use.

What's the best number of leisure batteries?

Leisure batteries are used to power 12v lighting and appliances. Logic implies that more batteries mean more power and longer between charges, and while this is largely true there is a sensible limit to how many batteries you need. General consensus is that four leisure batteries is the maximum sensible number. Remember, more batteries means longer charging times. It's impractical and costly to properly charge

more than four. With this ratio of charging and power production in mind, most boats have three leisure batteries. Moderate power usage will usually be rewarded with around 36–72 hours of power before recharging is necessary. If your power usage is low then two leisure batteries may suffice, and indeed many boaters find two batteries sufficient.

Why does my starter battery need to be kept isolated from my leisure batteries?

Your starter battery is used to start your boat's engine. Keeping your starter battery isolated allows you to deplete your leisure batteries whilst retaining the ability to start your engine. Most boats will use either a split charge relay unit or a more sophisticated battery management system.

Is it better to charge my batteries with the engine in gear with the prop turning?

No. Running your engine whilst moored up is fine, so long as the prop isn't turning as this can cause degradation to the bank and is against CRT rules. This is true of all canal edges, whether wood, stone, pilings or raw edges. Bank degradation and breeches have been caused by this problem, whatever material is used for edging.

When the topic arose on a popular Internet discussion forum recently the consensus was that the practice lives on from the days when diesel engines needed to work hard in order to avoid damage and cylinder bores coking up. However, modern engines and oils have largely eradicated this problem. More importantly, it is commonly accepted that any build-up of coke in the cylinder bores will be flushed through during the next time the engine is run at high-revs.

Besidees, ou can run your engine and use higher revs, but out of gear without the prop turning. This protects the bank, gives the best charge, saves on fuel costs and protects your engine too, so the best of many worlds. Other solutions to avoid the issue altogether are worth considering too. Using a generator is cheaper, quieter, more efficient and less damaging to the land at the water's edge. An even better solution is to untie your ropes and go boating.

12v or 24v

Some boats have a 24v system, as opposed to the much more common 12v system. I understand that those who have especially opted for the 24v system do seem to have some complex technical reason for preferring 24v, but I have never been able to understand why it is supposedly better. I do know that most boatyards are more used to working with 12v systems and will have all of the right equipment to work with 12v. If you have a 24v system you might find it more difficult to get help when you need it.

Can I run 240v appliances (those with a conventional 3-pin plug) on a boat?

Although most boats' electrical systems are 12v (the same as your car) it is possible to convert 12v power into 240v power by using an inverter. This is wired to your 12v electrical system and converts the power so that you can use items that have a conventional 3-pin plug.

Below: The more luxurious your boat, the greater your power needs are likely to be.

Top tip: LED lighting

Change any incandescent lights to LEDs as these use much less power. LEDs are available for all light fittings and there are several types which give off a pleasing light.

Ignition key warning

Although your starter and leisure batteries are split when in normal use, your engine ignition will link the two sets of batteries in order to charge them. Be sure to switch off your engine ignition by turning the key fully to the off position. Otherwise you risk linking the batteries, draining them all during the evening and having no charge in the starter battery when morning comes.

It is important to note that the inverter itself uses power in order to do its job, so using 240v appliances is always a power-hungry option. Most boats also have a landline hook-up option which supplies 240v directly from the land-based mains to the boat, using a heavy duty cable. When plugged into the mains your boat will have a direct supply of 240v power, negating the need to use an inverter.

Which appliances use the most power?

Anything that relies on 240v power will drain your batteries quickly. These appliances won't be much of a problem for those boats that are plugged in to a shoreline electricity source, but if you're out and about or reliant on your batteries and an inverter then 240v appliances will quickly drain your batteries. Most appliances are available in 12v models and these are usually a better option if you want to conserve power. Here's a list of the worst power-hungry offenders, along with some tips on how to conserve your valuable power supplies.

Top tip: protecting your engine

'There are a number of serious engine problems that might be caused by running at very light load.

- Bore glazing: a hard varnish that forms in the cylinder.

- Bore polishing: the cylinder becomes too smooth and shiny.

- Ring sticking: a sticky gum stops the rings moving and pressing against the cylinder wall.

- Bore wear: not many people appear to worry about this and it's the most serious problem.

'These things can all cause poor compression and burning of engine oil (blue exhaust smoke) because the cylinder wall needs an amount of microscopic roughness to work correctly. It's not easy to work out just how much light running really contributes to these problems, there are many experts (some real experts and some self-appointed experts) and they have different views. So, some boaters run in gear to load the engine just to be safe. As mentioned above it's against the rules and anti-social.

'The best approach is to fit a reasonably large alternator and a temperature gauge. A big alternator will load the engine as much as the propeller. Run the engine quite fast at first until it gets up to temperature then ease off to a bit above tickover. If you're running for a long time then maybe give it a few revs every hour. An engine running at tickover will most likely never warm up and this is a bad thing.'

Dave: Nb Vox Stellarum

Appliance	Power-saving tip
Fridge and freezer	A three-way fridge can be run using 240v, 12v or gas. Using the 12v option is better than 240v, but running the fridge on gas is less expensive and does not drain your batteries.
Microwave	Most boats do without, but if you must use one then try to do so when the engine is running.
Television	Many boats do without, but 12v TVs are available.
CD players	Using an MP3 player, such as an iPod, uses far less power than playing a CD.
Games consoles	Rechargeable handheld consoles are a better option.
Laptop computers	Many laptops can be run through a 12v adapter but make sure you get the right one for your unit. Running the laptop using its own integral battery will not only save your boat battery power but will extend the life of your laptop battery too.
Vacuum cleaners	You might find that your inverter is not powerful enough to run your vacuum cleaner. This can sometimes be remedied if you run your engine while using the appliance, but this trick doesn't always work. 12v handheld cleaners are available, although they're really only good for small clean-up jobs. If you have the option you might like to forgo the vacuum cleaner in favour of a broom and mop combo.
Power tools	In similar fashion to the vacuum cleaner above, many power tools cannot be run through an inverter. It's wise to use a shoreline electrical hook up to a 240v power supply on land when using power tools.
Water pump and shower gulper	There's not much that can be done to limit or forgo use of these appliances, but you can use them wisely. It makes sense to use them during the daytime while the engine is running, saving your battery power for the evening. Seriously frugal boaters might entertain a 'navy shower' where water is run to wet the body before turning off the tap to lather up with soap. You can switch the water back on again to rinse. Navy showers usually use water for no longer than two minutes. Enjoy!
Hair dryers and straighteners	Both appliances are available in 12v models. Another option might be to get your hair cut short. It works for me.

Use technology wisely to save power.

FEELING THE HEAT: STOVE MANAGEMENT FAQ

Almost every boat on the waterways has a multi-fuel stove and for many, this is the sole source of heating. There are many reasons why stoves are so popular. They are easy to use and easy to maintain and provide a great deal of heat. However, I think most boaters would admit that the best thing about a stove is the comforting glow of a fire that makes a boat a snug sanctuary to be in when it's cold outside.

What kind of stove should I buy for my boat?

Most boats are pretty small, compared with a brick house, and so most stove units will provide enough heat. Indeed, the biggest consideration is ensuring that you can regulate the heat from your stove efficiently enough to avoid overheating. You'll regularly see boats with all of the doors and windows open in the bleakest days of winter – a sure sign of an overheating stove.

The Morsø Squirrel is, perhaps, the most popular stove you will find aboard, but there are many other units and manufacturers to consider too. Squirrel units are relatively expensive, but many boaters feel that they are worth the money. If you are going to look for a different unit then you might want to consider these points before making your decision.

- Does the flue fix to the top of the stove? You might not have space for a flue that protrudes from the back of the unit.
- Are spare parts available for the unit you are considering? New grates, glass and closing fittings are often required.
- Does the unit have internal fire bricks for insulation and efficiency?
- Does the unit have a 'riddler' to easily remove ash from the grate?
- Is the ash pan big enough for the grate, or will ash fall around it? (This is a headache that will mean your ash pan won't slide in easily, forcing you to remove ash from the area regularly.)
- Can the unit run on wood, coal and nuggets?
- Is the flue diameter compatible with your roof collar?

Can I use any type of fuel in my stove?

That depends on the stove, but usually the answer is no. The most frequent problem is caused by buying the wrong type of coal nuggets. 'Petro-coal', of the variety you will often find for sale on petrol-station forecourts, burns too hot for most stoves. This can cause your stove to overheat, warp and break the seals. The damage can be so bad that, sometimes, a new stove is required.

There are many other types of coal available that are entirely suitable. The debate rages about the best type to buy with many boaters being partial or partisan to a particular type. You'll find that there is a fine balance between price, heat output and the amount of ash that is produced. In essence, you'll get a coal that is good at any two of these features. Burnwell, Taybright, Excel, Homefire Ovals and Phurnacite are popular brands, but there are many others too.

As for wood, you shouldn't use MDF, melamine, ply or other composite wood types as they exude poisonous gasses when burned. Painted, varnished, and any otherwise-treated wood has associated poison risks too and you should also avoid yew and rhododendron for the same reason.

Can I collect wood from the towpath for my fire?

Officially, no, as the wood does not belong to you. In reality, most boaters do and most land owners don't mind. However, there are some ecological issues to consider if you are going to collect firewood.

Deadwood and foliage provide important food and habitat for many plants and animals. Over-collection, such as can occur in small wooded areas near marinas and popular moorings, can desecrate the habitat. Many boaters use the towpath rule – if you can reach the wood from the towpath then it's OK to collect. Any wood that you can't reach from the towpath belongs to Mother Nature.

I'm having trouble lighting my stove

Building a relationship with your stove takes practice and most people find that the relationship begins with the calling of a truce. Your stove will only allow you to cut so many corners before it fights back and refuses to light. Offer your stove some loving care and attention; clean the grate and empty the ash from the pan. Start your fire in stages. Try using firelighters or well-scrunched newspaper to light a few skinny sticks of dry kindling. Once that is alight you can add more substantial kindling pieces before adding a layer of coal. Make sure the stove vent is open so that it can draw in air.

When you have a good glowing start to your fire you can add a healthy layer of coal which should burn nicely and slowly if you are practised enough at using the stove vent. Knowing how much venting to use takes practice. It's a dark art that differs with each boat, each stove and each phase of the moon; or at least that's how it seems. You can cut corners here and there, but if you take too many liberties then you are

Did you know...?

That ash from your fire can be used to pack the seal gate of a dry dock? If you are moored near a boatyard with a dry dock they will probably be pleased to be offered your ash. Re-use and recycle!

likely to have to start all over again with a clean stove.

I've done all that, but it still won't light

Check that you don't have a problem with your stove. Poor maintenance can create issues that make your fire difficult to light. However, the failure to light well is probably the least of your worries as this is potentially a symptom of a more dangerous problem. Carbon monoxide poisoning and overheating stoves that create a fire risk are the two major issues to be wary of. Stove maintenance is essential as failure to do so is a major health and safety risk.

Blocked flue pipes and damage to any part of the unit can make your stove difficult to light or otherwise behave strangely. Check the baffle plate, the piece that sits below the roof of your stove between the flames and the flue. Ash can gather here, blocking the flue. While you're at it, ensure the flue and chimney are clear too. Either buy a flue brush or lower a rope down your flue, tie the end of the rope a towel inside your (cold) stove, close the stove door and then pull the rope and towel up the flue pipe. Do this several times.

Check the entire unit for holes, burst joints and other seals. These can make your stove overheat and become a significant fire hazard.

Check behind the stove and flue. Wait until your stove is cold and put a torch into the unit. Look for light leaks. This test is, of course, best conducted at night.

What other stove maintenance should I do?

In addition to the checks above you should:

- Check door seals are sound. Ensure that stove rope seals around the door are securely in place and that the door closes and seals fully.
- Check the seals around any other opening, such as cooking pan plates etc.
- Check the fire bricks are still in place and in one piece.
- Check your grate hasn't warped from overheating. A blue petrol-spectrum colour is a good indication of a problem.
- Check and replace broken glass.
- You might also want to paint or polish your stove ready for the next season. Use heat-resistant paint or a polish, depending on the level of refurbishment that is necessary.
- Check the fire cement or other sealant around every seal.
- Check the collar attachment on the roof is watertight. Refit and reseal if necessary.

Can I cook on the stove?

You'd be silly not to! Boiling a kettle using the stove makes great sense as you save gas and money by doing so. Many boaters cook soups, stews, curries and other hotpot recipes on the top of their stove with great success. It works best if you are adept at regulating your stove's heat output in order to avoid burning the meal at the bottom of the pan. Some even bake potatoes in the embers of their stove, although most who try this seem to get either burnt or undercooked spuds.

What's the best way to keep your fire in overnight for a warm boat when morning comes?

This is another example of the 'getting to know your stove' process and there isn't a cure-all answer. You'll find that keeping a stove warm throughout the night requires careful juggling of several factors – fuel type, vent use, how much fuel you will use and how much ash is produced. The most significant of these is the amount of coal you use to bank up the fire as most failures are caused by using too little. The use of the vent is a significant factor too. You should leave it open just enough to keep the fire lit, but not so much as the fuel burns hot and gets wasted fast before the night is through. Practice makes perfect!

A stove with ecofan fitted.

Tony's towpath tales: A stove emergency

I'm always very careful when using my stove. I know the risks and take all of the precautions I can to keep them to a minimum. One thing I'm particularly wary of is the risk involved when lighting the fire. Like many boaters, I'll get the kindling and coal going by opening the bottom hatch where the ash pan fits, allowing lots of air to be drawn in. This gets the stove going very well indeed, but you must be sure to close the hatch when the coal is well alight; otherwise the stove will continue to draw lots of air and can overheat very quickly. Many stoves are designed to stop this practice, but mine relies on common sense and vigilance, so I'm particularly careful when I light my fire in this way.

I'd been to the local supermarket to buy supplies before meeting up with a friend for coffee. Arriving back to the boat I opened the side hatch to be greeted by the sight of water spurting from behind my stove and a faint smell of smoke. Stepping aboard I could see that there was water about three inches deep in my bedroom, so the leak had been spraying for some time. After switching off the water pump and the supply from the water tank I investigated the problem.

The plumbing from my water tank runs down the port side of my boat, past my stove to the taps, shower and toilet. As the pipework runs alongside my stove it is shielded by a section of wooden trim which, when I looked, had obviously been on fire, leaving a scorched hole the size of a small shoe.

Checking the plumbing pipework I couldn't immediately find the leak, so I switched the water back on and found the source – a tiny hole; so small that it looked like it had been made with a nail. And when I looked at the floor near the stove, there was the nail! I was confused.

It took inspections from four other people before we deduced the series of events that had caused the problem. It appears that the ash-pan door had either come open, or been left open while I was away from the boat. The stove had overheated and set fire to the wooden trim that protected the plumbing pipes that ran alongside.

But here's the interesting bit. At some point in history, before I bought the boat, someone had, apparently, accidentally nailed through the wooden trim and punctured the plumbing. While the nail sealed the hole, there was no problem with leaks. However, when the trim set alight, the nail became hot, melting the plastic plumbing pipe surrounding it and allowing the nail to work loose. Water then squirted from the hole left by the nail in exactly the right place to extinguish the burning wood. It's the only explanation.

I'm 99 per cent sure that I closed that ash-pan door, so if it came open for whatever reason it was unlucky that it did so while I was out. I made a note to myself to double-check the latch when I use that door. I also no longer use the ash-pan door to increase the draw of air, relying instead on the smaller vent that is meant for exactly that purpose. It's slower to start the fire, but much safer. But the most significant thing that I have learned from all of this is that it is the little tiny details that can cause or cure disasters. Someone, somewhere accidentally nailed through my plumbing in exactly the right place to extinguish the fire that could have destroyed my boat. Having repaired the damage, I often wonder if I should nail through the pipe again.

WATER, WATER EVERYWHERE: WATER MANAGEMENT FAQ

The water you use on your boat can be obtained for free from any of the purpose-provided taps along the waterways system. You pay for the service through your licence fee. Many boatyards and marinas will also let you fill your water tanks there too, although some places in remote rural areas may not. This is because they rely on boreholes with a finite supply.

The water system on your boat requires a little care and attention to ensure it remains drinkable and to manage your supplies sensibly.

My water turns brown when my tank is almost empty. Why?

This is because the tiny particles that are found in all mains supplied water have settled at the bottom of your tank, making the last few centimetres of water cloudy. All water supplies have tiny particles and impurities. With the supply from land-based taps being constantly renewed and flushed through, these particles are usually invisible to the naked eye, entirely harmless and present in such small quantities that they cause no problem.

However, on a boat your water supply is stored in a tank. Over time the particles will settle to the bottom and form a layer that clouds the bottom of your tank. It is advisable to empty the tank occasionally to remove this cloudy layer before it becomes a significant issue.

The water tank is rusty and my water is cloudy. What do I do?

It's probably time to treat the inside of your tank. Emptying the water, preparing the metalwork and repainting it with a specialist coating will refurbish your tank. It is a good idea to do this every few years but your needs and individual circumstances will be your best measure.

Why have I got two water tanks?

This is probably because someone has taken exception to the quality of water in the integral tank and fitted a plastic tank to supply one tap, usually specifically for the purpose of drinking. This works well if the tank is used often and is impermeable to light. Otherwise, the tank could grow slimy mould, negating any benefits.

Should I treat my water before I drink it?

You can, and many boaters recommend treating your water tank with purifying tablets at regular intervals. Others routinely clean and treat their tanks to stop the build-up of impurities discussed in the first question of this list. A growing number are installing filters in the plumbing line below the tap in the galley.

There is a school of thought that says treatment is unnecessary and that the impurities in your water supply are helpful in strengthening your body's immune system. Whilst this is largely true, it is dependent on degree and assumes that the people drinking the water are fit and healthy.

What do I need to know about my hose?

There's not much that can go wrong with your hose, but a few common sense practices are recommended.

- Don't let your hose (or any part of it) fall into the canal.
- When filling your tank, run off the first few seconds of water into the canal. This ensures that the water in your tank is fresh and hasn't been standing or stored in your hose for any length of time.

A valuable collection of hose connectors.

- Be careful of letting dogs run on your boat roof if you store your hose there, otherwise it is likely that they will urinate on it.
- It's a good idea to gather a collection of various hose fittings, preferably a few of each type. You're bound to need them and you'll occasionally leave them behind at water points. If you find one of mine that I left behind, you're welcome to it.
- Having two hose reels is a good idea for those times you can't moor close enough to the tap. That said, other boaters will usually be happy to lend you their hose to use as an extension in that situation.

I think I'd rather use bottled water. What do you think?

I can understand the reasoning of boaters who want to use bottled water. The benefits are obvious. However there are some significant downsides to consider too. Most obvious is the cost. Some estimates say that bottled water is 2000x more expensive than tap water, despite having no discernable benefits. Indeed, there are plenty of reasons that bottled water is a worse choice, besides the fact that you'll need to store and transport it.

First, and most significant, is the cost to the planet, with plastic being one of the main litter contaminants of our canals, rivers, seas and landscapes. The manufacturing process involved in producing bottled water is significantly harmful to the planet too. A better idea is to transport tap water in opaque re-useable containers as this saves cost and is better for the environment.

But if that isn't reason enough to forgo bottled water (shame on you!) then consider that your stores of bottled water could go yucky if they're not kept somewhere dark and cool. The taste, colour and smell will change.

Why does my water pump sometimes buzz a short cycle, even though there are no taps on?

There are several reasons why this might be, but in 99 per cent of cases it is an indication of a leak in your plumbing system. As water leaks from the system the pressure in the pipes is reduced, inviting the water pump to add more water into the pipe to restore pressure. That's probably why your pump is going off at intervals.

First, check the inspection hatch that allows you to see into the bilges under the floor of your boat. It will likely be somewhere near the stern. If there's water in there, you could have a leak.

Next, check for any obvious leaks. If you find none then it will require a process of elimination to find a leak, if there is one. If your plumbing line has been conveniently fitted with shut-off taps then you can determine which section of pipework the leak is in by strategically shutting these off in series. Otherwise, strategic use of paper towels along the plumbing line will do the same job. Remember that water runs downhill and so finding a puddle might not necessarily mean you have found the location of the leak. If you've eliminated leaks as the cause, then your problem is likely more complicated and probably requires expert help. (I've assumed that you're not an expert already, if you're reading this section!)

Is it OK to drain the water from my sink and shower into the canal/river?
Legally, yes. 'Grey water' from sinks, baths and showers can be drained into the waterways (unlike 'black water' from your toilet, which must be stored and disposed of correctly). However, many experts feel that the increasing popularity of boating and concentrations of boats is affecting water quality in our canals as larger volumes of grey water are drained into them. If this concerns you then you might wish to do something about it before it becomes a problem and changes in grey water disposal are forced upon us.

- Use ecologically friendly dishwashing detergents and bathing soap products.
- Dispose of fats carefully in your domestic waste. Use paper towels to wipe plates and pans. Allow used cooking fat to cool before decanting into a container for disposal.
- Don't scrape plates into the water or rinse food down your plug hole. Put it in the bin instead.
- Consider fitting a filter to your system before it becomes a legal requirement.

Do you have any tips for saving water?
- Turn off the shower whilst you lather your body.
- Turning off the tap while you brush your teeth saves four gallons per minute.
- Use grey water and the water from cooking to water your plants instead of fresh water from the tap.
- Collect rain water for your plants.

- Make sure your hose does not leak.
- Choose low water-use plants or native species for pots and gardens.
- Fix dripping taps. One drip every second wastes five gallons per day.
- When filling your water tank, keep an eye on it and don't let it overflow.

FULL TO THE GUNWALES – SAVING SPACE ABOARD

Whether you live aboard or you're a fair-weather boater, one issue that affects all boaters is the limited storage space available on boats. The best solution to this problem is to take less stuff aboard, but there's a fine balance between hardcore roughing it and the liberating comfort of having just enough.

Then, when you've decided on the things you absolutely must have on board your boat, the next step is to prioritise the stuff you use most and make sure it is accessible when you need it. It's a trial and error process that takes time, but you'll eventually have all of your stuff right where you want it.

Here's a list of space-saving tips to get you started, including some tried and tested methods from seasoned boaters.

Use the space under the gunwales
This area is often just the right size for CDs and books. Install shelves under the gunwales and save using space elsewhere. Other ingenious boaters store fold-up chairs and tables here ready for when you have more bums than seats.

Under the bed
Beds on boats will generally have lots of storage beneath but, unless it is cleverly designed, the

Clever storage – folding chairs fit under gunwales.

space is practically inaccessible. Removing your bedding and mattress to get to your tool kit will soon become a chore that makes even the most righteous curse. Clever design fixes will work wonders for your patience and storage issues alike. A bed-base fitted with pull-out drawers or baskets is a simple and obvious fix, but more adventurous boat designers include pulleys and lift systems to elevate the mattress to give easy access to the space beneath. If you're designing your boat from scratch you might want to consider your options carefully, as the amount of storage space under your bed is invaluable – if you can get to it.

Make it accessible
While we are talking about the space under your bed it is worth considering the items that can be

stashed there. If your under-bed storage space is hard to get to (that's most of us then!) then it's a good idea to stash stuff there that you won't need very often. Camping gear and out of season clothing are two obvious choices. Power tools that you need only occasionally are another.

Put stuff you use regularly in drawers and cupboards, under furniture or in the step near your cratch. Your everyday tool kit should be close to hand; otherwise that new picture frame will never get hung. Some boaters even keep a Leatherman-style multi-tool on a shelf for those quick and easy jobs you could do right now. First aid kits, bad-weather gear and sun block should all be kept somewhere you can get at them easily.

Everything in its place
When you need something, you usually need it right away. It can be a real pain if you have to search your whole boat because you can't remember where you stashed the pump-out key or that piece of hose that was just right for the job. Make sure you keep everything in the allocated place and make sure that everyone knows to put stuff back when it lives. If you only use your boat occasionally, it's easy to forget where you stashed things last time you were aboard. Some boaters (such as me) are so particular that we have a list of where to find things, just in case we forget.

Embrace technology
Despite the fact that our canal system is centuries old, the joys of the modern world can make boating easier. Substituting CDs for an MP3 player saves oodles of space. A tablet is less cumbersome than a laptop. An e-reader device cuts down the number of books you keep aboard; although we would never get rid of every book we own. That would be unthinkable!

Reject technology

Do you really need a TV aboard your boat? Do you want to be working on your laptop when you're supposed to be enjoying your boating break? Can you unplug completely and leave your phone at home? If you can, that's boating Utopia!

One in, one out

You have a finite amount of space on board, particularly in places such as bookshelves and wardrobes. Try running a 'one in- one out' policy: if you buy a new shirt, then one must go. Want a new book to read? Then you must relinquish one that currently takes up space on your bookshelf. It can work with anything; shoes, board games, grandchildren... (OK, maybe not grandchildren.)

Space-saving furniture

When purchasing furniture for your boat, consider if it can be used for storage. The right type of footstool will have integral storage. Chests make excellent coffee tables. Even some chairs, sofas and sofabeds have storage built in. It's worth considering!

Containerise

Putting stuff in boxes, crates, bags and baskets makes it easier to work with. It's easier to pull out a few tubs than it is to rifle the entire contents of a badly-organised cupboard. Store similar stuff together and label the containers if appropriate or necessary.

Top tip: boating Zen

If you're using or moving aboard a boat for the first time, take only the bare minimum of things that you need to get by. Only bring more stuff aboard when you absolutely need it. Don't take stuff aboard that you might need; it will take up space and never get used. Trust me, you can get by with much less stuff than you think, and you'll be happier for doing it.

Top tip: nice drawers

Install drawers instead of cupboards. Drawers allow you to easily reach the stuff at the back and help to avoid less stacking too.

A sofabed with drawers offers excellent additional storage space.

8 BOAT MAINTENANCE

If you want to fully enjoy boating you will need to be proactive about boat maintenance. Like any equipment, narrowboats are more reliable and less troublesome if you keep up with the necessary jobs that need doing. Burying your head in the sand will only delay the day of reckoning, and by then you'll probably be facing a much bigger job that delays or cancels your cruising fun. An ounce of prevention is certainly better than a pound of cure when it comes to boat maintenance.

INSIDE THE BOAT

Water pump

Your water pump should ideally be considered a consumable item. The pump will rarely warn you before it is about to break so it makes sense to have a spare pump on standby. That said, a new pump is not always necessary. There are some user-serviceable parts that can easily be maintained by the layman. New impellers and filter blockages are easy to sort if you have a spanner and a screwdriver handy.

How long it takes:
- Replacing an impeller: One hour.
- Clearing a blocked filter gauze: One hour.
- Replacing the whole water pump unit: One hour.

How much it costs:
- New impellor: £30–£50.
- New water pump: £100–£150.

Smoke, gas and carbon monoxide alarms

Some boat features, such as stoves, cookers, water heaters, gas lamps and candles, require risk assessments and alarm systems in order to minimise risks. In addition to the usual common sense precautions, be sure to install alarms to alert you should the worst happen.

How long it takes:
- Installing three alarms: one morning.
- Testing alarms: seconds, repeated weekly.
- Common sense precautions: a lifetime.

How much it costs:
- Carbon monoxide alarm: £30.
- Smoke alarm: £20 or free from your local fire service.
- Gas leak alarm: £50.

Boat Safety Scheme logo.

Boat Safety Scheme

Independent and authorised BSS Examiners are there to carry out BSS examinations and to ensure that your boat meets their minimum legal safety standards. A BSS examination must be conducted at least once every four years.

How long it takes: one morning.

How much it costs: usually less than £200.

Toilet seals

Whether pump-out or cassette, the seals in your toilet will one day deteriorate, releasing smells or affecting how your loo functions. Replacing them is not a pleasurable job, but it is easy enough for most boaters to tackle.

How long it takes:
- Cassette toilet: two hours.
- Pump-out toilet: one morning.

How much it costs:
- Cassette seals £5–£10 each.
- Pump-out seals £20–£35 each.

Water tank

Plastic water tanks require no servicing until they break completely. You might want to add water-purifying tablets occasionally, but otherwise plastic tanks are best left well alone. Steel tanks will need recoating with a specialist

Boat maintenance is a never-ending job.

coating to eliminate rust. The time between treatments varies, dependent not least on the owners' ability to turn a blind eye. Both steel and plastic tanks will accumulate an amount of 'dirt' at the bottom of the tank as tiny debris in the water supply sink, settle and build up over time. It makes sense to have a full clean out at least yearly, but this is only possible if your water tank has an inspection hatch of the appropriate size.

175

How long it takes:
- If your tank is empty and dry, half a day, but longer if the boatyard has to empty and dry the tank.

How much it costs:
- Around £150, assuming the tank is empty and dry, otherwise more.

Stove maintenance

Stoves need and deserve regular attention to ensure they work properly and are safe. The common maintenance issues include repairing seals, keeping the flue clear and blacking the cast-iron body for aesthetic reasons. You should check your stove and flue for cracks, leaks and rust holes regularly. This is most easily done by two people in the dark: one shines a bright light inside the stove belly while the other looks for light leaks on the outside. You should also check visually and manually, though, looking and feeling for any issues.

How long it takes:
- Replacing stove rope around the door: 30 minutes.
- Clearing old rope and applying new rope: one hour.
- Re-sealing flue junction: one morning.
- Removing and resealing flue collar: up to one day.

How much it costs:
- New stove rope and glue: £20.
- Resealing flue junction: new stove rope plus cement or heat-resistant silicone: £20.
- Flue collar replacement: new stove rope plus cement or silicone: £20.

OUTSIDE THE BOAT

Bottom blacking

Applying bitumen (or other specialist coating) to the hull of your boat will help protect the steel against rust. It's an important precautionary measure as the only remedy for a rusted hull is over-plating, and that is not cheap. Opinions vary, but most recommend blacking your hull every three years.

How long it takes:
- At least three days, although experts advise the process should take 50 man hours. This is because it will usually take five days to prep the boat, paint the hull and let the coating cure. To do the job in three days means not waiting for the coating to dry. It's usually boat owners who undertake the process themselves who cut short the curing process in a bid to save money on dry-dock hire costs. Professionals and indeed the manufacturers of the blacking paint products recommend that the coating is allowed to dry properly before putting the boat back in the water.

How much it costs:
- For a professional job at a boatyard you'll pay around £10–£12 per foot plus VAT. You can save money by hiring the dry dock and doing it yourself, but it's hard and dirty work and not worth the saving, in my opinion. Besides, boatyard professionals have the experience to do the work quickly and efficiently. You're unlikely to be as fast or efficient. Most boaters undertake the job only once before deciding better of it the next time around.

Surveys

While a Boat Safety Scheme examination is required every four years, it doesn't cover some very important maintenance points.

There are two main kinds of survey. A hull survey looks at the structural aspects of the boat, such as the integrity of the steel and the stern workings to ensure the boat will remain afloat. Steel will usually deteriorate at a reasonably predictable rate, especially if you have kept up with regular bottom-blacking maintenance, but a hull survey will reassure you that a breach is not imminent.

The other type is a pre-purchase survey which also considers the onboard systems in addition to the structural aspects of the boat. Both types of survey will require dry-docking, cranage or slipway removal from the water.

How long it takes:
- Pre-purchase survey takes around a day to complete.
- Hull survey takes around five hours floating

How much it costs:
- Pre purchase survey will cost around £10 per foot.
- Hull survey costs around £8 per foot

Note that the cost of dry-dock/crane/slipway must be added which can add £200–£300.

(Prices as quoted by Mike Boulton at Blue Star Surveys in Yorkshire – other surveyors may differ.)

Survey for insurance

If your boat is over 20 years old then your insurer might require a hull survey before they will cover you. Each hull survey is usually valid for five years before a new one is required.

Anodes

Sacrificial anodes attract the electrons that would otherwise corrode your hull. They're usually checked and replaced when your boat is being blacked, if necessary. There are usually four in place, one on each side of the boat, fore and aft.

How long it takes:
- Less than 30 minutes during the bottom-blacking process.

How much it costs:
- £30–£60 each (most boats need four).

Survey recommendations

Most boatyards will not recommend a particular surveyor for ethical reasons, but most local yards and surveyors will know each other and have a good understanding of how the process works. Ask other local boaters for a recommendation.

Galvonic isolaters

Also consider fitting a galvanic isolator, particularly if you are moored near other boats with shoreline electrical hook up. These hook ups increase the amount of corrosive electrodes in the water and protection is recommended. Be aware, though, that you'll only be bouncing the electrodes onto another boat of some poor sucker who doesn't have a galvanic isolator. It's a bit like pass the parcel, except whoever is left holding the electrons when the music stops doesn't get a prize.

Ropes, poles, hooks and gang plank

These items are useful boating tools so it makes sense to keep them in good condition. Painting your poles will help to protect them from the elements, and this is important as rotten poles are useless at best and extremely dangerous at worst. If your pole snaps while you are pushing off with it, you could end up in the water if you're lucky. If you're unlucky you might end up impaled on the sharp, snapped end. Boating is impossible without good ropes but a new set will usually last for many years.

How much it costs:

- New pole: £40.
- New hook (with pole): £30.
- New plank: £70.
- New ropes: £50–£100 for a set of three ropes.

Fenders and ropes are expensive, but they usually last for a very long time.

Fenders

Fenders are usually lost long before they wear out, but it is worth treating this as a maintenance issue anyway. By far the most common way to lose fenders is to cruise with them still fitted to your boat. Fenders serve little to no useful purpose when underway and can actually cause a hazard. Fenders can get caught up when locking, causing boats to tip or even sink. They also cause drag, therefore adding to your fuel costs. It's always better to remove them when you set off and refit them when you tie up.

How much it costs:

- Inflatable vinyl fenders start at £5 each.
- Rubber tube fenders are around £9 each.
- Attractive traditional rope fenders start at around £15 each.

Anchor

An anchor should last for ever, but you should check the rope it is tied to for wear. A good anchor is useless if the rope snaps, and that's the last thing you need in an emergency situation that requires an anchor.

How long it takes:

- Less than a minute, annually.

How much it costs:

- New anchor: £40–£100, depending on size and type.
- Less than 20 for a new length of anchor braid rope, if necessary.

Life-saving rings and throwing devices

Again, these are not something that require maintenance, but checking they're present aboard needs to be a conscious part of your boat maintenance schedule.

A typical anchor.

A variety of flotation devices.

How long it takes:
- Seconds, ideally before each cruise.

How much it costs:
- New life ring: £40–£60.
- New life jacket: £50–£60
- New throw line float: £20–£30.

Horn and bow light

Horns and lights are more useful than essential, but in certain circumstances you're going to need them. Most tunnels are easier to navigate if you have a bow light that works. Without a horn you risk meeting boats on sharp bends and at bridges.

How long it takes:
- Replacing a faulty bow light or horn should take no more than an hour, assuming a more complicated electrical issue is not the fault.

How much it costs:
- New horn: basic model horns start at £10.
- New bow light: from £50.

Paint job

An ageing or poorly-executed paint job will devalue your boat and, in the worst cases, cause deterioration of the steel. A new paint job will last around 8–10 years, depending on the quality of the initial work and how tolerant you are of dull-looking paint. Again, a professional job will cost more than if you do it yourself, but for many boat owners the difference is clear and well worth it. It is entirely possible to do it yourself but be prepared to put in the time and effort required to properly prepare the job. Again, a professional boat painter will have plenty of experience and will confidently produce a good job. If you do it yourself it will likely require a very steep learning curve, which probably accounts for the fact that most self-paint jobs range in quality between the decent and truly awful. A new paint job can be cheap, easy or good. But you can only pick two.

How long it takes:
- Around six weeks.

How much it costs:
- Depending on the design a new paint job will probably cost around £80–£110 per foot. Coach-lines, harlequin, door design and sign-writing are the things that will push up the price.

CASE STUDY: A BRAND NEW PAINT JOB

It comes to us all at some point. The dull or scratched paintwork, coupled with patches of rust become too much to bear, until eventually it is time to bite the bullet and have the boat painted. I went to discuss my options with Jo Dortona at Snaygill Boats in Skipton, North Yorkshire.

A narrowboat paint job can cost as much as a new small car, and so I was looking for ways to keep the costs down as much as possible. Jo advised me that there were two ways to achieve this. Getting the boat back to bare metal gives the best finish, but by sanding the existing paintwork flat and applying fresh paint over it would reduce the workload significantly, whilst still producing an impressive finish. I could save still more money by doing the bulk of the preparation work myself. After comparing the costs I decided to adopt both cost-saving recommendations.

The dates for the dry dock at Snaygill were booked, so it was important to ensure the boat was ready in time. I grilled Jo for advice about how to go about prepping the boat and which tools would be the best ones to use for the job. Next, I called in some favours and recruited the help of several friends to

assist. It was hard and dirty work, but after around 30 man-hours we'd done as much as we could and the boat was ready for inspection.

'Oh no!' said Jo. 'Oh dear! That's a real problem.'

My heart sank.

In our efforts to remove the rust patches we had sanded through the layers of paint, creating craters that were up to a millimetre deep. These craters would show through the new gloss paintwork, regardless of how precisely we tried to apply body filler. (Apparently it would be better to chip out the rust patches with a chisel to leave 'cliff edges' rather than the craters we had created.)

'How do I fix it?' I asked.

'Let me introduce you to The Scabbler!' replied Jo.

The Scabbler is actually a concrete polishing tool that has been re-purposed for unlikely use in the boat-painting process. It's a mean-looking power tool with a rotating disk head filled with rotating wheels of metal teeth. In less than four hours The Scabbler had stripped the paint on my boat back to bare metal. Going back to metal increased the cost of my paint job significantly, but the finish would

Nb The Watchman *was in desperate need of a new paint job.*

Boat prep is hard and dirty work.

Andrew of Snaygill Boats with The Scabbler.

Andrew with The Needler.

be better for it and at least the boat would be ready for the allocated slot in the dry dock. I called Jo to appraise my work.

'Not bad, for an amateur!' she said.

'What do you mean?' I asked.

'I was expecting there to be much more work left to do than this,' she replied.

'You mean it's not ready yet?'

'Nowhere near. Let me introduce you to The Needler.'

The Needler isn't as mean-looking as The Scabbler; in fact it is not at all dangerous unless you drop it on your toe. However, it is an amazing tool that can be used to reach all of the tricky areas on your boat that you might otherwise spend hours sanding by hand. Corner welds, where one sheet of steel meets another, are notoriously tricky to prep. The bobbly weld would take hours to sand by hand, but The Needler made short work of them. After

another week of work I was done. Really done. I'd had enough.

'Please just take over, Jo! I can't do any more!' I pleaded.

'You've done a good job, better than we expected.' said Jo. 'We'll take it from here.'

From that point I was banned from visiting the boat until it was finished, four weeks later. Not only would this stop me from churning up dust that would blemish the wet paint, but also allow the painters to do a 'Big Reveal' when the job was finished.

Reflecting on the work involved in prepping the boat, I'm convinced that if I had to do it all again I'd simply hand over the whole job to the experts. Although doing the prep was ultimately fulfilling, at many times throughout the work I was discouraged and worried I was doing something wrong.

CASE STUDY: A BRAND NEW PAINT JOB continued

Making progress – in the wrong direction.

The Scabbler makes short work of removing the paint from Nb The Watchman.

Rust around leaking windows needs careful attention.

Power tools

Preparing your boat for painting will require the use of several different power tools. Sanders and angle grinders are readily available and easy to use, so long as you pay attention to the risks involved in using them. The Needler is also safe and easy to use; your boatyard might let you borrow theirs, if you are lucky. The Scabbler/concrete-polishing tool might not be so easily available. Even if your boatyard has one, they're unlikely to lend it to you. It's a large, heavy and powerful piece of equipment and both you and your boat could come to significant harm if you don't use it correctly or if something goes wrong.

The work was very hard too. Removing the windows was an awful task and one that I would not have been able to do without help. My windows seemed to have been welded in place, creating many hours of work to remove them, clean the frames and treat the rusted steel on the boat where they had been.

Making sure that you get into all of the nooks and crannies is almost impossible for the layman too. Even after days of meticulous work, there was still plenty of prep left for the boys in the workshop to do before Jo could start work with the paintbrushes. Drain holes, under gunwales, hinges, fittings and fixtures and every corner, upright and edge will need to be prepped. You're guaranteed to miss something, and once the painting has started, there's no way you can get the sander out again.

And the dust! So much dust! Despite my best efforts, the inside of my boat was coated in a thin layer of dust that took forever to clean up. I was sure when I began that I'd done my best to seal the inside of the boat from the mayhem of dust that we were creating

Silicone nightmare

When removing windows be sure to clean all traces of silicone or sealant from the steel before using any sander or grinder. Otherwise you'll spread the silicone across the steel, creating speckles of silicone that cannot be painted. Use a silicone removal fluid to avoid this problem.

Nb The Watchman *stripped almost bare.*

on the outside, but apparently not. I'm assured that the professionals are much better at creating a seal, not least because they don't keep going into the boat to find the right tool or to get a clean pair of jeans or another cup of tea.

But the most compelling reason for me to not undertake the work again would be because I just don't have the right tools or enough experience to do the job as well as an expert. Remember, I only did the prep and nonetheless, it was evident that my expertise and experience was not up to the job. Heaven forbid I should try my hand at the painting itself. No, in future I'll leave it to the experts. The boat that they delivered back to me once the work was done is so spectacular I am embarrassed to think that I could come anywhere near the standard of work that they produce. And anyway for the time I spent doing the work myself and making a saving, my time would be better spent earning a living or going on holiday. Never again.

When preparing edges and corners you might need some help from The Nibbler.

Top tips for keeping the cost down

- **Have a small boat**: paint jobs are priced primarily on the amount of space that needs covering.
- **Don't take it back to bare metal**: You won't get as good a finish as if you did, but it will be pleasing enough.

Undercoated and ready for painting.

CASE STUDY: A BRAND NEW PAINT JOB continued

Snaygill's Brett Selby knows how it should be done.

The first colour to go on.

Nb The Watchman *sign writing close up.*

- **Don't take the windows out**: Only an option if your windows don't currently leak. If they do leak then there is every chance that there is rust beneath the frame that will eventually become visible through any new paintwork, so take leaky windows out and treat the area beneath. Also be aware that if your windows don't leak now, there is still a chance that they might start to leak the week after your painting is done.
- **Keep your colours**: Implementing new colours and coach-lines can be difficult, depending on how well the new colours cover the old ones. Get advice from the painter regarding the design, as some colour options will cost more to achieve than others.
- **Keep extras to a minimum**: More colours, design extras and 'Oh, can you just' additions will bump up the price.

Top tips for preparing a boat for painting

- **Have the right tools**: A good sander and angle grinder are a must. Use the right grade of sandpaper and flap disks. And don't press too hard with either as this can either score the metal or quickly ruin the tools.
- **Get some advice**: There's so much that you could do wrong that might increase the work and costs of your paint job. Get some specific advice at regular intervals through the job.

ENGINE HOLE

Engine servicing

A standard engine service will include replacing all of your engine fluids and filters. A more advanced marine service will also include other perishable items such as stern gland packing, weed hatch seals and suchlike. Of course you can save money and do the work yourself if you have the time and the skills. Servicing your engine should happen yearly.

How long it takes:
- Standard engine service: ½ day.

How much it costs:
- Standard engine service: from £200.

Batteries

Battery management can be something of a dark art and many myths abide when the topic of battery management arises. Regardless of how well you care for your batteries, they will need replacing at some point.

How long it takes:
- This depends on access and on the number of batteries you have. Replacing the bank of three batteries tucked into the smallest darkest recesses of my boat can take up to an hour. Your mileage may vary.

How much it costs:
- 110ah batteries cost around £90 each.

Weed hatch

These will rarely need any maintenance, but it is vital that you regularly check for wear around the weed hatch seal. If in doubt, change it. It costs pennies, takes only a few minutes and can prevent sinking.

How long it takes:
- Checking the seals takes only a few minutes.
- Replacing the weed hatch seals takes less than an hour.

How much it costs:
- Less than £10.

Engine fluids

Keep an eye on coolant, engine oil and gearbox oils, preferably before each cruise.

How long it takes:
- Check and top-up takes around 15 minutes.

How much it costs:
- Coolant: £15.
- Engine oil: £20.
- Gearbox oil: £10.

Bilge pump

These expire rarely but having a spare can be a lifesaver. I check my bilge pump works before each cruise.

How long it takes:
- Replacing a bilge pump can take less than an hour if all goes well. I usually allocate at least two hours for the job.

How much it costs:
- New pump is around £30.

Check your engine fluids regularly.

Stern gland packing and grease

The propeller that drives the boat is outside the hull. The engine that turns the propeller shaft is inside the hull. The hole where the prop shaft leaves the boat is the threshold between the dry bits and the wet bits. The thing that stops water from getting inside the boat is called the 'stern gland' and it must be packed tight around the prop shaft to limit water intake to an absolute minimum. This is done by tightly packing the gland with specialist rope and grease. The collar around the stern gland can be loosened and removed to gain access to the stern gland rope that has likely worn away. By picking out the old rope and replacing it with new, the gland is made almost watertight, although there is often an occasional rogue drip to annoy you when you think you've done a great job.

How long it takes:

Depending on access and the dimensions of shaft, hole and rope, the job can be frustrating and fiddly to one degree or another. A tight gland will require you to fight for every mm of packing rope you wedge into the hole. It can take a couple of hours and lots of swearing if your boat is being uncooperative.

Stern gland packing kit.

Top tip: proper packing technique

Most boats will use three 'rounds' of stern gland rope around the prop shaft. Each round should begin and end at a different place. Do not line up the rings of rope with the cut ends together as this gives a clear channel through which water can easily run. Don't be tempted to coil the rope around the prop in one piece either. This method will invariably drip as the water follows the route through the corkscrew.

How much it costs:

- New packing rope: less than £10.
- Grease: less than £10.

Diesel bug

All diesels within Europe must, by law, contain a percentage of eco-friendly bio-diesel. The ratios change from time to time, invariably increasing the percentage of bio-diesel required. Unfortunately the ever-increasing amount of bio-diesel can promote the growth of bacteria that is colloquially known as 'diesel bug'. All diesel contains the diesel bug bacteria, and, in ideal conditions, this would not cause a problem. The issue arises when the bug is able to breed, and for this it needs two things – warmth and water. The warmth is provided by your engine or by the weather, and the water is usually provided via the production of condensation. Limiting the warmth is largely impossible, but you can take steps to limit the production of condensation by keeping your fuel tank full. This limits the amount of air and water vapour that could condense, thereby denying the diesel bug the necessary medium in which it likes to breed. There are also several treatments and preventative additives that can help address the problem before it gets out of control, but a serious contamination will always mean draining and cleaning the tank. Throwing away 150 litres of diesel is both frustrating and expensive. (And by 'throwing away' I mean properly disposed of at a regulated recycling point.)

How long it takes:
- Draining, cleaning and refilling your diesel tank and the fuel lines can take around one day.

How much it costs:
- Around £300 to remove and dispose of your diesel and clean the tank. (Add to that the cost of refilling.)

Boaters' tool kit

If you own a boat then you should be prepared to get your hands dirty. Second-hand boats demand seemingly constant attention and even a brand new vessel will require maintenance. Even if your boat is

Various items for the boater's toolkit.

in A1 condition, the occasional trials and tribulations of cruising will have you reaching for your tool kit. Thankfully, boaters are generally resourceful folk and happy to take on many of the common boating jobs. A list of every tool that you might ever need would be endless, and if you already know how to use a MIG welder then you can probably skip this section. For the rest of us, here's a guide to the must-have kit that you should keep aboard. You'll likely already have a tool kit containing some of these items, but perhaps there are a few you might like to add?

The standard boating tool kit

These everyday multi-purpose tools should be in everyone's tool kit.

Tool kit
Cordless drill/driver
Flat-head screwdrivers
Phillips/Pozidriv-head screwdrivers
Electrical screwdriver
Spanners – imperial and/or metric
Allen keys
Adjustable spanner/AJ
Mole grips
Wood saw
Hacksaw and junior hacksaw
Stanley knife or similar
Tape measure
Pliers
Long nose pliers
Socket set
String and rope
Cable ties – various sizes
Jubilee clips – various sizes
Electrical tape

Tool kit additions for the well-prepared boater

This list of tools is usually owned by those who have already tackled the common boating repair jobs once or are sufficiently prepared to anticipate them.

- **Gaffer tape:** if it moves and it is not supposed to, use Gaffer tape.
- **WD40/lubricant:** if it is supposed to move, but it doesn't, use WD40.
- **Jump leads:** one day you'll wish you had some.
- **Oil/suction pump:** for removing water, oil and other fluids from hard to reach places.
- **Spare bilge pump:** for removing water, oil and other fluids, usually after a big spill, plumbing problem or emergency.
- **Electrical cable lengths:** for that extra few feet when you really need it.
- **Spare fuses:** these can solve a small problem that causes a big headache.
- **Flexible cable/pipe unblocker:** for sinks, showers, inlets and outlets.
- **Telescopic magnet:** for when you drop that nut in your engine bay.
- **Flexible grabber:** for picking up non-magnetic items from your engine bay.
- **Jerry can:** for that day when you accidentally run out of fuel.
- **Hose lengths:** for those jobs that need just the right piece of hose.
- **Stove rope and glue:** fixing the seal around your stove door is a five-minute job that can save your life.
- **Heat-resistant silicone:** fixing seals around your stove flue and flue collar can save your life too.
- **PTFE tape:** to stop a drip from turning into a dribble.
- **Latex gloves:** because sometimes you need to do dirty jobs before you can go for lunch in the pub.

The tools you might not own at home

The specifics of boating call for a few well-chosen tools and other items. These will usually bail you out of a tricky situation or make boating that little bit easier.

- **Axe or hatchet:** Every boat with a stove should have one.
- **Carabina:** These are often used for quick release of fenders, but they're useful for so many other things too. I've seen them used for hanging tools, emergency dog lead repairs and even as a handle to carry logs in those horrid nylon string bags.
- **Feather duster:** Boats are a haven for spiders at certain times of the year. The warm, humid on-board environment is an ideal home for these creepy crawlies. I use my feather duster all year round, except at the end of October when the cobwebs become decorations thanks to Halloween.
- **Shoreline electrical extension:** No matter how long your shoreline is, you can guarantee that one day you'll find a mooring that requires a longer one.
- **Sea magnet:** These mega-strong magnets can be used to retrieve those things that you accidentally dropped into the water, so long as the items are made from a ferrous metal. They're one of those tools that you'll rarely need, but when you do need it, you *really* need it.
- **Fishing net:** If you drop something that floats into the water, retrieving it can be a pain in the neck. Often you'll need to drop to your belly on the towpath or the back of your boat,

Top tip: screwdriver options

A ratchet screwdriver is really handy for most screwdriver jobs. You can even get jointed screwdrivers for those boat-typical hard-t-reach spots. Make sure you use the right size for the job. A screwdriver with a changeable bit will save storage space, but beware of cheap, poor-quality versions that break too easily.

Top tip: spanner options

An adjustable spanner is OK for quick and easy jobs but a proper spanner that is the right size will usually be a better fit. Ratchet spanners are enormously useful on board for those hard-to-reach jobs where space is limited. Otherwise you might opt for short-handled spanners instead.

*If it moves and it's not supposed to, use gaffer tape.
If it doesn't move and it is supposed to, use WD-40.*

muddying your clothes as you watch the item float out of reach. If only you had a kiddies' fishing net handy.

- **Hose adapters and fittings:** A selection of these is a real godsend. Whether you're looking for the correct fitting to use the water point or patching together two hoses for extra length, having the right connector can save a whole heap of hassle. If you're anything like me then it's a good idea to have duplicates. I'm forever leaving them attached to the water-point.

- **Alcohol handwash gel:** You can catch some nasty diseases from canal water and from the mess you find on the towpath. The really nasty diseases are rare, but even a stomach upset can ruin your boating fun. The best solution is to thoroughly wash your hands with soap and water. Make sure you do it properly too, otherwise you may as well not have bothered. The average person washes their hands for just 6 seconds, but it takes at least 15 seconds of hand washing with soap and water to kill germs. That's approximately the time it takes to sing 'Happy Birthday to You' *twice*. If you're on the tiller and can't get to the sink, a good blob of alcohol hand gel will do most of the job.

Obviously!

The one tool that you won't need aboard your boat is a spirit level. The shelves that I fitted when I moved aboard still remind me of this mistake to this day.

Top tip: the fast access mini-kit

You won't need your tool kit very often and so most people keep them somewhere hidden out of the way. It can be a real pain to pull out a big box of tools to do a small simple job. You might consider keeping a mini-tool kit in a drawer.

- Mini adjustable spanner
- Ratchet multi-bit screwdriver
- Mini hammer
- Mini mole-grips
- Mini tape measure
- Tub of assorted screws and tacks

MY FAVOURITE BOATING TOOLS

Katrina: Nb *Explorer*
COMMUNITY BOAT SKIPPER

Favourite tools: Bread knife and nappies

It's not until you have to dig around in your weed hatch that you realise how painful and incapacitating cold water can be. Hacking tangled rope, fabric and weeds off the prop happens often enough for me to be prepared. The best tool for the job I have found is a bread knife taped to a length of wood. It means you can cut away at the problem and keep your hands mostly dry.

My other favourite bit of boat kit is a supply of disposable nappies. If you've had a spill or a plumbing leak of some type then you'll usually use a bilge pump to clear up most of the water. However, that last inch or so is a nightmare to clear up. I just drop a couple of nappies into the puddle and come back after I've drunk a cup of tea. Sorted!

Brett: Dutch barge *Boadicea*
LIVEABOARD BOATER

Favourite tool: Head-torch

The most important item in my tool kit is my head-torch that gets used several times every day. A hand-held torch is OK, but sometimes you need both of your hands free. Besides, most torches are simply a storage device for dead batteries. From crawling around in the engine room to carrying bags along a dark towpath, a head-torch is the best tool for the job.

Carol Jones: Nb *Caelmiri*
RETIRED LEISURE BOATER

Favourite tools: Flask and wind-up torch

Not quite a tool, but extremely useful nonetheless, is my flask. This flask has been everywhere with me and it's been useful beyond measure. Having a cup of hot tea on when you're at the tiller is lovely but you don't always get chance to get to the galley, particularly if you are single-handed. Besides, boating is much too much fun to be going indoors all the time. But the real value of a flask is when something has gone wrong or if the weather turns a little sour. Then a flask full of tea is the greatest thing in the world.

Other than that I'd list my wind-up torch as the most useful tool I own. You can always rely on a wind-up torch.

Steph: Wide-beam *Roisin Dubh*
LIVEABOARD

Favourite tools: Foldaway trolley and sunblock

Our mooring is quite a walk from the carpark and it can be quite muddy on the site. The foldaway trolley is perfect for getting stuff from the car to the boat, and when the job is done it tucks away flat on the back deck.

Also, you should always have sunblock handy somewhere near the tiller as it's too easy to get sunburn should you forget to rub some on.

MY FAVOURITE BOATING TOOLS

Tony: Nb *The Watchman*
LIVEABOARD BOATER

Favourite tool: Leatherman multi-tool
My Leatherman multi-tool sits on a shelf and is used very regularly too. It has a blade, pliers, screwdrivers and a bottle opener; enough for most of those quick and easy jobs. It means I don't have to open a tool box and hunt for the right bit of kit very often at all. Be careful if you buy one of these and make sure you get a good-quality one. There are plenty of cheap ones on the market but they invariably fall apart very quickly. Mine has been used regularly for almost a decade and it is still as good as new.

A Leatherman tool – almost all you need is here.

9 LIVEABOARD LIFE

Living aboard on the inland waterways has become increasingly popular over the last decade for many different reasons. If you've ever thought about doing the same then this chapter will give you a taste of what to expect.

Taking the decision to live aboard your boat is the start of a steep and lifelong learning curve. There is plenty of help available for new boaters, and reading this book is a great place to start. You will quickly realise that there are a great many different ways to achieve a pleasurable liveaboard life, and the choices you make at the start of your journey will greatly influence your liveaboard lifestyle in future.

The first questions to ask yourself are 'Why do I want to live on a boat?' and 'Will boat life suit me?' Most people who choose to live aboard will cite increased freedom, reduced living costs

All sorts of folk choose to live aboard these days.

and a less complicated lifestyle among their reasons for choosing a boat for a home. Boat life can certainly deliver these rewards, but they come at a price. Living aboard can be hard work, complicated and frustrating and has the potential to seriously affect your bank balance with expensive repairs and by restricting your earning potential. It's not all rolling countryside and the easy life. It is important to conduct some research beforehand and to be prepared for the ups and downs of life aboard a boat.

> ### The Liveaboard Guide
>
> If you're thinking of living aboard, be sure to read *The Liveaboard Guide*, also by Tony Jones.

It is all too easy to end up being bound to a complicated and expensive boating headache if you are not adequately prepared. The decision to live aboard is not one that should be made lightly or quickly and there is much to learn and consider if you intend to avoid the many potential pitfalls. But for those who have the right outlook on life and are willing to do their homework, a rewarding and peaceful lifestyle awaits.

THE LIVEABOARD COMMUNITY

In every community there is a broad spectrum of characters and circumstances and boat life is no different. However, boating does seem to attract people of a specific type and there

Liveaboard communities thrive on the cut.

are some commonly-encountered profiles. For example, it is common for boaters to live alone, mainly because of the space constraints of life aboard, but there is also a rambling 'free spirit' inherent in the lifestyle. Another reason for the prevalence of single boaters is that living aboard is sometimes a consequence of a divorce, leaving one partner (statistically usually the husband) with a share of equity large enough to buy a boat. That said, it is common enough for couples to live aboard too, especially as boat folk are often easy-going types who can rub along in the confines of a boat quite happily. Although not particularly common, you may find whole families living aboard. Usually these are small families comprising only two, three, and rarely, four people.

Young people may also become liveaboard boaters as they look for cheap places to live, while at the other end of the scale boat life is often the refuge of the retired looking to downsize their life, sell their home and see out their days on the equity. Many of these retirees become constant cruisers, making good use of their new-found free time. However, growing old and infirm aboard a boat can be difficult and eventually very dangerous, so it is important to have a contingency plan in place for when and if boat life is no longer a viable option.

Boat folk are a varied and eclectic bunch with many differing circumstances and lifestyles, but you will see that there are a few common threads that unite us all.

There are lots of reasons why people choose to live aboard.

You'll occasionally find whole families living aboard.

LIVEABOARD MOORINGS

It is often said that finding a suitable mooring is one of the biggest challenges facing residential boat owners and with living aboard becoming an increasingly popular lifestyle choice, suitable moorings are in high demand.

Official residential liveaboard moorings are costly and extremely rare. Marinas wishing to offer residential moorings need to apply for and be awarded proper planning permission, and in many areas this type of planning status for 'dwellings' is prohibited. Even when planning permission is granted, it is often applied specifically to a single boat or a specific mooring spot and is not transferable – just because a marina has planning permission for residential mooring in one spot, they usually need to reapply should there be a need to change either the boat or the specific mooring spot. Those boaters who do secure a residential spot potentially have all of the amenities of a land-based home including a postcode and postal service, a telephone landline and sometimes the opportunity to pay council tax too. However, liability for council tax is ambiguous where liveaboard boaters are concerned and the Residential Boat Owners' Association has defended several cases where liveaboards have been faced with a bill. The general rule is that if the terms of your mooring stipulate that your boat is likely to be moved to a different mooring spot, then you will not be liable for council tax.

Most moorings providers though do not offer official residential moorings and whilst some will strictly enforce a no-liveaboard policy, others will 'unknowingly' accommodate discrete liveaboards. Even some marinas owned by CRT offer a 'Class A' or 'Class 1' mooring which entitles boaters to stay on their boat all year. The definition of residential is so ambiguous that it is easy for marina owners to find a loophole, especially when, as is usually the case, most boats leave the marina for some weeks or months during the course of any given year and so cannot be accurately described as permanent residents.

It is wise to do some research before meeting with the owner or manager of the site to look for signs that people live aboard. Ask other boaters about the local liveaboard options, but avoid asking boaters from the site you

Face to face

It is rarely fruitful to enquire about moorings by phone or email. It may be necessary to set up an appointment by phone, but don't enquire about costs or space, and certainly do not declare your liveaboard status. Face-to-face meetings are always preferable, particularly when the mooring provider has a policy of vetting new arrivals.

Overstaying on visitor moorings will eventually attract attention.

are coveting until you know how the land lies. When a meeting has been arranged, be careful about asking 'Can I live aboard here?' as the answer is often an official 'no', but there is usually a way to achieve an unspoken understanding. Some will ask outright if you live aboard and explain that living on site is not allowed and that you must vacate your boat for a set number of days per year, whilst others have a higher tariff for 'high-use' boats. Answering questions honestly and complying with the rules laid down by the site is always the best policy to avoid issues further down the line. It may be that you can comply with

the regulations by taking your boat out to cruise the local waterways for a few weeks or months each year. This is a most agreeable means of toeing the line and so long as you do not hog popular visitor moorings you are unlikely to attract the attention of CRT agents. (Boaters with a permanent mooring seem to attract less attention than those registered as continuous cruisers for some reason.) Perhaps your partner is based locally and you spend occasional nights there? A few weeks of holiday later and you will almost certainly have negated any enforceable definition that you live at your marina.

Moorings providers are not obliged to give you a mooring and so you should make your application as attractive as possible. Some places, clubs and private marinas especially will discriminate against untidy-looking boats with the view that these will 'lower the tone' of the establishment. A boat roof lined with piles of firewood, pushbikes, loud unruly dogs, a TV aerial and bags of rubbish can hint that not only are you likely a liveaboard, but likely a messy one at that. Presenting a good image and reading between the lines when discussing moorings can make the difference between their site being full and them being able to squeeze your boat in somewhere.

MOVING FROM HOUSE TO BOAT

Once you introduce ambiguity to your residential status by moving aboard a boat, you can slip through the gaps in the network of modern society. Most offices of officialdom will ask for your name and address and unless you can give an answer that is acceptable to their computer system, you'll likely experience problems. Everything from your driving licence to your access to healthcare and financial services can be affected and unless you want to hide from the world entirely, you need to be prepared to find a solution. Submitting a tax return, registering to vote, claiming benefits and even getting an OAP bus pass is complicated for those without a recognised conventional permanent address, but there are ways to deal with the issue. Continuous cruisers are most vulnerable to the problems that living aboard can cause and often the only answer is to rely on the safety net provided for those who are homeless.

One solution is to use an address that is accepted as your official residence, such as that of a charitable friend or member of your family. Whilst this may seem the most simple and suitable answer, the location of that address and its proximity to your current mooring defines how effective a solution it actually is. Postal services, couriers, registering with doctors and the electoral register are all problematic if your official address is nowhere near your mooring spot.

Residential moorings are rare, but there are alternative options.

Renting boats for residential purposes

Buying a boat to rent is not to be taken lightly. Every year there are tragic accidents, from carbon monoxide poisoning to fires to boats sinking. As the landlord you will have a duty of care to your tenants and, if anything goes wrong, then you will be held responsible. If you can't demonstrate that you've met all the legal requirements, including having a non-private boat safety certificate, commercial insurance and proof that you've gone through the handover procedure correctly, you may end up with a serious criminal conviction.

On a practical note, on waterways looked after by the Canal and River Trust, you will need to hold a Residential Letting licence to let it out for residential use. You can only get one of these if you have a home mooring with planning consent for residential use. If you don't have a home mooring you will not be to able rent out your boat for residential use, for holiday use or as a hotel or B&B, and you'll be in breach of the terms and conditions of your licence.

To anyone thinking of renting a boat, whether to live on or for a holiday, please do your research and make sure the boat is above board. If it doesn't have a business licence, then it's not. And if it doesn't have a home mooring, then it can't have the right kind of licence, so if anyone offers you any kind of rental or letting arrangement on a continuous cruising basis, you can be sure that it hasn't met the proper regulations.

Doctors and other medical services

Of course you can get treatment in an emergency at any local hospital with an accident and emergency department, but you can still experience problems if you need to call an ambulance or have a doctor visit you aboard. Although it is rare, there have been occasions of both ambulance crews and GPs refusing to board a boat for health and safety reasons, despite the health of the patient being seemingly at greater risk. Even registering with a doctor can be difficult (see below) so be ready to find a way to fit into the system they have in place.

Some local NHS districts offer walk-in Health Centre facilities akin to GP services for non-registered patients although these are not available everywhere and your nearest centre may still be some distance away. Some large cities have similar private sector clinics but these will inevitably charge for the services and convenience they provide. Another option for minor injuries and illnesses are the NHS Walk-in Centres. These are staffed by nurses and you do not need to register or have an appointment to visit them. Their services overlap those offered by doctors and hospitals, covering infection and rashes, fractures and lacerations, emergency contraception and advice, stomach upsets, cuts and bruises, and burns and strains. However they are not set-up to deal with ongoing health problems or life-threatening emergencies.

Tony's towpath tales: Finding a doctor

I'd been at my new mooring for a couple of months when I fell ill and needed to visit the doctor. On arrival at the surgery I was asked for my address which, when I told them I lived on a boat, caused something of a commotion. My official address was in another county and the address of my boat club mooring was not listed on their database, so they were not sure that they could accept me as a patient unless I could prove that I lived in the area. It was eventually suggested that unless I was intending to be in the area for a 'decent period of time' that I should not register and instead visit my old GP instead, some 120 miles away. I explained that being a boater it was likely that I would be moving around quite a lot and so I could not guarantee that I would be in the area for 'a decent period of time' – whatever that might be. However, as I was obviously sick right now and they were currently my local surgery, I would be grateful if they could register me there and arrange for me to see a doctor. Still there appeared to be some reluctance and they were clearly not comfortable for me to register. In the end I told them that I had just decided that I would be staying in the area for the rest of my life and gave the address of my local friend. I was seen by the doctor, and consoled myself that, although their system didn't accommodate my circumstances, I had still managed to get the treatment I needed.

Post and courier deliveries

Although most moorings providers do not offer residential moorings, some have provision to receive mail for those with boats moored there. The risk here is that by receiving mail to a mooring address it can be perceived as evidence that the mooring provider is breaking their planning terms by accommodating liveaboards, and so many marinas draw the line at providing this service. Some though still do and a little detective work can help you to spot when mail services are available at a mooring provider site.

In most places it is possible to use a 'Poste Restante' service. French for 'post remaining' this is a free service that was popular historically and is intended for those without a specific address. It enables itinerants to collect mail from a post office or sorting office near to their current location. It is rather a pot-luck process to find a post office or sorting office that still remembers, understands and offers this service and some will simply bluster or downright refuse to accommodate it. Usually the mail is addressed to the recipient using the address of the collection office or sorting office and marked 'Poste Restante', but others use the address of the recipient's mooring, knowing that the letter can go no further than the most local sorting office. In either case it is imperative to establish an understanding with the local staff at the office to ensure it all goes smoothly. Some marinas have had this system in place for many years with boaters and office staff being on first-name terms.

Courier deliveries for those without a specific address can be even more problematic as the service is more sporadically utilised and relationships are more difficult to nurture. Often couriers will arrive at a postcode looking for a house with an interesting name. Unless the recipient is on constant watch for the puzzled courier then the parcel will go back to the depot, and with nowhere to leave a calling card, you'll never know that they have been. Occasionally a long-serving delivery driver will keep the same patch for years and get to know the contact details for local boaters, but this is a rare occurrence and cannot be relied upon. There are a couple of common solutions, the first being to request that the sender lists a mobile phone number on the address label of the package. This is a reasonably reliable work around, but occasionally the sender manages to omit the number from the label or the delivery driver misses the number or doesn't want to call it from his own mobile phone. A more reliable option is to have the parcel delivered to your place of work or to a local friend if these options exist. While it would not be acceptable to use such addresses for official address purposes, most employers (and friends) are happy to receive the occasional package.

Banks and other service providers

Not being able to get mail delivered to your mooring can cause significant problems when being asked for proof of your address. The requirements of banks and other service providers such as mobile phone services vary greatly. Some require proof in triplicate of a registered address that they have listed in their database, whereas others have a more flexible approach. As a general rule it can be considered much more problematic to set up a new account with a new organisation than it is to change an address with an existing one. This though compels boaters to stick with a company not through loyalty or because they offer the best product or service, but because the prospect of changing supplier is so fraught with difficulty. Again, the easiest solution is to have one single registered land address where all formal correspondence is delivered. The problems of proximity are negated in most cases, as statements, bills and invoices can be viewed online. Internet banking is fast becoming the norm too and most bills and transfers are easily done on the Internet.

The matter gets complicated when companies require several different proofs of address. If you use different addresses for different services you may find that you do not have enough to give a proof of address for one specific place. Most will expect to see utilities bills, but as boaters do not use gas, electric or water supply companies these are not an option. Most companies will not recognise correspondence from CRT as an official proof and the lack of landline, broadband and TV service providers narrows the field even more. Given the headaches proof of address requests can cause, it is worth keeping a log of all of the organisations you need to notify when you change your mooring. Keeping them up to date with your current whereabouts will ensure you have as many options as possible when providing proof of address. Thankfully, most commercial organisations (such as mobile phone companies) are keen enough to attract and keep customers that they are happy to go the extra mile to accommodate those with unusual circumstances. Explaining your liveaboard lifestyle to the operative taking your application will usually bring about a satisfactory result, thereby providing another proof of address you can use in future.

Claiming benefits

It is possible to claim benefits as a liveaboard boater. Claiming housing benefit to cover mooring fees appears relatively simple and some boaters have even managed to have their licence fee awarded too. Once claiming these benefits it would make sense to claim Council Tax Benefit too, if indeed you are one of the very few boaters

who actually pay it. And therein lies the problem. By claiming housing benefit and council tax, your liveaboard status becomes very noticeable, official and undeniable. A mooring provider that does not have the relevant planning permission for residential moorings would understandably take exception to any official statement that they are harbouring a liveaboard, often resulting in them tightening the mooring rules. The consequences for liveaboards down on their luck and reliant upon benefits might be severe, as the likelihood of losing a mooring must not be underestimated. Whilst there are many cases of liveaboards finding a niche in the system where claiming benefits is possible, there is inevitably an inherent stress and vulnerability that comes with the situation and extreme caution should be employed.

Tax credits are the responsibility of HMRC rather than the local council and there appears to be little communication between the two agencies.

TV licensing

There are no specific rules regarding TV licensing for liveaboard boaters and even those who attempt to obtain one do often run into problems. If you have a land address with a TV licence then your viewing aboard is covered under this. If you have a residential mooring where you are permanently dwelling you will need (and can easily acquire) a TV licence specifically for that bona fide address. However, those boaters without a specific address seem to slip between the gaps of the licensing regulations.

Interestingly, TV licence inspectors have very few powers to investigate licence evasion, even when investigating those watching TV in a land-based house. Ownership of a TV, aerial or set-top box does not require a licence. A licence is only required to receive and view a TV broadcast programme and so unless it can be proved that someone was watching a broadcast TV programme, enforcement of the licence regulations is very difficult indeed. Licensing officials have no right to enter property without a warrant and ownership of TV broadcast-receiving equipment is no proof of licence evasion.

Dating

Liveaboard boaters often live alone, not only because of the constraints of space, but also as a consequence of a rambling 'free spirited' nature. However, that's not to say boaters are inherently sad and lonely. Many boaters live aboard with a partner and occasionally whole families live aboard too. Neither are most boaters single. In fact the novelty of living aboard is often an attractive positive in the dating stakes and, given that most boat folk are 'interesting' people, there is usually no shortage of dating opportunities. On the flipside, it can be difficult to reconcile a constant cruising or itinerant boating lifestyle with a house-living, land-loving partner and usually something has to give.

Clean clothes

Due to the constraints of space, power and water, most boats do not have a washing machine or tumble dryer on board. Unless you know a friendly neighbourhood washing machine owner you will need to take your dirty washing to a laundrette. Prices vary a little but probably outweigh the cost and inconvenience of running a washing machine on board.

'I always leave my laundry as a service wash, says Darren from Nb Dunster. I have much better things to do than spend two hours watching my underwear go round. I'd rather pay an extra couple of pounds and collect it later, washed, dried and folded.'

Liveaboard boating can be very civilised indeed.

203

Laundrette list

The Aylesbury Canal Society publishes a list of laundrettes conveniently locatednear canals and rivers. Find out more at aylesburycanal. org.uk

Some mooring providers, usually the more expensive and luxurious ones, have self-service laundry facilities on site, but these are rare. Usually these are coin-operated laundrette-style machines, but sometimes they are simply standard household models and cost a couple of pounds in cash paid to the marina owner. In a bid to solve the problem of not having access to a tumble dryer some boats even have collapsible clothes lines installed near the tiller on their boat.

Transport

Cruising is great so long as you are not reliant upon a car for the duration. Otherwise it can be quite a headache to ensure that both car and boat are in the same place. Once your day of boating fun is over you will need to factor in some way of collecting your car from where you left it, which can mean getting a lift, using a bicycle or using public transport. Either way, collecting a car will cost you time, money, favours or energy and possibly a combination of each. Once again, preparation is key. Finding out about local bus and rail services is probably the easiest solution, so long as the services are local and reliable. Weekends and evenings can often make a mockery of the timetables, especially in rural areas. Cycling back to your car might be an option if you only moved your boat a short distance, and those fit enough to undertake longer journeys might not need to use a car in the first place.

Boats and bikes play together nicely.

You can easily store a bike on top of your boat and it is the cheapest and easiest mode of transport.

Tony's towpath tales: Getting around

About three years ago I gave my car away to a fellow boater who had more need for it and I haven't missed it one bit. As a writer I work from my office aboard my boat and do not need a car for commuting. I'm lucky that my mooring is within walking distance of a local train station and there are shops and a couple of small supermarkets less than a mile away. When I do need a car for long journeys or multi-stop trips I will generally hire one.

The combined cost of public transport and occasional car hire is far less than the cost of owning a car, even when that car was parked up and unused for the most part of the year. On the whole I found driving and car ownership to be a stressful and expensive headache and not at all suited to my boating lifestyle and philosophy. Tax, insurance, repairs and fuel were eye-wateringly expensive. Road rage and city driving send stress levels through the roof and so help you if you inadvertently fall foul of one of the many motoring hazards. Parking fines, congestion charges and speed cameras are all expensive and stressful things to consider, and even the most conscientious drivers can get caught out. But the worst danger is the risk of death and injury if you have an accident. The risks are just too high and to my mind, the odds are not favourable. Even if you are not hurt the stress and financial implications of an accident makes car ownership an unpleasant prospect for my liking.

My favoured mode of transport these days is a bicycle. For less than £50 I have a reliable and extremely cheap transport option that is suitable for the vast majority of my needs. It keeps me fit and is infinitely better for the environment too. I can fix most things myself and should the worst happen and I need to buy a new one, they are widely and cheaply available. I'm with H.G. Wells when he said, 'When I see an adult on a bicycle I do not despair for the future of the human race.'

The Residential Boat Owners' Association

The RBOA represents all boaters living on the UK inland waterways, including liveaboards, continuous cruisers and holiday boaters. They can offer mediation and advice on all legal aspects of boating, from residential moorings, council tax disputes, benefits advice, diesel VAT issues, taxes and other HMRC related questions.

Contact them at http://www.rboa.org.uk/

10 PETS ABOARD

With Britain being a nation of animal lovers, it is little surprise to see boats with pet passengers. Amongst the commonplace dogs and cats you'll find all manner of furry, feathered and fanged animals. Some pets take better to boating than others, but as you'll see, where there is a will there is a way!

DOGS ON DECK

Dogs are by far the most popular pet to bring aboard and the joys of boating and dog ownership are too numerous to explore in detail here. Dogs certainly tend to be easier to acclimatise and most make good boaters. They learn the ropes quickly enough and know how to stay safe and dry, usually after a couple of unplanned dips in the canal. Once they learn to stay on the dry bits there's not much else that can go wrong for a well-behaved and well-trained dog. It's usually the mischievous ones that will cause frustrations. It's worth remembering that some breeds of dog typically cannot swim. The most common non-swimmers are breeds with flat muzzles, such as bulldogs, pugs and boxers. Others with disproportionate body dimensions, such as big-headed staffies and short-legged dachshunds can have trouble too.

Boaters usually have small dogs, but not always!

Do ...
- Think about using a lead when walking the towpath. Read the law about controlling your dog in public here: https://www.gov.uk/control-dog-public/overview
- Have a generous supply of dog poo bags, for use with your own dog and to offer to others who 'forgot'.
- Make sure your boat is well-ventilated on hot days.
- Provide regular fresh water, especially on hot days and after exercise.
- Provide a raised bed that is insulated from the cold floor, particularly during the colder months.
- Use a gate or other means to stop your dog escaping from your boat when moored.

CASE STUDY

Tony Jones:
Nb *The Watchman*

'My dog, Puck, is infamous on the canals around Bingley Five Rise Locks on the Leeds and Liverpool Canal. Everyone seems to know him and he manages to make friends wherever he goes. He's quite at home trotting up and down the roof of my boat as we cruise along, stopping only to pee on my chimney or plant pots. He has a group of friends, local dogs, who walk the same routes in the area. Puck always gives them a bark "Hello" as we cruise past, as if to say "Hey! Check me out! I'm on a BOAT!" He's such a show off, but he's loads of fun.'

A buoyancy aid is useful for dogs that can't swim or are new to boating.

Don't ...

- Risk a 'dog overboard' situation. If you're underway, the last thing you need is a dog in the water. If they're likely to chase after wildlife, livestock or other people's pets, then keep them indoors.
- Tie your dog to the boat. If they fall overboard you risk strangulation, drowning or injury from the propeller.
- Allow your dog to walk or jump onto a scorching hot steel roof.
- Let your dog near frozen canals. Ice is one of the biggest risks for dogs and their owners during wintertime. Frozen waterways can look a lot like solid ground to a dog, particularly when the ice is covered with snow. Every year several dogs die after falling through ice and some owners also die in their efforts to rescue them. Pet owners are advised to stay on dry land and call emergency services instead.

You'll see lots of dogs aboard.

'Our dog didn't understand the difference between green grass and green pondweed covered canal!'

Ivan Cane via facebook

207

CATS ON THE CUT

Boating cats are usually in the care of liveaboard owners who rarely leave their home mooring. Fair-weather boaters and hire boaters are understandably reluctant to take their cats cruising for fear that their pet will not find their way back to the boat. However, some cats seem to adapt quickly, exploring new areas and returning each evening for their dinner. It's a case of trial and error and some cats adapt better than others.

Do …

- Keep your cat indoors for a few days before letting them out into a new area.
- Provide a ramp so that they can escape from the water should they fall in.
- Assess prospective mooring spots with your cat in mind before you tie up. Look for unknown dogs, busy roads and very busy towpaths. If any of these are present, you might want to find another place to moor.

Don't …

- Take your cat cruising if you have to stick to a tight schedule. They may stay out longer than you are able to wait.

CASE STUDY: CATS ABOARD

Polly Player: Nb *Springy*
VETERINARY NURSE

'Cats roam away from a new point concentrically, and unless they get scared, they are really unlikely to fail to return or find their way home. I have wind chimes on the boat to orient them, though I am not convinced that this does anything that they cannot do themselves. Some people think that a litter tray will act as a homing scent for cats exploring new places. Of course, each cat will be different but most don't tend to approve of the smell of their own funk! I'll generally put a litter tray on the stern deck until the cat gets comfortable in a new area, but apart from that I don't use them otherwise.'

- Forget to have your cat spayed or neutered before they go wandering into another cat's territory.
- Automatically assume that an older cat will not take to boating. If you slowly and carefully introduce them to the sound of the engine and the feeling of movement, most cats are happy boaters.

Cats love boats too.

Hamsters make great boat pets.

SMALL FURRY FRIENDS

Rabbits, hamsters, guinea pigs, gerbils, mice and even rats are kept as pets aboard. They're a great pet choice as they will usually be either supervised or in their enclosure. Cleaning and feeding is easy and they don't take up too much space, need walking or murder the local wildlife. Keeping them out of your bilges is probably your only worry. You might be surprised by the number of pet rabbits on the cut. Most are kept indoors as 'house rabbits', but some bunnies get to roam on deck or are even taken for walks on the towpath!

CASE STUDY: RABBIT AND HAMSTER

Holly Barker: Nb *Gertruda*

'I have a rabbit called Ziggy and a hamster called Trabby on board. Trabby is fine on the boat and it's not much different to looking after a hamster in a house, although he bumps into things in his ball more often. The rabbit does just fine too. I've even heard of people letting their rabbits swim in the canal but I'm too scared to see if Ziggy would.'

CASE STUDY: BUNNY ON A BOAT

Kerry Dainty: Nb *Linnet*

Kerry lives aboard a historic wooden boat called *Linnet* and sells coal and diesel from another historic boat called *Ariel.*

'Paddy wears his harness when he's on the roof and I hook the lead onto the speedwheel just in case. But he's a good lad and he remembers his training. It took months of solid training and dozens of Weetabix to get Paddy trained, and there are still days when all the Weetabix in the world won't budge him!'

Paddy the bunny about Nb Linnet.

CASE STUDY: ROVING RABBIT

Sarah Henshaw: *The Book Barge*

Book shop by day and liveaboard vessel by night, Sarah's boat is also home to a lop-eared rabbit named Napoleon Bunnyparte.

Sarah is also the author of a splendid book called *The Book Shop that Floated Away*.

'When my boat was a full-time book store I used to bring Napoleon with me to work each day. When we moved onto *The Book Barge* I initially worried he'd miss the space (and courtyard) he'd enjoyed when he lived in a house. However, I didn't count on the compensatory closeness narrowboat living affords. Rabbits are sociable animals and they rather like having a human around. Napoleon definitely enjoys this proximity. The boat is open plan and he seems to revel in the lack of privacy and close quarters where my boyfriend and I sometimes struggle.

'Problems arise because the boat still doubles as a bookshop. Having a rabbit here puts stock and potential sales in constant jeopardy. He has a taste for expensive antiquarian book spines and an unpredictable bladder. On the flip side, he's occasionally rather brilliant customer-luring collateral. His ear-washing routine has earned Napoleon a dedicated fan base of under-fives, who visit the shop regularly to 'awww' over him, parents (and their purses) in tow.'

Napoleon Bunnyparte: boating can be tiring.

Top tips for boat-bunny keepers

- Get a bunny playpen for travel-grazing.
- Invest in a good comfy basket for roof travel time.
- Get a rabbit harness so that they can eat grass on towpath or in parks.
- Make sure they can't escape. Block your door if your rabbit can jump or climb steps.

CASE STUDY: GUINEA PIGS

Laura Darling: Nb *Saving Grace*

'I live aboard with my boyfriend Owen, a cocker spaniel called Jonty and two guinea pigs – Bean and Pea. We had the guinea pigs before we moved aboard and were planning on re-homing them but thought we would see how it worked out. We're glad we did because they seem to love life aboard! We open the cage in the daytime to let them run around in the bow and they get plenty of grass cuttings when the grass nearby has been mowed. We have been on a few cruises with them. Passers-by stop and smile when they notice that we have guinea pigs in the bow. Jonty the dog tends to ignore them.'

MINI BEASTS ABOARD

It's good to see that boaters are generally fond of most animals. We've heard of several unusual pets on boats, including fish, parrots, hedgehogs and even giant stick insects.

CASE STUDY: BIG SPIDEY

Sue Law: Nb *Billy G*

'We have a boating tarantula! Sidney is a female Chilean Red Tarantula and she's quite gentle. She lives in a large fish tank and eats crickets, which can get on your nerves as they chirp constantly. When people come to visit they expect to see fish when they look in the tank. Some visitors stay and some make an excuse and leave. She did go missing once when she dug the cork out in the corner of the top of the tank and decided to climb the curtains. She wasn't impressed at being put back in the tank! We also have two dogs and a budgie called Naughty Boy.'

The author's dog, Puck, enjoys life aboard in all seasons.

11 BOAT SAFETY

From driving a car to walking across icy lock beams, there is risk involved in every aspect of life. The sensible ones amongst us take precautions to negate and minimise these risks in order to enjoy the benefits of those activities. Boating is a relatively safe pastime compared with many, but it is still important to be aware of the dangers and to avoid coming a cropper.

SLIPS AND TRIPS

These are the most common ways to get injured on a boat. Wet surfaces, mud, ice and diesel are just a few of the lubricant hazards that can upset your transition from shore to boat and back. Jumping aboard or ashore is asking for trouble and it should be protocol to always have the boat close enough to step, rather than jump. It is good practice to step squarely onto your boat, keeping your weight above your feet. Side-stepping onto a boat can cause your feet to slip sideways from under you.

Wooden surfaces are particularly hazardous and often surprisingly so. Wooden pontoons, stern decking, lock beams, waterside edgings and even wooden swing bridges are frequently the cause when boaters come a cropper. Wet and wintery weather will, of course, exacerbate the risk so be sure to exercise extreme caution and err on the side of paranoia. The biggest worry is the risk of falling between the boat and a hard

place given the multitude of ways that this could end badly. A good solution for the slip risk posed by wooden walkways is to cover the surface with chicken wire stapled in place. If you're authorised to do so it is well worth taking the time to do it. Walking across lock beams is rarely necessary and downright foolish when the weather is bad.

Ropes, plant pots, mooring pins, dogs and rooftop bicycles are some of the most common trip hazards for boaters. While some of these items are a necessary part of boating it is worth taking time to minimise the risks where it is possible. Creating a roof-top clearway to reduce the need to slalom around obstacles is a useful pre-cruise precaution, and coiling ropes is a good habit to get into. Towpath trip hazards can be a problem too. Thankfully almost every moored boat on the cut has its mooring pins highlighted with hi-vis tape or carrier bags to improve visibility. On that note, given that most canals are not well lit, a head-torch is one of the most useful pieces of kit a boater can own.

Canal towpaths are rarely well lit.

Anti-slip safety tips

- Many boaters have a whistle attached to their boat keys in the hope that should they slip and need help, the whistle will attract attention.
- Locks and bridges, particularly hazardous and it goes without saying that extreme care should be exercised.
- Spilled diesel and oil are severe slip hazards and should be cleaned up immediately.
- Never jump onto or off a boat. Step aboard or ashore comfortably, and if this is not possible, move the boat closer.
- Never jump onto the roof of a boat from a lock or from another boat.
- Highlight mooring pins with hi-vis material or white plastic bags.
- Keep ropes coiled and out of the way and the roof free of trip hazards, particularly when cruising.
- Clean the roof regularly as leaves, mud, soot and slime will increase the risk of slips.
- Step squarely onto wet boats and pontoons as sideways momentum can cause your

You might want to clear your roof of obstacles when you're underway.

foot to slip from under you in wet or slippery conditions.
- Never become blasé about the risk of slips and falls on a boat. Falling onto a steel boat can break bones and cause head injuries. The risk of falling into the water while unconscious is very real.

Steel boats are very slippery – particularly in conditions like this.

It's important to know exactly where you are.

Don't get beat up off the beaten track

Remember that canals rarely offer easy access for emergency services if you get injured, so the risks are increased should you need to get medical help quickly. With that in mind, always keep track of exactly where you are on the waterways as you'll need to give good directions in order to be found by those more used to roads. Should you need to contact the emergency services and give directions to your location, make sure that you stay there and don't move. Keep your phone charged and nearby. Or better still, take every precaution not to get hurt in the first place.

Single-handed boaters are particularly at risk when slips and trips occur, because help might

not be immediately available. A simple trip can turn into a life-threatening situation if you hit your head and end up unconscious in the water. It is recommended that single-handers wear a self-inflating life jacket when boating.

This section would be incomplete without making mention of the effects of alcohol. Enjoying a glass or two of your favourite drink is a most enjoyable way to end a day of boating, but good sense and precaution should always prevail. Unlike when driving a car, there is no law against boating and drinking, but rest assured that if an accident were to occur as a result of intoxication it is likely the person affected could be found at fault and made liable.

Watch out for that cill.

OUT AND ABOUT

Canal boating appears a very long way down the list of 'Dangerous Things To Do' and, as with all things in life, you'll probably be just fine if you employ a little care and common sense. Features such as swing bridges and winding holes are relatively risk free once the slip and trip hazards listed above have been considered. Although tearing cratch covers or breaking a window on a badly-negotiated bridge can be expensive and frustrating, it is not a life-threatening issue. Using locks, however, is an inherently risky business and it is vitally important to keep your wits about you to avoid trips and falls, particularly in poor weather conditions.

Hanging your boat on a lock cill is all too easy if you take your eye off the ball. Inadvertently leaving the boat engine in gear as the water level drops is a common cause of this, and being distracted whilst at the tiller comes a close second.

Hanging your boat up on bollards can be a problem when filling and emptying locks too. The potential for error is clear in the case of emptying the lock, but even when filling, rope problems can still occur. A boat that is tied on a short mid-line rope can be tipped as the water level rises higher than the rope length will allow. Be careful of fenders becoming snagged in locks too. Removing the fenders before you set off is an easy way to avoid this issue, plus you won't be wasting diesel by dragging your fenders through the water as you cruise.

The voice of experience

'Three things cause most of the accidents we see on boats: inappropriate footwear, alcohol and the lack of a torch,' says Troy Dortona from Snaygill Boats in Skipton on the Leeds and Liverpool Canal. 'Wearing high heels on the way to the pub when it is still light is not a problem, but later in the evening when it is dark after a few drinks, these three ingredients can be a recipe for disaster.'

A head torch is one of the most useful pieces of equipment.

Another lock worry is if the lock's gate paddles are opened before the ground paddles as the torrent of water from above can sink a boat in seconds. This is usually the result of inexperienced lock-monkeys, so be sure to train them fully before letting them loose with a windlass. Well-meaning 'gongoozlers' are another common locking hazard as they try to help out, sometimes armed with their own trusty windlass. It is usually better to politely decline their assistance by saying that you

'have a system' and you don't like to break your pattern.

Believe it or not, mooring can be a risky activity where sinking is a risk. Mooring too tightly on a waterway with variable water levels is an easy mistake to make, causing your boat to tip as it rises or falls with the water. Allowing a hull skin fitting (such as an exhaust or vent) to fall below the waterline can easily cause the unthinkable to happen.

Well-meaning gongoozlers can cause problems.

Wield your windlass safely!

Always keep a hold on the windlass when operating locks. Letting go of the windlass leaves paddles at the mercy of gravity, causing the windlass to spin wildly as the paddle drops and the spindle turns. If you cruise a lot you'll regularly see instances of near misses where shocked lock-monkeys lurch backwards to avoid a spinning windlass. Occasionally you'll see them get whacked on the hand or the arm and once in a while you'll see someone get hit in the face by a spinning windlass. The ruination of your day's boating will be the least of your worries should that occur.

Communication is key when locking.

Cleaning the weed hatch

Be careful when clearing debris from around your prop through the weed hatch as fishing twine and hooks are commonly found there.

An unsecured weed hatch cover is another common error that can cause serious water ingress. Having removed the items that have fouled the propeller, boaters are often eager to get underway and either replace the cover badly or sometimes not at all. Getting this wrong can quickly become an emergency as there is a real risk of sinking. Be sure to check the integrity of the seals around the hatch as you replace the cover, and then check for water getting through while you are underway if possible.

While you are in the bowels of the boat it might be worth casting an eye across your stern gland. Being the threshold between the inside of your boat and the water outside, this gland needs occasional attention and regular inspection. Look for drips, dribbles and leaks and the resultant water filled bilges. Replacing and re-packing a stern gland is an untidy and unpleasant job, but it is well within the DIY capabilities of most able-bodied boaters.

GAS, FIRES AND CARBON MONOXIDE

Propane and butane gas are highly flammable and therefore the risks are obvious. Most of the problems caused by gas are a result of poor maintenance or amateur fit-outs. Compliance with the Boat Safety Certificate scheme will negate most of the risk here and a new certificate will offer peace of mind. However, a

Gas bottle storage

Never store gas bottles on their side on your boat. They must be stored and used upright as lying them down creates the risk of liquid being released at pressure. The liquid gas will behave differently to gas with the potential to create squirting jets of burning liquid.

There is also potential for a 'hydrate' to form; a blockage of 'iced' gas. If this happens you may think that the bottle is empty or somehow switched off. When the hydrate clears the gas flows again, it could ignite.

Storing gas bottles anywhere but inside a safety-scheme compliant locker is also considered risky and will fail a Boat Safety Scheme inspection

test pass today will not necessarily eliminate a problem occurring tomorrow and boaters should remain vigilant. A gas alarm unit will alert you to any leaks that might unexpectedly occur and it is wise to have an expert check your gas system just once each year. Remember that propane gas is heavier than air and so may not be noticeable to your sense of smell at head height. Most gas alarms sold for use in houses have instructions stipulating that they be installed high, as domestic gas is lighter than air. Propane gas used on boats is heavier than air and so these alarms should be installed near the floor aboard a boat.

Despite the usual boater's inclination to do it yourself and make do and mend, don't be tempted to install gas appliances yourself or let other unqualified persons do so. The risks are too great for you to later realise that it has not been done properly, and only an experienced expert can be sure. Check the connections, taps and hoses on the gas line each spring as winter weather can cause movement and deterioration.

FIRE

Most boats have a stove of some description fitted and there are plenty of great reasons why they are so popular. It is recommended that neither stove (nor cooker for that matter) is lit when cruising and regardless be well secured to the floor in case of a bump with another boat, bridge or lock. However, most cold-weather boaters do keep their stoves lit whilst cruising, ignoring the guidance about lit fires, so if you are one of these be sure to take extra special care. Once again, common sense will dictate the safe usage of your stove, but for the sake of stating the obvious as a reminder, here are some dos and don'ts.

Do ...
- Ensure that the door of the stove is closed and secure when lit.
- Exercise caution when passing the stove as boats will rock and flue pipes are not good grab rails.
- Be aware of the risks associated with carbon monoxide – see later in this chapter.
- Make sure that the hearth is big enough to catch any falling embers.

Do not ...
- Vent the fire for long periods. Drawing the fire with open vents can help to get the fire going, but pay attention and do not let the stove overheat.
- Dry fabrics near the fire where they might fall and become ignited.
- Dry wood too near the stove.
- Use unsuitable fuels as these can burn too hot and damage the stove. (Petrol station coals are a frequent culprit.)
- Burn unsuitable wood types. Ply, MDF, melamine, yew and rhododendron are bad choices.

Carbon monoxide

Appliances where fuel is being burned, such as engines, generators, gas cookers, boilers and multi-fuel stoves, all produce carbon monoxide gas. Carbon monoxide is colourless, tasteless and odourless and it kills, on average, one boater each year. It does this by restricting the oxygen from reaching vital organs. Even at low levels it can affect concentration, cause memory loss and dizziness. Higher doses can kill in a matter of minutes.

A booklet produced by the Boat Safety Scheme and the Council for Gas Detection and Environmental Monitoring is available to download from www.boatsafetyscheme.org. It explains how to recognise the symptoms of carbon monoxide poisoning, what to do in an emergency, how to spot danger signs on your boat, preventing risks, and fitting a CO alarm. A carbon monoxide detector with an alarm should be a standard feature in every boat and there is no sensible reason not to own one. The alarm aspect of the detector is most important as it is vital to be made aware of the hazard in order to take action. A small beige dot turning grey as you fall asleep for ever is no substitute for a detector with an alarm.

Maintaining your equipment and appliances is vital.

* Check exhausts and fixings on all appliances to ensure that they are still in place and free from cracks and holes.
* The flame from most gas appliances should be blue and a yellow or orange flame can indicate the production of carbon monoxide.
* Keep all ventilation clear. Unintentionally blocking vents with furniture or intentionally blocking vents to reduce draughts is worryingly common and frighteningly risky.
* Ensure stove door is well sealed with rope.
* Check the construction of the stove has not been compromised by overheating. The joins between the sides and the top of the stove can dislocate if the stove gets too hot.
* Check stove flue seals at the union with the collar and the unit.
* Check stove flue for rust holes and damage.
* Clean the flue, chimney and baffle plate inside the stove. If your stove won't easily light or is belching smoke then a blockage is the most likely problem.

HEALTH

Most boaters will be unfortunately familiar with a towpath health hazard that is all too common. The prevalence of dog poo and the associated risk of disease is an infuriating aspect of boating, but it can be hazardous to your heath too. The greatest risk is from a disease called

Candles

Using candles on a boat is much more risky than it is on land. Boats rock, increasing the risk that the candle will fall over. Also, the confined space within a boat means there is an increased likelihood that fabrics or other flammable materials will come into close contact and possibly ignite. Extreme caution is recommended.

Internet memes claiming that it is possible to heat your boat with four tea lights under a plant pot are so full of holes that it's difficult to know where to begin. Not only is the power output nowhere near what is required for comfort, but the paraffin used to manufacture the candles is unpleasant and toxic to inhale. Any perceived environmental benefits are outweighed by the air-miles that likely carried the tea lights to this country. Add to that the increased fire risk and, all in all, it's a non-starter.

Keep a first aid kit handy.

Weil's disease symptoms

- Headaches
- Fever
- Chills
- Malaise
- Vomiting
- Muscle pain – particularly in the calf muscles
- Bruising and bleeding beneath the skin

Toxocariasis, an infection caused by round worm *Toxocara canis*. These are passed out in dog poo and can live for up to three years in the soil. The disease is most easily transmitted via the mouth when hands have become contaminated by dog mess. The elderly, children and those with a weak immune system are particularly at risk, but the disease can affect anyone.

There are two types of toxocariasis: *visceral larva migrans* (VLM) and *ocular larva migrans* (OLM). In VLM, the *Toxocara canis* larvae reach the liver, causing symptoms such as abdominal pain and fever. OLM occurs when a migrating larva reaches the eye. It causes inflammation of the retina and in severe cases, blindness. There are around 12 new cases of OLM in the UK each year according to the government Department of Health. Good hygiene and vigilance are the only means to negate the risk of toxocariasis (and indeed many other boating-specific diseases) by washing one's hands before touching food, keeping unwashed hands away from the face, eyes and open wounds. Items such as ropes and windlasses should be considered contaminated as a matter of course.

Canal water itself is home to some particularly unsavoury stuff too. Although most water-borne contaminants will result in only a mild

stomach upset, boaters should be aware of the specific danger that is Weil's disease. Weil's is transmitted by animal urine which has come into contact with broken skin. Boat life being what it is, open wounds and scratches are a regular occurrence and so being alert to the possibility of contracting Weil's is quite sensible.

All contact with canal water should be considered a risk – from falling into the water, working in the weed hatch and even handling wet ropes. The symptoms of Weil's are listed above but as most are akin to those you get when you have a cold or flu, it is easy to forget the possibility that you may have contracted Weil's. Be prepared to see your doctor and to stress your concerns to them.

WATER QUALITY

Most of the water provision for boaters is supplied via the same water mains that supply homes and businesses across the country. In homes this water is constantly renewed, with fresh water rushing through the pipes each time a tap is turned. There are some small and harmless impurities in this supply, sometimes so big that they can be seen with the naked eye, but given the constant flow of water these are insignificant.

Aboard a boat, these are different. Boats carry their water supply with them inside the water tank. Those small, usually imperceptible, impurities aren't being flushed through the system while the water is being held in the tank. Instead, these particles sink to the bottom and, over time, build up to form a layer of murky, gritty water at the bottom of your tank. As the water level in your tank drops you will eventually reach this bottom layer and, when you turn on the tap, the water that comes out will be brown. It's time to overhaul your water tank.

The impurities in mains water are not a problem in the minute quantities that are found in the mains supply, but ingested in concentrated quantities that can build up in a boat's water tank there becomes a risk of illness. Emptying and cleaning your tank will defer the job, as will using water purifying treatments, but eventually you will need to repaint the inside of the tank with a suitable coating.

Boat water tanks need monitoring and maintenance as any bacteria will have the opportunity to multiply while the water is in storage. Thankfully most problems are restricted to sickness, diarrhoea and upset stomachs. An inline filter (in addition to the gauze in the water pump) will help matters considerably and a water-purifying treatment should be a part of your routine maintenance.

Some boaters get around the issue entirely by using the water tank only for showering and relying on bottled water for many other applications. If you're using bottled water, be very careful where you store it and for how long. Always store it somewhere dark as light causes major problems for stored still water. If you've ever left a bowl of water outside, the green slime that built up will convince you of this.

ANIMALS

Dogs are one of the great joys of the waterways with many people regarding them as a great place to walk their pet. Most dogs and their owners are conscientious and friendly but, as always, there are some that cause a problem. Apart from the ever-present hazard of dog poo, the rare risk from aggressive or untrained dogs is worth considering, particularly if you have a dog of your own. Interactions between dogs can occasionally turn nasty, and on the canal towpath there are less options for escape. Most dog owners are familiar with the problem and know how to deal with any issues that arise.

Other animals that are commonly found on the waterways cause occasional problems, but the risk is so slight and so unlikely that they hardly warrant a mention. Nesting swans can cause alarm. Escaped farm animals might block your path and people are occasionally killed by stampeding cows. The best defence is to keep out of their way and exercise common sense and caution.

Ice hazard

Every winter a few people die attempting to save pets that have fallen through the ice on canals, rivers and other bodies of water.

CRIME

Including a section on crime in a book about narrowboating is admittedly incongruous considering the waterways are one of the best places to go to avoid the problem. Towns and cities and even the countryside have their own common types of crime, but the inland waterways are thankfully largely free from the problems. Burglary happens very rarely. Opportunists with an easy target or drunken stupidity are usually the rare culprits. The usual common sense advice applies, keep valuables out of view and keep anything of value locked inside the boat when you are not aboard. Items such as laptops and generators are the most obvious items that attract the attention of thieves. A generator running on the towpath or a laptop seen through a window might be too tempting to a passing thief with a plan to return when you're not aboard. The ever-rising price of diesel has seen an increase in diesel thefts,

Porthole power

Portholes are more secure against break in than the larger types of window which are usually very easy to remove. Louvre windows are particularly vulnerable to break in.

but the issue is still rare and the risk is greatly reduced with a locking filler cap. Theft of solar panels is rarer still and there is little to be done to negate the risk. Sensible precautions aside, the spirit of narrowboating recommends that you don't stress about what might happen, especially given the fact that in reality, it probably won't.

Burglar alarms for boats are available but few boaters find them necessary. Some of these alarms have motion sensors attached which emit an electronic beep as you near the boat, highly irritating for those moored nearby. Canvas covers

Keep dogs away from icy canals as they may confuse the ice for solid ground.

WORDS OF WARNING

Andy: Nb *Summer Wine*

I once shared a lock with a gentleman who was single-handing. Tackling one set of paddles each we worked as a team, letting the water out slowly until the boats were settled at the bottom of the lock. I pushed open the gate to let him out first and was horrified to see him gearing up to jump onto the top of his boat from the side of the lock! It was too late to call a warning as he launched himself into the six-foot drop. Thankfully he only slipped enough to land on his backside on the roof of his boat, narrowly missing falling between his boat and the lock wall. I think he must have been a little hurt (although he denied this) as he moored up shortly after the incident.

Tony: Nb *The Watchman*

I was once moored at a boatyard abreast another boat with a cruiser stern, awaiting work to be done on my boat. Having stepped across their cruiser stern to reach my boat earlier in the day you can imagine my surprise to find myself in a heap at the bottom of their engine bay as I made my way ashore later that evening. Someone had removed their decking boards sometime earlier and, being dark, I had not noticed this until it was too late. Thankfully no bones were broken and the cuts and bruises eventually healed. Nowadays I always wear a head-torch.

Darren: Nb *Dunster*

My top tip is to keep your boat keys in your pocket until you are safely aboard – at least then you still have them if you fall in.

at bow or stern provide nominal protection for items stored within, but also provide cover for intruders to work unseen on your security. Good padlocks seem to deter all but the most determined burglar but it must be accepted that it is easy to get into any boat if the intruder is determined enough. Given that there is little space or inclination to collect high-value possessions most boaters are more fearful of vandalism than of burglary, but remember neither experience is common on the waterways.

The most common type of 'crime' is caused by drunken or mischievous miscreants and is usually limited to causing a nuisance. Most of the time the problems can be avoided with a little friendly banter or by simply ignoring it; after all, better a little annoyance than to escalate the problem. Choosing the right mooring places can help a lot too. If you moor in the centre of a town with

a busy nightlife then you might be occasionally disturbed by rowdy banging or climbing on your boat roof or, as in the case of one boater friend, a late-night reveller peeing in their plant pots. Occasionally you might hear stories of broken windows, stolen boat poles and mooring lines being untied or cut, but the odds of it happening to you are unlikely.

Violence on the towpath is amongst the rarest of all waterways crimes. Towpaths may be sometimes dark and often secluded, but that in itself makes them one of the safest places to be as there is usually nobody else around. Violence on the towpath is usually caused by boater disputes or run-ins between other waterways users. Inconsiderate boaters, fisherfolk, cyclists and the like can annoy to the point where violence could occur. Avoid the problem by being neither inconsiderate nor reactionary.

Axe and hatchet safety

Most boaters with a stove fire will own an axe of some description, but many will not know how to use them safely and efficiently. Brett Selby is a boater and also a bush-craft and survival expert. Here's his advice on how to use an axe without tears or bloodshed.

Before you start chopping firewood ask yourself these two questions:

- What is the safest way to use these tools? Best practice is not to use them at all. If another method is available, use that.

- Are you tired or cold and is it dark? If any of the answers are yes, put the sheath back on the blade and do the job at a more suitable time.

Brett Selby.

Some myths dispelled:

- A blunt axe isn't safer than a sharp one; the edge will not bite into the wood, causing it to glance off in an unpredictable way. If this happens, even if you avoid a serious cut, fractured or broken bones can result. Keep your axe razor sharp, making it a pleasure to use at the same time as instilling a healthy respect for its capabilities.

- A hatchet is not safer than an axe. The shorter hatchet shaft means that any uncontrolled swings will tend to come back towards you. The longer shaft of an axe takes the head in a longer curve which actually increases your 'safety zone'.

Safe techniques:

- Concentrate.
- Stop working if distracted.
- Always cut away from yourself and others.
- Avoid using the axe in a big movement from above your head. If you don't hit the target cleanly it could glance off into your foot or leg.
- As the axe approaches the work-piece, push the hands downwards so that the shaft and cutting edge move parallel towards the ground. This removes most of the dangerous arc.
- Use chopping blocks whenever possible. They provide a barrier, stopping the axe-head moving if things go wrong.

12 PRE-SEASON CHECKLIST

As a liveaboard boater I live quite close to nature. I watch the seasons change from the window of my onboard office, and as the leaves turn to brown and golden I know that it is time to prepare for the forthcoming winter season. I watch as the days get shorter until I know that the last fine days are past and it is time to hunker down with a good supply of coal and a list of jobs that I postponed during the warmer months. I dig in and count the days until spring is here and I can enjoy being outdoors again. Winter on board has its pleasures, but I do so love the emergence of spring that when it finally arrives I am chomping at the bit and desperate to start my engine and get boating.

This winter my boat, my dog and I hunkered down at Snaygill Boats in Skipton, North Yorkshire. The good people who run the hire fleet and boatyard there had done a sterling job of remedying my failed efforts at boat maintenance. 'I love it when you work on your boat!' said Troy who owns the business with his wife Jo. 'When you work on your boat it means I am going to earn some money by fixing the mess you make!' he teased.

It was during one such DIY rescue early in the New Year that we began to talk about my plans for cruising as soon as the weather improved. 'You need to start getting your boat ready now!' said Jo. I expressed a little surprise and explained that my preparation plans included little more than filling up with fuel and water before starting my engine to set

off into the big wide open. 'No no, no, no, NO!' admonished Jo. 'I'll make you a list and we can tick them off as we go.'

ENGINE SERVICE AND SPARES

It is prudent to replace the filters on your oil, fuel and coolant lines to begin the season with a clear conscience. Check hoses and connections for wear and corrosion and replace them if necessary, as a small leak now will invariably become worse. Boats that use canal water for cooling their engines should be closely checked for blockages in the line and filter, and while you are there you should make sure that your header tank is topped up with antifreeze too. Finally, a check on fan belts and cables and you're ready to move to the next section.

It's a beautiful day for boating. Are you ready?

Extra checks

- Does your boat have a water separator installed on the fuel line? If it does, be sure to drain it off and check it at least monthly when you are underway.

- Check your stern gland for leaks and re-pack it if necessary. This will usually need doing every three to five years, so if that time is approaching you might want to get the job out of the way and ticked off. I realise that we should be working in kilograms now, but an ounce of prevention is still better than a pound of cure.

- Take a look in the weed hatch to check your prop for hitch-hiking debris. Check too that your weed hatch is re-secured properly and the seals are doing their job well. Not replacing the weed hatch properly (or not replacing it at all) is a common mistake and can lead to engine damage or even sinking.

- Check your engine mounts are still in one piece.

Be sure to check your plumbing and hardware after each cold winter.

Spares

Having a few spare parts in storage can be a godsend when something goes wrong in the middle of nowhere. Preparation now will stand you a better chance getting underway quickly and with less fuss, instead of wasting time and money hunting for the right parts in unfamiliar territory. The following items should be in your locker:

- Drive belt
- Fan belt
- Throttle/gear cable
- Engine oil
- Gearbox oil
- Antifreeze
- Grease

UTILITIES

Cruising will test your boat's mettle more than being safely tucked up on your mooring. Murphy's Law says that you'll discover a problem when you are out and about, so be sure to check the facilities that you rely on before cast off into the unknown.

Electrical issues are by far the most common cause of all boat breakdowns according to Jo at Snaygill Boats. After spending the winter months hooked up to the mains, many boaters find that their batteries are fried and no longer reliable. If you only check one thing before setting off on the first cruise of the season, it should be to check that your batteries are up to the job and holding a charge, replacing them if necessary.

Clean away

Cleaning the battery terminals and connectors is a sensible precaution that can save lots of time and headaches.

Another common electrical fault lies with fuses, with your 12v system and inverter being the usual culprits, so check those first. Bilge pumps, bow thrusters, horns and headlights probably won't have been used over the winter period and so you may not know if they are still shipshape. Make sure you have spare fuses, bulbs, cable and an adequate tool kit before you set off.

Water

Plumbing issues and leaks are a common seasonal affliction for boats that have been moored up during cold weather. Of course most boaters will have prepared their boats for winter and therefore will have negated most of the risk, but it can never be eradicated completely. Burst pipes will make themselves evident sooner or later, so it makes better sense to check plumbing now rather than find a big watery mess when you put the system under pressure.

Hardware can suffer in the deep freeze too, so check that water pumps and shower gulpers have made it through the winter unscathed. The units themselves and the plumbing attached to them can spring a leak if they get frozen. Similarly, both hot and cold water tanks can be damaged by freezing too so that's another check to cross off the list before you get going. Once you're sure you're free of leaks it is time to fill your tanks in readiness for the cruise ahead.

Gas

Servicing gas appliances every year is recommended and should be carried out by a qualified and registered gas engineer. It doesn't really matter when this service is done, but it seems logical to do it before the high-usage season starts.

As for DIY gas jobs, you'll want to check all of your gas connections for corrosion and replace them where necessary. Check too that all connections are tightly done up as the expansion and contraction caused by changing temperatures can slowly cause them to undo.

Finally, now would be a good time to check that you have enough gas for your next cruise. Half-cooked dinners and cold showers are enough to dull anyone's boating enjoyment, and we wouldn't want that.

Toilet

Given the horrors that might become apparent, checking the toilet is usually the last job on the list. If you have a pump-out system you might want to get the tank flushed out to displace and remove anything that might have settled and hardened while your boat has been left undisturbed. Some boatyards offer a jet-wash service and getting someone else to do the dirty work sounds like a good idea, whatever the price. Cassette owners might like to conduct a similar deep clean, albeit on a smaller scale, but be sure to check those seals and valves to avoid nasty spills and vapour release blow-backs. Once your throne is fit for a king, you can stock up with chemicals and toilet roll and you are good to go, so to speak.

KIT CHECK

So, you're almost ready to get underway and likely chomping at the bit to cast off your ropes and get boating – but take a few moments to do a quick kit check. Checking your waterproofs might only save you a soaking, but missing a check on some of the other items on this checklist could seriously damage your health.

- Check that ropes and fenders are in good order.
- Check that your bilge pump still works, and that you have a spare for those little emergencies.
- Check any bilges that are accessible through an inspection hatch. Some boats have several along the length, others have just one near the stern before the engine bulkhead.
- Check that your engine covers and deck boards are still sound.
- Test your carbon monoxide and smoke detectors and replace batteries (or the whole unit) as necessary.
- Make sure that your hose pipe is in good working order and give it a rinse through with sterilising fluid.
- Check your wet weather gear for mould, holes and other wear and tear.
- Check poles, boat hooks and planks are free from rot and slimy mould.

Now it's time to stop reading and get boating.

GLOSSARY

Air draft	The height of the boat taken from the waterline to the highest fixed point on the boat (so you won't hit a low bridge).
Bow	The front of the boat.
Counter	The flat area below the water line above the swim.
Draft	The amount of the hull that is below water.
Freeboard	The distance between the waterline and the lowest deck level where water can enter the inside of the boat.
Gunwale	The top edge of the hull where it joins the cabin side, lateral gun wall (but pronounced gunnel as in tunnel).
Hull	The main part of the boat that sits in the water and gives a boat its buoyancy.
Keel cooled	A closed system, with a slab tank (narrow and baffled) is normally welded to the inside of the swim; engine-cooling water is then circulated through it. (It does the same job as the radiator on a car.) Important note: the engine and cooling system can easily have anti-freeze added to prevent frost damage.
Port or port side	Left-hand side when standing at the stern facing forward (towards the front end) of the boat.

Raw water cooled (direct)	Canal water is drawn in via a mud box (normally a watertight container large enough to allow the incoming water time to settle) before being pumped around the engine to cool. It is then returned to the canal. Important note: the engine and every part of the cooling system must be completely drained during cold weather to prevent frost damage.
Raw water cooled (indirect)	Canal water is drawn in via a mud box (normally a watertight container large enough to allow the incoming water time to settle) before being pumped through a heat exchanger mounted on the engine; it is then returned to the canal. The engine's own coolant is also pumped through the heat exchanger but is kept separate inside the heat exchanger enabling the engine to be protected with anti-freeze. Important note: the raw water side of the heat exchanger and unprotected parts of the cooling system must be completely drained during cold weather to prevent frost damage.
Skeg	A steel horizontal bar welded to the base plate (normally in channel form) and protruding from the stern to carry the lower end of the rudder post and bearing. It also gives some protection to the propeller.
Starboard or starboard side	(From the Norse steerboard referring to the oar that was used to steer the boat.) Right-hand side when standing at the stern facing forward (towards the front end).

Canal boats at sunset.

Stern	The back end of the boat.
Sterngear	The propeller, propeller shaft, sterntube, sterntube bearing and stuffing box or packing gland (an adjustable gland to help keep water out of the engine space bilge).
Swan's neck	The S-shaped steel bar welded to the rudder post to which the tiller bar is fitted (the brass shiny stick with a wooden handle on the end) on a motor boat.
Swim	The after (back) underwater part of the hull that goes to a point to allow a cleaner flow of water over the propeller.

Tiller bar (or extension)	Fits on the swan's neck of a motorboat to give extra leverage. (The brass shiny stick with a wooden handle on the end.)
Transom	The after (back) part of the boat (normally a rounded shape) above the water where the person steering the boat stands.
Tumblehome	The amount a cabin side slopes inwards (to give more bridge clearance).
Waterline	The line on the boat's hull where it floats.
Windlass or lock key	A cranked handle for opening and closing lock paddles.

BIBLIOGRAPHY AND RESOURCES

Books and magazines

The Liveaboard Guide by Tony Jones, Adlard Coles Nautical, 2012
Everything you need to know about living aboard on the UK's inland waterways.

Boaters' Handbook, British Waterways
A brilliant concise guide to boat handling and safety. Available as a free booklet from British Waterways and free download at http://www.waterscape.com/media/documents/1784.pdf

Narrow Boat by L.T.C. Rolt, The History Press, 2014.
A book about life on the English canals that was originally published in 1944, it has been continuously in print since. At the outbreak of the Second World War, Rolt took a four-month canal trip with his new wife. The book is credited with a revival of interest in the English canals, leading directly to the creation of the Inland Waterways Association which spearheaded the restoration of the canals and promoted their use for leisure boating.

Narrowboats: care and maintenance by Nick Billingham, Helmsman's Books, 1995.
A useful breakdown of boat maintenance, and although written in 1995, not much changes on the cut.

Voyaging on a Small Income by Annie Hill, Tiller Publishing, 2006.
It's about yachting, but contains some fabulous advice and was the inspiration for my first book, *The Liveaboard Guide*.

Buying a Boat: how to get started, British Waterways
A good place to start with the basics with practical advice and resources. It is available free from British Waterways

De-Junk Your Life by Helen Foster, Aurum Press, 2002.
Not specifically aimed at boaters, but the philosophy is well suited to liveaboard life.

Towpath Talk
A popular free monthly newspaper about the UK waterways, it features the latest news, trader ads, waterways stoppages and events.

Waterways World
The longest-established inland waterways magazine.

Canal Boat
A magazine championing our wonderful waterways and boating for well over a decade, providing news, views, boat tests, practical advice, cruising ideas, updates on canal restorations and keeping everyone in touch with everything that's happening on the UK's canals and rivers.

Narrowboat
The Inland Waterways heritage magazine.

Clubs, societies and other organisations

The Residential Boat Owners' Association
Established in 1963 the Residential Boat Owners' Association is the only national organisation that exclusively represents and promotes the interests of people living on boats in the British Isles. Representing all those who have chosen to make a boat their home – whether that boat is static or cruises; is based inland or on the coast; has a permanent or temporary mooring (whether residential or not) or continuously cruises – all are residential boaters.

The National Association of Boat Owners
NABO is dedicated to promoting the interests of private boaters on Britain's canals, rivers and lakes, so that their voice can be heard when decisions are being made which might affect their boating.

The Inland Waterways Association
The IWA is a registered charity, founded in 1946, which advocates the conservation, use, maintenance, restoration and development of the inland waterways for public benefit.

Online resources

The Considerate Boater
www.considerateboater.com
Aims to promote considerate boating and good boating etiquette on the inland waterways.

Canal Cuttings
www.canalcuttings.co.uk
A free online boating magazine with more than 750 pages of information and features about canals, navigable rivers and their usage including classified and waterside property ads.

Granny Buttons
www.grannybuttons.com
An entertaining and illuminating blog by boater and journalist Andrew Denny with the strapline, 'My own private thoughts and ignorance about the canals and waterways. (And no-one else's, except as quoted.)'

Low Impact Life on Board
www.liloontheweb.org.uk
The LILO website is where you'll find information about the eco-boating community in Britain.

Large boat brokerages

Boats and Outboards
www.boatsandoutboards.co.uk
Online brokerage with thousands of boats for sale and other boating related ads.

Apollo Duck
www.apolloduck.co.uk
Online brokerage. It is a large site with thousands of boats and related items for sale.

ABNB Boat Sales
www.abnb.co.uk
A friendly, well-run boat brokerage with a focus on customer service.

Whilton Marina
www.whiltonmarina.co.uk
The company has been buying, selling and caring for narrow boats since 1971 and have a large selection of narrow boats for sale at the marina for viewing.

Other organisations

Canal and River Trust
www.canalrivertrust.org.uk

Boat Safety Scheme
www.boatsafetyscheme.org

British Marine Foundation
britishmarine.co.uk

The Environment Agency
www.gov.uk/government/organisations/environment-agency

Other related organisations mentioned in this book

Lambon Boat Builders
www.lambonboats.co.uk

Snaygill Boats
www.snaygillboats.co.uk

Carefree Cruising
www.carefreecruising.com

Hainsworths Boatyard
www.boattransporter.co.uk

St Mary's Marina
www.stmarysmarina.co.uk

Braunston Marina
www.braunstonmarina.co.uk

River Canal Rescue
www.rivercanalrescue.co.uk
Breakdown and recovery for river and canalboats.

Lee Sanitation
www.leesan.com
Supplier of marine sanitation equipment.

Canvas Man Boat Covers
www.canvasman.co.uk
Makers of bespoke boat covers.

Sofabed Barn
www.sofabedbarn.co.uk
Suppliers of sofabeds and storage solutions for narrowboats.

Craftinsure
www.craftinsure.com
Marine insurance brokers.

Blue Star Surveys
www.bluestarsurveys.co.uk
Marine surveyors.

Canal Junction
www.canaljunction.com
Online boating resource.

INDEX

Acknowledgements

For Massie, Wenny and Maya.

Photography by Tony Jones, Chris Beesley, Steve Rayner, Mark Wilson, Tim Coghlan, Chris Sailsbury, Angela Schorah, Duncan Stephens, Jo Bowling, Polly Parrot, Kerry Dainty, Margaret Holmes, Sarah Henshaw and Cabal.

Other photography courtesy of Getty Images, Shutterstock, Narrowboats of Distinction, Aqua Narrowboats and Tek Tanks.

Thank you to all of the boaters and experts who provided insight and case study data for this book, and particularly to Troy and Jo Dortona and all the gang at Snaygill Boats for their help and friendship. Thanks to Carol, Nina and Phil for bailing me out every time anything went wrong. Thank you to my editors Lisa Thomas and Janet Murphy for their patience and support in the production of this book.

Finally, thank you to Wee-V for your help and support. Without you this book might never have happened.

Happy boating!